Your dog will never lie to you, deceive you, criticise you, intentionally hurt you, judge you, let you down or belittle you. Instead, your dog will give you an amazing welcome every single time you come home, even though you left him. He will never hold a grudge but will show you incredible loyalty by always being by your side, especially at your bleakest times, when he will comfort you and lift your spirits.

Front cover; from left to right; Mabel, Tilly, Nero (AKA Wasabi), MR. Darcy (AKA Doug the pug), Dexter (AKA Wasabi)
Courtesy of Mark Wilson, North West Film Locations Ltd

Back cover; Brece at her 14th birthday party

Prologue

At the age of fifty, and after three decades of loyal service working for an insurance company, I found myself being pushed out of the office. This left me at a daunting crossroads in my life with no idea which road to take.

After a short unsuccessful stint working as a volunteer, I decided to follow my heart by setting up my own business as a professional pet sitter. As well as sharing my home with my beloved 9-year-old Golden Retriever 'Brece' we now had to make room for a plethora of other dogs which came in all shapes, and sizes, each with their own unique personalities. Whilst I dealt with the new customers, Brece earned her keep by vetting the hounds, filtering out any anti-social visitors, and thereby ensuring doggy harmony under our roof.

For the next five years I was to live with only dogs. I started to learn some important things about their behaviour within the pack; the key observations being the realisation that dogs do not want for material things, they live in the here and now and show compassion to others. By doing so the dog, instinctively follows many of the Buddhist beliefs. Such as living in the 'here and now' and not wanting for material things, making for a simplistic yet contented life.

'Trials and Tribulations of a Pet Sitter' describes the immense joy that the animals have brought into my life and how my business has grown from strength to strength. Not forgetting the fantastic dog owners that I have met along the way who love their pets unconditionally. But there were low points too; from the everyday challenges faced in ensuring the dogs are happy and safe, to the trauma of committing the cardinal sin of losing a customer's beloved dog!

Chapter 1

Frisco 1975

As a child, my two younger siblings and I were fortunate enough to own shares in the family pet dog, a female Alsatian Labrador cross called Frisco, whom we loved with a passion. Frisco was quite a character, a free spirit who frequently escaped from the back garden and was rather partial to taking herself off for a stroll around the local picturesque lake. The lake was within half a mile of our house and situated across the other side of a busy main road at the end of our sleepy street. Getting herself to the lake involved jumping over the garden wall, walking down our street, then carefully crossing the main road.

Our independent agile dog loved her strolls around the lake, after which she liked nothing more than to while away her time sat in one of the canoes, moored by the lakeside. And there she would happily chill without a care in the world, that was until she caught sight of a flock of geese coming in to land. Once they had landed she excitedly jumped out of the canoe and felt compelled to give chase to the birds, barking ferociously the whole time. When she tired of tormenting the local wildlife, she made her way home, at the same time getting a chance to practice her foraging for street food skills. She was good at this. The food came in various forms, usually scraps left by picnickers or walkers, but her best source of sustenance came from Mrs. Clegg who lived on our street at number twelve. Mrs.

3

Clegg was an avid baker, who every morning without fail rustled up tantalising culinary delights. It didn't take long for Frisco to catch on to the baking activities going on at number twelve. Gravitating towards the welcoming aroma, she always called in for a pit-stop before returning home. Sat outside Mrs Clegg's door, she barked incessantly until the lady herself appeared and fed our peckish dog with a home-made scone. Once this was devoured, it was then back to our house in time for lunch. Afternoons followed a similar pattern.

Like a lot of dogs, Frisco appeared to possess an inbuilt clock and always made sure she was home in time to greet us from school. Taking the scenic route home from school one afternoon I witnessed her returning from one of her lake escapades. Earlier than usual I caught her unawares and watched as she sat at the curb with her back to the lake. Looking to her right she waited for a gap in the traffic, oblivious to the fact that I was spying on her. When a gap appeared, she strolled into the centre of the road, then sat down again waiting for the traffic to clear to her left.

At this point, she was sat in the middle of the road with cars passing behind and in front of her, yet she remained calm. After about a minute the traffic to her left cleared, allowing her to calmly walk towards the other side of the road. Once safely across the road she picked up her step and headed off towards home, still unaware of my presence and of how completely in awe I was. Jaywalking was just another one of her many talents!

In the time-honoured tradition, Christmases were always spent at our grandmother's home. In her youth grandmother attended catering college in her home-town of Darwen, Lancashire and graduated as a first-class cook. Her confectionery masterpieces were legendary, she could give Mrs. Clegg a run for her money any day of the week. The festive season was a time for her to show off her infinite culinary talents, in particular her desserts which were nothing less than ambrosia to the palate. Frisco's maiden Christmas at grandmother's was bound to be a glorious experience for our greedy young pet, she would love being on the front line in grandmother's kitchen. However, we were proved wrong.

Following our usual schedule, we all arrived at grandmother's on Christmas Eve morning, full of excitement and festive cheer. That evening at about 6 pm my mother received an unexpected phone call from Mrs. Clegg alerting her to the fact that Frisco was outside her front door barking for her scone! In all the excitement we had failed to notice that Frisco had done her disappearing act, yet again.

The whole family tried to recall the last time we saw her. When we arrived that morning, we remembered her getting out of the car and then watched as she made her way straight through the house and into the kitchen where grandmother was busily preparing food for our Christmas Eve visitors. Frisco was doing her usual begging thing and in the process getting under grandmother's feet. Grandmother was clearly irritated and told Frisco to "Scarper", and that was the last anyone saw of her. Frisco had taken grandmother at her word and 'scarpered' all the way back home. Like some sort of big furry homing pigeon, she made the seven-mile trip back to number twelve to try her luck there, snubbing grandmother in the process.

The clever dog would have achieved this remarkable feat by following landmarks and also drawing on her incredible sense of smell. Frantically covering as much ground as possible and trying to pick up the scent of something to lead her back home, or more importantly to Mrs Clegg's. It's truly amazing how dogs can do this, it's as if they have an inbuilt sat nav. There is now research to suggest that dogs may be able to search by using magnetic fields in a similar way to migrating birds, for further information refer appendix A.

Surprisingly, my mother always seemed relaxed about our dog's escapologist antics, but I was always left with a sense that it wasn't quite right. In those days (circa 1975) stray dogs were not an uncommon sight, dog wardens had not yet been invented, it was the job of the police to herd up any strays. To set the scene back then; although pet dogs were not as commonplace as they are today, the streets were always strewn with dog poo. For the pre-decimal sum of seven shillings people were legally required to purchase a license in order to own a dog. You needed sixpence to make a telephone call, and people smoked everywhere; puffing away in pubs, restaurants, cinemas and even the workplace.

Frisco continued with her lake adventures until the inevitable day when we got a visit from a member of the constabulary. The policeman had diligently followed her home after one of her tours and came knocking at our door. Standing on our doorstep, he informed us that the police were aware of Frisco's escapades but were accepting of her as they knew she had good road sense!

Even at a young age, it seemed weird to me that the police didn't object to a dog wandering around alone and crossing a busy road; surely this must have been a hazard to drivers? The policeman did however inform us that the owner of the lake was not quite so accepting, especially in relation to her behaviour towards the geese. From that moment on, sadly for Frisco (but not the geese), she was grounded. Under police instructions, my mother was ordered to make our garden secure; it was the end of an era for our nomadic pet.

Like most siblings, we didn't always see eye to eye with each other, we squabbled and fell out amongst ourselves on a regular basis. But we always had something in common and that was our love for Frisco, our beloved dog. She was the glue that bonded us together. I will never forget the love that we all shared for our clever, peckish dog.

As a family we owned other pets; a cat, hamsters and a budgie, but Frisco was the jewel in the crown. All animals fared well apart from the budgie. One cold winter's day someone let the little bird out of its cage. It frantically flew around the lounge before bashing into a wall, concussing itself then dropping behind a blistering hot radiator. Despite our best efforts to rescue the bird, we failed miserably, and the poor thing perished.

Looking back to my youth having pets, and in particular a dog, probably formed a blueprint for a large part of my life and for this I will always be grateful. From a young age dogs have always made a massive impression on many aspects of my life. It wasn't just the family dog that I adored I started to appreciate all dogs. The sight of a dog enjoying its walk in the street, happily wagging its tail has always filled my heart with joy. As I pass the dog, I constantly turn around to glance back at it, just to see its contented face for that bit longer.

Almost all dogs appear to be extremely happy when out on a walk, perhaps with one exception- the Greyhound. With their bowed heads and rigid tails, they never appear to be enjoying their walk. Perhaps they aren't, maybe they really are 'lazy hounds' preferring to stay at home relaxing. Amongst my multitude of canine thoughts, I often wonder if dogs weren't so pleasing to my eye, would I love them the same way? Probably not. I can't imagine myself having the same feelings for an animal that isn't quite so aesthetically pleasing. Snakes and lizards just don't do it for me, fur over scales and feathers all the way!

Chapter 2

The angelic creature 2003

Mike moved into my house at Heyhouses Lane in 1994, a modest three-bed semi built in the 1940s. He was eight years my junior and worked as an IT Business Consultant. Academically, he was highly intelligent and boasted a first-class honours degree and PhD in Maths and Artificial Intelligence. He also understood several computer languages, but unfortunately, his computer brain did not always lend itself to matters of common sense. In appearance, he looked older than his years, he was twenty-eight when we met but looked a decade older. Much to his annoyance people seemed to have a compulsion to compare his appearance to that of a plethora of famous people. The comparisons started off with a poor man's Antonio Banderas and Robert De Niro, then moved on to Taylor Hicks (winner of American Idol many moons ago).

"Why can't I just be me? I don't want to look like all these other OLD men."

Mike was always greatly frustrated when people made their unwanted comparisons.

Eight years into our relationship we were at the checkout in the local supermarket, when the till assistant remarked;

"Do you know who you remind me of?"

Mike sighed.

"Don't tell me, Robert De Niro?" His Antonio Banderas days had long since gone. Mike was noticeably irritated at this point.

"No, Father Ted."

An uncomfortable deathly quiet swept down on us and accompanied us for the entire time spent at the checkout. The till assistant's observations amused me no end, but of course I had to enjoy my amusement in silence. Mike had gone from resembling Antonio Banderas to Father Ted in eight years of being with me. Needless to say, he was completely underwhelmed with the sales assistant's comments, grabbing the groceries, he indignantly scuttled out of the supermarket. *God he was mad!*

Things between the pair of us were good but we both recognised that there was a gap in our lives, which neither of us particularly wanted to fill with an off-spring. Of course, I wanted to fill this gap with a dog; in fact, I was hell-bent on inviting one of God's creatures to come and live with us. Mike was not quite so enthusiastic about the prospect, but after a little gentle persuasion I managed to convince him that he would also love being part-owner of a dog. It would be a common interest and responsibility for the pair of us to share and enjoy.

Purchasing a dog became our new project, we had to get it right. Never having owned a dog before, Mike grew excited at the prospect; *little did he know what was in store for him.* In 2003 we agreed that we were going to buy a Golden Retriever. Having previously seen one in the back of someone's car I was struck by what I considered to be a beautiful yet subdued looking dog. Admittedly, it seemed a tad odd to be drawn to an animal that looks forlorn, but maybe that was part of the attraction. I had immediately fallen in love with the breed and could think of little else. The Golden Retriever began to consume my thoughts.

Fortunately, Mike was happy with my choice; in fact, he did all the research and found a Golden Retriever breeder on a North Yorkshire farm, who was selling a litter of seven puppies. It was important to us that we didn't buy a dog from a puppy farm. It is no secret that mass-produced pedigree dogs can sometimes suffer serious hereditary health problems. In addition, it's no life for the bitches. We decided to pay the breeder a visit to check the place out; not that we had much of a clue what we were looking out for in terms of spotting a puppy farm. All we really knew at that point was that it was important we saw the mother and that she was in good health.

Arriving at the farm we were greeted by a pleasant lady in her late forties. She introduced herself as Angela and led us to an outbuilding which was being used as a nursery. Walking into that outhouse I was taken by surprise. The place was strewn with newspapers, not unexpected, but the second thing that caught my eye was the vast amount of dog poo lying around the place. Obviously, with seven puppies, there was going to be a lot of mess but it surprised me that Angela hadn't had a quick spruce up ahead of our visit. She finally proceeded to clear up some of the dog mess. As she did so, I looked away over to a corner of the building where mummy Retriever was laid in her bed feeding her gorgeous little puppies; a sight to behold. The little rascals were clambering all over each other, in one intertwined fluffy mass. Sticking limbs in each other's faces without any sense of concern or irritation, they seemed to enjoy the contact, need it even.

Angela was quite forthright in telling us that she did not operate a puppy farm, not that we had asked her, but I was glad that she had shared this information. Apart from the hygiene conditions, Angela seemed genuine enough, so we took her at her word. She explained that some of the puppies had already been sold, but at just six weeks they weren't old enough to be taken away from their mother and required another two weeks of nurturing. The litter consisted of four darker puppies and three lighter coloured ones, known as champagne colour. Personally, I preferred the darker coloured pups, but couldn't pick one over another, all four were sublime. As Mike was indifferent to colour, I asked Angela to keep one of the darker ones for us, to which she agreed.

A fortnight later, as arranged, we returned to the farm with Mike in the driving seat. On arrival we were once again greeted by Angela, who proceeded to take us back to the nursery. On entering the outbuilding, I was surprised for a second time but in this instance, it was because there was only one pup left and it was a champagne bitch. My request for a dark coloured pup had clearly been ignored, this left me feeling disappointed. Part of me wanted to ask Angela what she had done with our darker coloured puppy but somehow it didn't feel right to put the question out there, sort of insensitive towards the remaining lone pup. Mike wouldn't be bothered one way or the other so I just let it go. Besides it didn't really matter now, we had our puppy, we would love her no matter what shade she was.

Still stood in the outbuilding and just when I thought I was over the disappointment, a string of niggling thoughts crept into my head; why was she the last one left, were the other puppies nicer than ours, was there something wrong with her, was she the runt? It was hard to know if she was the runt or not as there were no other puppies left to compare her with.

As Angela handed the lone pup over to me, for the second time I put my reservations to one side. It felt euphoric to be holding her, nothing else mattered now, my niggling doubts evaporated. After a couple of minutes of being transfixed on our pup I managed to prise my eyes off her and looked at Angela who was also attentively watching the pup. Angela's eyes were full of genuine affection that seemed tinged with a slight sadness. Although Angela didn't audibly share her feelings, I picked up on her worry and concern for what was about to happen to a puppy that she had bred. I imagined her to be wondering if the precious animal would enjoy a happy life, what would be in store for it? The expression on her face will always stay with me: I felt for her and wanted to swear some sort of oath that we would give our puppy the best life ever, but refrained. Angela promised to keep in touch and provide updates on the pup's siblings. Her last words as we left the farm were;

"Puppies must have fresh clean water at all times."

So off we went with her words of wisdom in our ears and pup in arms. Our beloved new puppy sat on my lap all the way home. I immediately loved her with every fibre of my body. Having never felt maternal before I imagined the feeling to be similar to what I was experiencing at that moment. Mesmerised by her for the entire journey I was unable to take my eyes off her, they were glued. This was the first time she had been separated from her mother and also her maiden voyage in a car with complete strangers; a big deal for an eight-week-old puppy.

Playing with my adorable creature in the car made me incredibly happy, my dopamine levels went off the scale, I was completely enthralled. Watching her cute furry face, silky ears and little black button nose filled and satisfied just about all my senses. Her soft fur was amazing to touch. I couldn't help but repeatedly kiss and sniff her, she smelt gorgeous. With each inhalation I imagined my serotonin levels to be multiplying, literally making me increasingly happier. Even the sound of her bark was adorable, a sort of a high-pitched cute yelp. The only sense that she didn't satisfy was taste; but even looking at her I almost began to salivate, perhaps she really was good enough to eat! She settled well during the three-hour journey home never once crying or even having the slightest accident. As she cuddled up in my arms, I felt an instant connection, we had bonded.

That first night away from the only home she had ever known she slept alone in her cage covered with a blanket. Mike had read that placing a blanket over the cage would ensure the puppy felt more secure. During the night she appeared to be calm, a couple of little yelps when we first left her but then silence. Unusual for a puppy's first night away from its mother, she had settled better than expected. It was a restless night for me though, tossing and turning in a turbulent mixture of worry and excitement. Mike on the other hand slept like a log.

At the crack of dawn, I descended the stairs feeling apprehensive; things below seemed quiet, a bit too quiet. I was expecting crying and whimpering, but nothing. The silence began to fill me with dread. I became terrified at the thought that she may have died in the night due to lack of oxygen caused by the blanket. Surely this couldn't be the case, people wouldn't make such recommendations if there was the slightest risk of pet asphyxiation. I knew the logic but it did nothing to alleviate my fears. Arriving at the cage I stood in front of it in trepidation. Still no noise came from beneath the blanket, increasing my concerns even further. She should have heard me by now! I quickly snatched the blanket in the same way a magician removes the cover from the cage of his prized illusion. And there looking up at me with her beautiful brown eyes was one happy little puppy, wriggling silently with excitement. Thank God we hadn't managed to kill her on that first night!

Coming up with a name for her was a long process which took a considerable amount of time. At that time in our lives, we owned a cottage on the north-west coast of Brittany in Northern France close to the seaside town of Brece. The cottage, a traditional Normandy long-house, was built from stone and set in half an acre of land in rural surroundings. There was a massive field populated with cattle to the back of the cottage, and fields dotted with hens and chickens roaming freely to the front. Quite 'The good life'.

I wanted to call our pup Brece (pronounced Bressay) after the town, it meant a lot to me, as did the place itself. But Mike wasn't too keen on the name, I put it to him that it was either that or 'Santa'. The name Santa evolved when one morning a little uninvited Cocker Spaniel walked into my house at Heyhouses. It was summer, the front door was wide open, and the stray dog couldn't resist a peep inside. After a quick inspection of my home and much sniffing I checked the dog's tag which was inscribed with the word 'Santa'. I took a real shine to the name, but Mike was not of the same opinion as me, he hated it, even more than he hated the name 'Brece'. After much deliberation, we decided to call our pup Brece. Our French neighbours must have thought we were mad, calling a dog after the town; a bit like calling a dog Blackpool.

The decision to call our dog Brece did not come without its problems. Most people struggled with the pronunciation, she was either called Brejay, or Breese. The receptionists at the vets seemed determined to call her Breese and in time I gave up trying to correct them; it didn't really bother me what they called her. When out and about and people asked me her name, I started telling them she was called Bessie. Calling her Bessie avoided all the usual questions surrounding the origin of her name, which meant I saved a fair bit of time.

Chapter 3

The not-so angelic creature

Brece was an angelic looking creature but looks can be deceiving. She was by no means an easy puppy to look after. If the truth be told, she was a real handful. I had completely forgotten what it was like to have a new puppy tearing the place up; our very own bull in a china shop. Most of her time was spent swiping all objects off the coffee table and other low surfaces; no ornaments escaped her decluttering activities. She created havoc from the minute she woke until the minute she crashed. With her around the place it was difficult to get on with chores or anything else for that matter. In contrast, it was also almost impossible to relax and do nothing; she demanded constant attention. When I was with her my sole focus was looking after her, constantly checking that she wasn't destroying anything or harming herself in the process.

Part-owning a dog was a completely new experience for Mike and, as such, he had little understanding of dog mentality. Our mad dog seemed to sense this and reacted towards him in a negative way. Typical example being that whilst he was relaxing on the couch after a busy day at the office, she would approach him and, and without warning, sink her razor sharp teeth into his face. I liked to think that her behaviour was innocuous but, deep down, I don't think it was. It wasn't the usual teething puppy sort of bite, but more of a vicious premeditated bite, with intent to hurt. At such times those nagging doubts entered my head again; Why was she the last puppy in the litter? Was there something not quite right about her that the others had spotted but we hadn't?

Mike continued to bear the brunt of her bad behaviour. He must have deeply regretted the day our new boarder shacked up with us. Not knowing what had hit him, he said it was like living with a wild animal. In fact, he wasn't too far off the mark; after all, dogs and wolves are 98% genetically identical, hence the dog evolves from wild animals. It takes careful training to domesticate a dog, and depending on the breed, some are easier to train than others. I had to agree with him though, she was rather wild. I also began to think we had been misled by some of the literature we had found when researching the breed. Everything we read pointed to the conclusion that Retrievers are lovely placid dogs, that will do anything to please their owner. I'm not sure what thoughts went through her fluffy head half the time, but I'm sure pleasing us wasn't one of them!

Continuing to ignore our commands and preferring to concentrate on developing her horticultural skills, she became a dab hand around the garden. In a relative short space of time she had dug most of the plants out of the flower beds, leaving only a few robust shrubs intact but lots of nice new deep craters. I was proud of the few flowers we had managed to salvage, in particular my crop of hardy Agapanthus. This spectacular flower starts life as a green pod protruding from the end of a long thin stem. The pod gets bigger and bigger, then eventually metamorphoses into a beautiful blue flower, like a butterfly emerging from its chrysalis. I always looked forward to the flowers coming into bloom; unfortunately, so did Brece. She was also attracted by the beautiful vivid blue colour and usually proceeded to kindly separate the heads from the stems for me. The flowers took about six weeks to bloom, then thirty seconds for her to guillotine them!

Her digging was beginning to get out of control. She was regularly found excavating the lawns to the back of the house. As if by magic, two large holes suddenly appeared overnight by the living room back door, one on each side. The more we tried to fill in the holes, the harder Brece worked to dig them out again, as if it was some sort of manic game. She dug so far down that eventually the footings of the house became exposed. Naturally, we didn't know how long her digging phase was going to last, but we hoped it would abate before the house started to subside.

Although still a puppy Brece was already quite a size and a force to be reckoned with, both strong and untrained, not a good combination. Visitors were frequently subjected to her rambunctious behaviour. She continually jumped up at people, almost knocking them off their feet when offering her overly enthusiastic greetings. Personally I preferred to think of her behaviour as boisterous as opposed to bad. She loved to see people and was unable to contain herself, always giving them a heartfelt chaotic welcome.

Mike's sister, Chloe, came to see us on a regular basis. One visit in particular sticks in my mind. It was summer, Brece was outside working on some finishing touches to her external renovations. A new hole had now appeared directly outside the back door, effectively joining up the two holes on either side. Although it was summer, it was a wet one. The previous weeks had provided heavy rainfall and a moat had effectively formed at the perimeter of the house.

Access to the garden now entailed jumping across the moat to avoid falling in it, a drawbridge would not have gone amiss. Although still in the garden the sound of Mike opening the front door alerted Brece to the fact that we had a guest. From my vantage point in the lounge I could see both Chloe at the front door and Brece tending to her duties in the garden. Chloe was always well groomed and well-dressed, even when coming around to ours in full knowledge that we had a mad crazy pup in our midst. On this particular occasion she was wearing a pretty green dress and matching green shoes. In contrast Brece was covered from head to paw to tail in mud, *not so well-dressed*. The second I saw the state of her I tried to stop her getting to Chloe but it was too late; our mad dog was on a mission to reach the object of her attentions.

With the force of a baby ox she immediately proceeded to bulldoze her way through the opened door, into the living room and across the modest hall to greet Chloe, front of house. After leaving a splattering of mud on the floors and furnishings, she jumped up at Chloe and wiped her filthy paws all over her pristine green dress, before head-butting her in the eye. As she reeled from the impact both her arms instinctively shot out to steady herself. Swaying like an aquatic plant, she nearly went down but somehow managed to regain her balance. Her left eye immediately began to swell and water profusely, causing her mascara to smudge. That poor woman, she had arrived at our house looking immaculate and left resembling a dishevelled green Alice Cooper. Thankfully Chloe took it all in good nature, even laughing as she left.

I don't particularly like to see a dog that has been 'over trained' to the point where it is void of personality, never putting a paw wrong. But I do think there should be a happy medium; a dog that is well trained but still has traits of its own personality. Brece did not fall into either of these categories. She wasn't your typical Golden Retriever whose traits are extremely friendly, intelligent, tolerant and forgiving of mistakes made by their owners. Brece was most of those things but she certainly was not

18

tolerant towards Mike. When it came to him, she operated a zero-tolerance regime. As well as her bad behaviour towards him, we hadn't managed to make much progress with her basic commands either. I had a little control over her, but Mike had absolutely none.

Although we had done our homework when deciding on which breed to get, it was becoming apparent that we hadn't done too much investigation into the training side of things. Perhaps I was complacent, my previous dogs had been a relative breeze in comparison to Brece. Besides Frisco, I previously owned an Alsatian bitch, which I acquired as soon as I left the family home. Whilst both my previous dogs had been boisterous pups, they had been relatively easy to train. Brece on the other hand was a completely different kettle of fish. It was time to do something about her errant behaviour, we needed some sort of demarcation, especially for Mike's sake.

When she was six months old, we decided to seek professional help with regards to her stubborn and wilful personality, and paid a visit to the vets, to discuss matters. With hindsight, I'm not sure why we didn't go to puppy training classes or why the vet didn't recommend classes but all the same the vet was most helpful. After we had explained the problems that we were experiencing with her, the vet informed us the main reasons for our problems were due to hierarchy in our pack; Brece saw herself as over and above Mike. Whilst she accepted me as the alpha (perhaps this was due to the bond that had developed between us on that first car journey), she saw herself as the beta and Mike as the omega. In other words, in her eyes, I was head of the house, closely followed by her, with Mike firmly rooted at the bottom of the ladder.

We were sent away with instructions on how to get Mike further up the ladder. The vet explained that Mike had to take control of the situation, he needed to be assertive with her and persistently work at his commands, never giving in to her. We were also given a plug-in, which once plugged into an electric socket was designed to release replica pheromones. Supposedly the same sort of pheromones emanated by siblings when in the litter, which create a harmonious, calming atmosphere. Mike was enthused that we now had a plan and set about putting his training tactics into place. But it was a battle of wills and Brece's will was clearly the stronger of the two. When he realised that he wasn't making any progress, he threw the towel in. With regards to the plug-in, it's hard to say if it had any effect on her behaviour or not, let's just say she continued to look at Mike as if he was a buffoon, rather than a dear puppy sibling.

We decided to do some research on the life-cycle of puppies for ourselves, *nothing like shutting the stable door after the horse has bolted!* We were to learn two key points. Firstly- in the litter the more dominant dogs will get more milk, while the submissive dogs will learn to wait, these are primeval instincts. Perhaps Brece was one of these greedy dominant dogs, but as she was the last dog left, we had no way of knowing for sure. With hindsight, perhaps we should have asked the breeder more questions, but at the time there was no way I was going to leave that farm dog-less, meaning that everything else was practically irrelevant. Secondly; generally speaking training should start at nine weeks. This is where we failed miserably, we didn't start her training until she was about four months. Ideally, we should have been on the case as soon as we brought her home. That is apart from house training. She picked that up quickly and never messed in the house from the age of ten weeks. For further details of the life cycle of a puppy refer appendix B

In my experience, a puppy doesn't tend to have much eye contact with their owner, the world is an exciting place, and they are too busy flying around causing havoc. Suddenly when Brece was just over eight months of age things started to change, she began to make eye contact with me. At around about the same time, her behaviour appeared to improve, she was now responding much better to my commands and taking more notice of me.

Life with Brece was beginning to get just a little bit easier for me but not quite so for Mike, but at least the 'biting his face off' phase appeared to be over. Although she still clearly didn't like him, Mike did not appear to take offence, He always did his fair share of caring, walking, feeding and so forth. Despite everything he never had a bad word for her, and always said that she deserved the best of everything. I quite admired his attitude towards her; somehow, if the shoe was on the other foot, I think I may have resented walking a dog that didn't particularly like me. He never seemed to notice her body language towards him, and I wasn't about to draw attention to it. Whilst she tolerated me more than Mike, she still wasn't 100% accepting of me either. My continual showering her with love and affection wore a bit thin at times. If I overstepped the mark, she showed her disapproval by gently growling at me. A subtle growl but all the same a warning. This was my cue to get out of her space and leave the little madam alone.

As time went by, we added names to Brece's title. I prefixed 'Princess', Mike added 'Madam' (for obvious reasons), then later she became 'Of Heyhouses' making her full title 'Princess Madame Brece of Heyhouses'. It was as if the more names we bestowed on her, the greater the measure of our love for her. However, we eventually decided that five names was probably enough!

Chapter 4

Dog boarding 2005

Thanks to the implementation of the 'Pet Passport scheme' Mike and I were able to take Brece along with us to Brece, Normandy. When the three of us visited France our days out usually consisted of walks in the many beautiful national parks, or along the river-banks with Brece swimming as we walked. We were also partial to visiting the historic medieval towns. The most notable trip happened when we visited the historic town of Mayenne on Bastille day 14th July 2005. It was memorable but no in a good way.

Mayenne is just one of many surviving Medieval towns. are few and far between in the country. Most of the medieval towns are built on both sides of a river with a bridge connecting the two sides together. The towns are always host to at least one church and of course the token château. That evening a firework extravaganza had been arranged in celebration of Bastille day. We decided to go along to watch the display but thought it best to leave Brece behind in the car. The display had already started by the time we left her but she remained calm, the noise from the firework explosions was not bothering her one iota. We thought nothing of leaving her in the little Renault.

We took our place amongst the crowds alongside the riverbank and directly in front of the château. The display was spectacular with the château making for a magnificent backdrop. Although the fireworks were stunning, they were incredibly loud, probably the loudest I had ever heard at the time. I wondered to myself if Brece would still be okay and tried to reassure myself that she would be fine, but I still had that niggling doubt. Returning to the car it soon became obvious that she had not been okay. We found her in an awful state of anxiety, crying and panting profusely. The whole thing had clearly been too much for her, she must have thought she was under siege. That poor dog she certainly had to call on her stash of 'Retriever Forgiveness' living with us two! From that point on, she was always terrified of fireworks, as are so many dogs. After all, the noise of a firework will sound about eight times louder to a dog than to us which can be a terrible ordeal for dogs and indeed most pets. For further details on the dogs hearing abilities refer appendix C.

Back in blighty in October of that year, one evening a couple of weeks leading up to before Bonfire Night, we went out and left Brece at home for a few hours. By the time we returned, it was obvious that she had been distressed, she was pacing up and down with a wild unsettled look in her eyes. We drew the obvious conclusion that fireworks had been going off in the vicinity. Although Mike and I had no way of knowing that it was going to happen, we felt awful that we hadn't foreseen that it might be on the cards. Expecting some damage to the furnishings, we checked the place out. We discovered that in our absence she had busied herself in the utility room by munching her way through the toilet seat. The adjacent washing machine had also come under fire and she had chewed the rubber seal from inside it. Not content with that; at some point in the proceedings she had taken herself off to the lounge and chewed her way through the artificial coals from the gas fire. She must have been terrified; we were full of remorse that she had suffered so. It was fortuitous that I had invested in a protection policy for my household appliances, but I did have a bit of a job convincing the washing machine repair man that the seal had simply perished!

Initially, I couldn't understand why her fears and anxieties drove her to do such random acts. Then I remembered Frisco, our old family dog who also had a fear of fireworks. At times of anxiety she had a penchant for getting into the bath which appeared to calm her to a point. Putting two and two together, I came to the conclusion that perhaps Brece was attempting to hide away from the fireworks, trying to find a small safe place, like an air raid shelter, a bunker even. If only everyone understood exactly what effect fireworks can have on animals.

When she was three-years old, we had another memorable day out with her, this time memorable for more positive reasons. Driving passed the local theatre on a regular basis Mike and I noticed an advert for a forthcoming event 'PDSA fun dog show'. We had no intentions of showing her competitively, but a fun dog show in the aid of charity seemed like a great idea. We decided to give it a go and see how she would fare on the doggy parade circuit, so I put her name down as an entrant. By this time, she was reasonably well-behaved, but she still had her moments, or character as I preferred to call it. Just to be on the safe side we decided to take some swede along with us for back-up, just in case we had any issues with her. Swede had become her favourite treat, she would do anything for a piece of the amber root vegetable. The big day arrived and the three of us trotted off down to the show with hearts full of hope and pockets full of swede.

The Doggy Parade was well attended; the place was packed with expectant dog owners with their happy pooches. It was not the chaotic scene that one might expect. The dogs were remarkably well-behaved, with no incidents or fur flying. Brece had never been in a place with so many people and dogs, as such we had no idea how she was going to react. For those first few minutes she was extremely hyper and just about the most excitable dog in the place. It wasn't looking as though she was going to behave well enough to do what was expected of her; not that a great deal was called for. All that was required from the entrants was a quick walk around the indoor arena, with their dog on lead, for a selected category. I expected Brece to calm down a bit once she had become acclimatised to her new strange surroundings, but she remained on high alert the whole time. She was acutely distracted by everything going on around her, continually pulling on her leash and trying to run off in the opposite direction. If someone came within two metres of us, she jumped up at them, taking no notice of our 'down' commands, that was until we revealed our secret weapon, the swede! Armed with the vegetable we now had control, giving us a certain amount of confidence about the forthcoming proceedings. She became transfixed on the swede, suddenly everything else that had previously enthralled her, became completely insignificant. I don't think I have ever seen a vegetable have such an effect on a dog.

After careful deliberation we decided to enter her into three categories, she did what was expected, and achieved great results. She came fourth in the waggiest tail category which struck us as slightly odd as she was sat down for the most part, and therefore unable to wag her tail. She got third in the bonniest eyes, and second in the prettiest bitch categories.

Even though it was a light-hearted affair we walked away with our three rosettes bursting with pride, it was if we had won best in show at Crufts. Returning home, we continued to bask in our sea of glory. After admiring the rosettes for many an hour, we eventually put them away in a drawer, but frequently went back to the drawer to indulge in yet another dose of pride. Brece seemed to understand that she had done something to be proud of, each time we opened the drawer she became incredibly excited. It was as if she was picking up on our emotions and knew that the rosettes had great importance attached to them. If we proceeded to get them out of the drawer, she started barking and jumping up and down, with her 'fourth waggiest' tail going hell for leather.

As a reward, I allowed her to sleep on my bed that night. This is a bad habit to get into, but I couldn't help myself. One night turned into two, then three and so on. With the three of us in that bed, things were getting a tad cramped until Brece came up with a solution. In her usual inimitable style, she started growling at Mike every time he tried to enter the bedroom. The problem was made worse by the fact that Brece and I used to turn in at the same time, whilst Mike preferred to stay up into the early hours playing computer games. By the time he came to bed we were fast asleep. Being disturbed didn't go down too well with me or indeed Brece, she demonstrated her opinions vocally. If he continued to approach towards the bed, her growling intensified, if that didn't deter him, she curled her lip. He usually threw the towel in at this point, conceded defeat, then made his way to the spare room. I knew I was condoning her behaviour, I should have banished her from the bed and let Mike in, but I didn't, instead I gave in to her. Looking back, this was probably the beginning of the end of my relationship with Mike; I was to pay the price.

A few months after the excitement of the Doggy parade Mike and I went on a two-week holiday without her. It was our first holiday abroad other than going to France, since she had come into our lives. The plan was to board her in kennels. In those days there weren't the home boarding options that there are today, people had no options other than entrusting their pets with family, friends or failing that boarding kennels. Booking her in at what we thought were 'superior' kennels, we felt reassured. The clue was in the name; 'Alpha Superior Kennels'. The name and their write up gave us confidence that it was a good establishment.

However, dropping her off at the kennels on the way to the airport, she appeared to know that something was wrong, she became highly worried and anxious. As we got out of the car, her anxiety increased even further. By digging her heels into the gravel, and refusing to budge, she made her feelings clear. But after a bit of a struggle, we managed to get her inside. Although she had previously never set paw in a kennel, she appeared to instinctively know that something was wrong, very wrong! Mike and I stood at the reception desk with Brece cowering behind us, determinedly attempting to make a run for it back outside to freedom.

The receptionist was a tall woman in her late twenties with short cropped hair, natural complexion and strong physique. By reading the name on the badge pinned to her oversized green sweat-shirt, I was able to deduce that she was called Jude.

Hoping for some sort of reassurance that Brece really would be staying in a luxury kennel, I asked Jude if we could see where our petrified dog was going to be staying. Rather surprisingly my request was flatly refused. When I pressed for an explanation, Jude curtly told me;

"Because it would disturb the other dogs."

At this point alarm bells were ringing loudly in my head, the dogs had to be disturbed at some point, so why not now? It was as though there was something to hide, but what could we do now? We were literally on our way to the airport. As I held onto Brece's lead, she stared at me the whole time, eyes trustingly boring into mine with a distinct look of fear in them.

Jude made her way over to us, taking the lead from me she tried to lead our dog away. But Brece refused to cooperate, staying rooted to the spot and continuing her frightened stare, still directed at me. With gritted determination, Jude managed to drag her towards the door that led to the elusive kennel *it was becoming apparent how Jude had acquired her strong physique*. As Brece was being dragged away, her head continually turned towards me, she never took her big sad brown eyes off me. To make matters worse, she was now whining incessantly.

The whole time there was no dialogue from Jude, she acted as if it was all part of the daily routine, par for the course, *perhaps it was*. Brece's reaction filled me with sorrow, my dog trusted me, I was failing her miserably. Mike and I had no words for each other, we left her in that place under an oppressive dark cloud saturated with guilt.

The two weeks passed slowly and we couldn't wait to go and collect her. I was extremely excited at the prospect and looking forward to being reunited with my dog again. Once again Jude was on duty, she brought Brece into the reception area to greet us. But it was not the reunion I had yearned for. She hardly seemed like the same dog; standing in silence her head was bowed, tail between her legs and she looked as though she had lost weight. I was expecting her to be happy to see us, but nothing could have been further from the truth, she was incredibly subdued.

On top of everything else she looked dirty, closer inspection revealed that shockingly, she stank of urine. It appeared that her instincts about the kennels were correct. What had we done to our beloved dog? In stark contrast to when we left her there, she was now refusing to engage in eye contact with either of us. I called her name and tried to give her encouragement, but it was ineffectual. Initially, I thought Brece was sulking with us for leaving her behind. But, knowing what I know now, I think her experience in the kennels had been a trauma for her. It was highly probable that she had suffered anxiety. Some dogs are quite happy to board in a kennel and there are some very good establishments out there, but it's not for all dogs. It was about two weeks before Brece returned to her normal self.

Feeling incredibly contrite about what we had done to our dog, Mike and I vowed that we would never let her stay in kennels again. We had a lot of making up to do to our dog. To this day I am still haunted by the fact that I went on holiday and left my dog in a place where I knew she was frightened and scared.

Months later whilst walking around my local neighbourhood with Brece, I got to know Gillian; a woman who lived about three streets away. Every time we bumped into her; she always made a fuss of my dog. In conversation I gleaned that Gillian looked after dogs in her own home, for a fee of course. Boarding dogs in private homes was an up and coming trend, and a much softer option than kennels. Gillian went on to say that if I was ever stuck, she would be happy to look after Brece for me. This was music to my ears, a great solution and definitely the way forward for us. For future holidays Her Royal Highness tended to stay with Gillian.

At first, I was slightly dubious about leaving her behind, probably because I was still mentally scared by the awful kennel experience. However, I need not have worried. Returning from holiday and picking our dog up from Gillian's, I was greeted by a happy Brece running down the stairs, barking and protecting her new surroundings. She had the run of the place, it was pleasing that she felt comfortable enough to want to protect her temporary home. Asking Gillian if my dog had missed me, I got a straight "No." I must admit a little part of me wanted the answer to be "Yes," but, all in all, it was far better for everyone that my dog hadn't missed me.

The reunion was, thankfully, a stark contrast to the previous one at the kennels. Our dog was extremely happy; it was if we had never been away and such a relief to us. Gillian later went on to tell me that Brece had taken to protecting her, to the point where she refused to allow her partner in the bedroom at night. Our dog had got herself into the habit of sitting by the bedroom door, growling and snarling as Gillian's partner tried to make his way to his bed. Without any hesitation, my fickle dog had replaced me with Gillian. She appeared to be able to happily latch herself onto a new pack leader. Dogs do this instinctively, in the wild, there are times when a new pack leader will take over, and the pack members must accept the dog in order to survive. Sometimes I suspect dogs are probably more accepting of a new leadership than humans are.

Chapter 5

Parting of ways 2007

Although my relationship with Brece was amazing, it was partly at the expense of my relationship with Mike. Our unique sleeping arrangements certainly had not helped matters. Sadly, after ten years together Mike and I parted company. Even though in a roundabout way I had put Brece before him, I still felt great sadness that things had turned out as they had. After our separation, there were many moments when I was down and in a reflective mood. Like most dogs, Brece picked up on my low spirits and comforted me by sitting by my side, and performing her repertoire of lovely cute tricks. These included sitting back on her hind legs with her front legs in front of her chest waiting for me to catch her paws. Her balance was quite remarkable for a dog of her size. For some unknown reason I referred to this position as 'Teddy'. She demonstrated 'Teddy' when ever we had visitors; it was always a crowd pleaser and never failed to earn her lots of attention. Every time she got into position, and she did it a lot, I felt happy and proud of her. When she tired of 'Teddy' she gave me her paw to hold, as if she was reaching out to me, her way of giving me a big hug. Like all dogs, she said so much without words. My sensitive dog always seemed to understand my feelings and genuinely appeared to care about me. Research has shown that dogs can improve our mental and physical well-being. Owning a dog can reduce stress, anxiety, and depression; that is, of course, if you are a dog lover and assuming you don't have a rambunctious dog in tow.

A few months after Mike had moved out of Heyhouses, my twenty-six-year-old niece, Sally, moved in. Previously she lived with my sister Anna in Hereford but found herself at a crossroads in her life and wanted a new start. The plan was to try her luck 'Up North'. Having her around the place was a Godsend; she paid her way, which was a great help with the massive mortgage I had inherited. I also enjoyed her company and so did Brece who immediately accepted her into the fold and showed her far more tolerance than she had ever shown to Mike.

Sally got herself a job working with children in care a few miles from my house. The children required round the clock attention which meant she had to work her fair share of night shifts. Never really having a handle on her shift schedule, consequently I never knew when to expect her home. We were ships that passed in the night, sometimes we didn't see each other for days on end. Although I didn't know when to expect her, Brece on the other hand always did. It didn't matter what time she came home; she instinctively knew the moment Sally had pulled up outside in her car. What's more, she also understood that Sally now lived with us, therefore, she didn't warrant the usual fanfare of barking. This was a blessing, as it meant there was no disturbance to me or indeed the neighbours, especially during the twilight hours. In contrast, whenever a visitor arrived, she barked incessantly, even if she knew them well. Amazingly, she was able to distinguish between Sally now living with me, and a visitor just calling in, without even seeing her. It's proven that dogs can learn to detect the noise of different cars. The likelihood was that by drawing on her senses, she recognised the sound of Sally's car and also her scent.

There may also have been other factors; some people think dogs have a third eye, an Extra Sensory Perception (ESP), claiming that dogs know when people are due home. The dog will sit in the window or by the door patiently waiting for his master's imminent arrival. But how does the dog know the arrival is imminent? A logical explanation could be that there is an environmental action that triggers the dog's behaviour. For example, a bus may routinely go past the house just before the owner is due home. The dog will get to learn this, realising that when the bus goes by the owner will return shortly after. Or it could be that some dogs do possess a form of ESP; I believe this is the case, and that Brece is possibly one such dog. One of the reasons I have come to this conclusion is that at times I swear she understands what I am thinking.

A good example is she always knows when it's her turn to go on a walk, even though the timings are completely random. This alone does not sound too astonishing, but the facts are that, as a dog walker, I am in and out of the house several times a day, yet only one of these trips is her time for a walk. Obviously picking up her lead would be a giveaway, but I never take her lead, she jumps straight into the car, then straight out onto the beach at the other end, so the lead is not the trigger. When it is her turn, as with most dogs, she is excitable, continually jumping up and barking. When it's not her turn, she gets it, and just sits there watching me leave. But how does she know? I'm convinced it's because the thought goes through my head; 'Right, it's Brece's turn for a walk now.' At the exact moment she seems to read my mind, there is no environmental trigger, therefore no other explanation.

Other dog owners have similar tales. A close friend has two children of school age. The children religiously phone their mother after they have finished school to let her know exactly what time they will be home.

Sometimes the children go home straight after school, on other occasions they go to a friend's house for tea, and don't return for a few hours. Regardless of how long the children are going to be, she always finishes the conversation with the same dialogue; 'Okay, see you soon.' If the arrival is not imminent the dog goes about things in his usual manner. However, if the children are coming home straight away, the dog runs to the window and patiently waits for the child. The only possible explanation for this is that the dog can read his owner's mind, again there is no other trigger. But of course there is no scientific evidence to support this theory yet, leaving many people understandably sceptical to such revelations.

Chapter 6

As one door closes 2010

I had spent most of my working career employed by a large insurance company based in my home-town of Lytham St. Anne's; a small town situated on the Northwest Coast directly south of Blackpool, Lancashire. The area comprises of Lytham and the second town of St Anne's, with Ansdell and Fairhaven nestled in between. The whole area is collectively known as Lytham St Anne's. The location is considered to be a pleasant coastal retirement destination, at least it is on the TV programme Coronation Street where the characters often refer to the area as 'The Opal of the North'.

In the 19th century, it was the wealthy mill owners from East Lancashire who built many of the affluent properties that pepper the town. Rich in golf courses, the resort boasts five links courses; one of which being Royal Lytham which is frequently home to the British Open Competition. I was born and bred in St Anne's, as were my parents, so not exactly a family of intrepid explorers.

After thirty years of loyal service to the insurance company and working as an IT Business Analyst, I was put 'At Risk'. Being 'At Risk' is a strange process whereby you are told that your job has effectively gone, even though you are still doing it. You are then encouraged to apply for other jobs that may or may not appear out of the ether. This all came as a massive shock to me although I don't know why as departments were continually being reviewed with the intention of cost cutting. The staff payroll is typically the biggest overhead that a large company incurs, and therefore a prime target for financial cutbacks. When it happened to me it was somewhat of a body blow, the company's decision left me feeling rejected, devastated even. How could they do this to me after decades of loyal service? Was I really that disposable, what about all the experience and knowledge I had accrued along the way: did that not count for anything? The feeling of being thrown on the scrap heap was tough to take.

In the past, many of my colleagues went through the same sorry ordeal. Some fared well, happy to take the settlement, then others not quite so well. One person in particular suffered from anxiety and depression after he was given the bleak news; sadly, he was never mentally the same ever again. I often wondered if the company had a real handle on how their decisions could affect people's lives, and in particular, their mental health.

After thinking long and hard about my situation and after a couple of weeks of feeling sorry for myself, I started to accept the situation. In a strange sort of juxtaposition I began to see things in a different light. I had now decided that I actually wanted to leave the company, take the money and run. It had slowly dawned on me that I now had an opportunity to do something completely different with my life. About time, after thirty years of working in the same place. Unfortunately, things weren't quite that straightforward. Just as I had come to terms with the situation, my manager suddenly told me that redundancy may not be offered to me, after all. I was then encouraged to apply for other jobs which had now miraculously appeared out of the ether. When I failed to do so, the jobs were offered to me. This left me in a weird situation where I was trying to persuade my managers not to employ me. In a strange twist of fate, the prospect of remaining in the office had now become an abhorrent idea.

Despite their redundancy strategies the insurance company had been a good place to work. It would have been better still if we had been allowed to bring dogs into the office. Sitting at my desk, I frequently daydreamed about Brece, imagining her running up and down the floor. She would have cheered us all up, I'm sure of it. Proud new parents were permitted to bring their new-borns into work, so why couldn't proud dog owners bring their dogs in? I didn't particularly enjoy seeing babies in the office, all it did for me was highlight my lack of maternal 'cuddling the baby' instincts.

Most of the other girls seemed to relish cradling the infant. We were all treated to a go, I dreaded my turn. Once the babe was in my clutches I tried to do and say all the right things, but always felt uncomfortable and fake. Even if the baby started crying, or worse vomited, the other girls still seemed to be in awe. I was more in tune with my male colleagues who just kept their heads down and pretended nothing out of the ordinary was happening. But a puppy on the premises, would have been a different matter, I would have been besotted, with no need for faked emotions, I bet even the men folk would have responded to a dog.

As employees, we enjoyed great benefits, affordable mortgage rates, final salary pension, oh, and the canteen. A magical place to enjoy good food with friends. In those days food was our God. The morning conversations with my girlfriends went along the lines of; "What are you having for lunch?"

In the afternoon the conversation unimaginatively evolved to, "What are you having for dinner?"

The males amongst us sometimes joined in the stimulating culinary conversations, that was if there wasn't a football match worth mentioning. On a Monday morning the footie fans arrived at the office to be greeted with,

"How did you do on Saturday?"

It amused me no end the way they spoke about the glorious game, as if they had been on the pitch themselves, and not just watching it on TV. It was as if people with an interest in football were members of some sort of elite club. Having absolutely no interest in the game myself, sometimes I felt slightly excluded from the prestigious group. Despite all the chatting that went on, as long as we reached our targets and goals, talking wasn't frowned upon. It was a mature and relaxed environment in which to work.

Eventually in December 2010 after much toing and froing, the company finally granted me a redundancy offer. With mixed emotions, I was now embarking on the next chapter of my life. I had enjoyed my career at the insurance company, making great friends over the years. But working in an office environment for such a long period of time was not dissimilar to being in a bubble. At times I felt like an ageing Alice in Wonderland, things could seem surreal and insular.

At the age of fifty, and still owing quite a hefty mortgage I needed some sort of income but had no idea how to obtain it. However, my satisfactory redundancy settlement would bide me some time, so there was no immediate rush to get back on that treadmill. In the meantime, I would enjoy my freedom. After thirty years of early mornings, of which I wasn't a big fan, lying in bed was going to be a marvellous treat. A few months elapsed, I was beginning to get bored of doing nothing, even lying in late wasn't all it was cracked up to be. It appeared that I had lost my talent for blissful sleep. Ironically, the older we get the less sleep we need. Just when we have the opportunity to slumber all day long, our sleep-inducing hormones reduce. Lying around in bed in the hope of regaining my sleep hormones, was futile. It was time to do something more productive with my life.

I found myself applying for a few part-time jobs. In the theme of doing something completely different to analytical work, I cast my net. Unemployment figures were high at the time, there was a lot of competition out there, but I continued my quest. The idea of receptionist work appealed, probably because it was completely different from my previous job. I imagined the role of a receptionist to be interesting, an opportunity to meet new people and have fun at the same time. An image of the receptionists in an Alan Partridge 'Knowing me, knowing you' TV comedy sketch sprang to mind; those receptionists had a ball. Fun was a big factor for me. I was happy to take on a little responsibility, but the thought of being anchored to an intense role, was by no means appealing. A junior role would suffice.

Dipping my toe in the turbulent employment waters, I applied for a couple of receptionist positions. It was no surprise to learn that I was unsuccessful in my applications, but a shock to discover that about 50 people were applying for the same roles as myself. Obviously, with no experience as a receptionist, I didn't stand a cat in hell's chance. I needed to come up with a plan B, so decided to turn my attentions to volunteering. Obviously, there would be no remuneration but the rewards would come in different ways. It would be light-hearted, good fun, with none of the pressures associated with working for a salary; this could be it, *or so I thought*.

After considering the various charity shops in the local town, I decided to offer my services at the Cancer Research shop. I had lost my mother to the disease the previous year, so working for Cancer Research seemed a logical choice; my way of doing my bit and also in memory of my mother. I did, however, feel slightly anxious about plan B. What if I was unsuccessful in getting a position, meaning that I couldn't even get a job working for nothing? How incredibly demoralising would that be? But it was a gamble that I was prepared to take.

As a child, I recall the great fear surrounding the disease. Nobody even said the word in full. It was always referred to as 'The big C'. If people felt brave enough to say the word in its entirety, it was whispered. In those days if someone was suffering from the illness, they were usually a goner. Once diagnosed, suffers weren't expected to survive for very long. These days the survival rates are greatly improved. A cancer patient is now twice as likely to go into remission than in the 1970s. But as we live in an ageing, increasingly toxic society, the disease appears to be on the increase. However, great advances in research are continually being made. The disease is now more treatable, although having to endure the treatment itself can be quite awful. Nowadays people no longer feel obliged to whisper or abbreviate the word 'Cancer'; it is said quite openly.

I was successful in my application at the shop, *thank God for that.* My duties immediately commenced, working two days a week. The shop was managed by George, a middle-aged, tall, slim Glaswegian, who enjoyed the benefits of a salary. Working in the shop it didn't take long to unearth from the customers, that paying charity workers a salary is somewhat of a controversial topic. There is a school of thought who believe all monies should be donated directly to the charity, whilst others say it has been proven that paid professionals increase the company profits. My thoughts on the subject were ambivalent, but I do know that George earned every penny he got. Working like a trojan he also expected the volunteers to do the same; this was the part that I had an issue with. The rest of the staff were unpaid volunteers without the same motivation or financial incentive as George. I was prepared to do a good day's work but at the same time I wanted to have some fun and not take things too seriously. Voluntary work at the shop wasn't quite the relaxed environment that I assumed it would be. It wasn't looking as though I was going to find myself too much amusement within the confines of the charity shop walls.

Working at the shop was quite an eye opener in many other ways, some people were incredibly generous with their donations, then others were just abhorrent by using us as a refuse bin. Early one midweek morning, George was rummaging through the large plastic bags of clothing donations, and I was working on the shop floor. Suddenly I heard a shout coming from George in the back. I shuddered to myself and wondered what had happened. Rushing into to the back, it was a relief to find that George was OK, well sort of. He was shouting out in disgust at the discovery of a used nappy, amongst the clothes! Then there was the time when the interior of the shop was being painted by inmates from Kirkham prison. One inmate fell off his ladder and although he emerged unscathed, he tried to sue the organisation for damages; After that event health and safety became a massive issue, another of George's tasks.

At times I took offence at some of the customer's comments. When on the till, some people tried bartering me down over the price of an item. All stock was at rock-bottom prices to start with and all for charity. But to me, the cardinal sin was the shoplifting! It was difficult to comprehend how some people could steal from a charity organisation. Of course, the shop was an easy target; with no security system in place we were like sitting ducks. During my time there I had witnessed an unattractive side of humanity; all things considered, I decided to leave the shop.

For a couple of months after leaving I did very little and quickly found myself getting bored again. Then slowly and organically, I started looking after my friend's pets while they were away on holiday. It was a pleasure to take care of their animals and something that I really enjoyed, filling both the nurturing and mirth voids in my life. This was what I had been waiting to land in my lap, pet care, but perhaps on a more professional basis. The thought of being paid to look after animals would be a win-win situation. After all, there was obviously a demand. With a quarter of all households in the UK owning at least one dog, I am certainly not alone in my love for animals. In fact, I would hazard a guess that in my local town the number of dog owners, is probably above the national average. Local people are crazy about their dogs; this affection extends itself to just about all dogs in the community.

People will do almost anything for a dog in trouble. The Lytham Beagle is a perfect example of the camaraderie that a missing dog can muster. The dog went missing and thanks to the marvel of social media, a large search party was immediately organised. There were several sightings of the dog but it was not found. The search continued late into the night but was abandoned shortly after midnight, the intention being to re-group early the next day. At 4 am the following morning the dog turned up on its own doorstep. The clever Beagle's nose, which was probably the thing that got it lost in the first-place sniffing for food, had led the dog home. The owners immediately alerted social media with the good news. Within twenty-four hours of the notification being posted, there were fifteen hundred messages of heartfelt relief published on the site. I don't think there are many other things that can muster up the good in people as much as a missing dog.

It is no secret that man has an incredibly unique relationship with his dog, there are many reasons why the dog is man's best friend. Apart from being loyal pets, dogs devotedly work for us in many ways and all they ask in return is food, affection, a walk and perhaps the odd ball thrown in for good measure. For details of the services the dog devotedly provides for people refer appendix D.

But of course, the most common role for the dog is as a pet. We have a great affinity with our dogs and love them for their incredible affection and loyalty amongst all of their many other attributes. A friend of mine makes the analogy that if he locked both his wife and dog in his car for hours on end, then let them out, he would naturally receive a stream of torrid abuse from his spouse. The dog, on the other hand would give him a tumultuous welcome, even though he had locked him up and left him. Personally, I think it is this unconditional love that attracts us to the dog, coupled with their ability to show great empathy towards us and, of course, their aesthetically pleasing appearance.

With all this in mind, I decided to do some investigating into dog-related job opportunities. Initially, my idea was to assist a Professional Dog Walker (PDW). So, in typical fashion, I googled 'dog walking', to see what was out there. K9Kreche Pet sitters appeared at the top of the browser, run by a lady called Carol who was based in Blackpool. Reading the blurb, I learned that K9Kreche was part of a nationwide franchise group, which was established in 2005 with over thirty branches across the UK. The group offers various pet sitting services, focusing on dog walking and dog boarding.

As luck would have it Carol was looking for someone to work in the St Anne's area, *right on my door-step, perfect*. At the time she was covering the location herself but as her business was growing, she was finding it increasingly difficult to cope with her workload. To my mind, this was a good indication that pet sitting was an expanding business. There was obviously an increasing demand for dog boarding in a home from home environment, as opposed to the more clinical environment of a kennel. People's preferences were shifting; a pet sitting boom had arrived on our doorstep, no doubt triggered by the ongoing research into dog behaviour. TV programmes on the subject of dogs had become commonplace.

One programme in particular that I tuned into, focused on separation anxiety in dogs. For the benefit of the programme, CCTV had been installed in the homes of several dog owners whilst they went out to work. Home alone the dogs were filmed. The programme revealed that approximately 70% of dogs suffered from anxiety when left, albeit at varying levels. Even owning multiple dogs did not always alleviate the anxiety in some pets. It was sad to see the owners watching the film back. One lady was in tears as she watched her dog crying and continually pacing up and down. Prior to the film she had absolutely no idea of the level of distress her dog suffered whilst she was at work.

The reason for the dog's anxiety is that they look upon their owners as the pack leader. When they are leaderless, they are instinctively worried and scared. My take on this is that in the wild the pack leader is with the dogs 24/7, he doesn't take himself off down to the office for a seven-hour stint, he is constantly with his pack, watching over them. The programme was quite an insight and a marvellous advert for the pet sitting fraternity.

I arranged to meet up with Carol and it all started from there. At the time there were a few other rival pet sitting franchises around. Some of them wanted quite a large sum of cash up front. The attraction of K9Creche being that there was no initial down payment and no payment required for the first six months. This seemed a reasonable amount of time in which to establish if things were going to work out, or not.

After the six-month period, the franchisor requested a royalty of seven percent of the franchisee's gross income. In return, K9Creche provided a website, supplied the public liability insurance at a cheap rate and offered support. In the early days, having the back-up from Carol, Sarah from South Shore and Michelle from Poulton was a Godsend. Initially it all seemed a bit too good to be true, and as we all know, things that appear too good to be true, invariably are. Even my family were dubious that there was going to be some sort of catch but I felt confident in what I was doing, Carol had given me that confidence.

I also received great support from the state in the form of a business start-up enterprise benefit, a Job Centre initiative intended to reduce unemployment figures. The amount payable was the princely sum of £50 per week for a three-month period. The state assigned me a support advisor, Terry, who helped me with a basic business plan. He also gave me accountancy assistance in order to help me complete my self-assessment online tax returns. Terry was always contactable if necessary, which was a great support in those early days.

I was ready to go. It seemed odd that no qualifications were required. Even dog groomers are obliged to undergo training, yet a dog boarder is permitted to care for a customer's dog for weeks on end without any sort of governance. Not even an animal first aid qualification was required. However, in some boroughs, dog boarders must apply for a council license in order to board dogs in the home environment. In those early days, I would have welcomed being vetted, as affirmation that I was on the right track and that everything was in order. But back in 2010 my local council did not operate such a scheme.

My only concern was that looking after dogs in my own home may be stressful for the animals, they might not settle when away from their own home environment. But then I remembered how comfortable Brece had been when staying with Gillian. Also, Carol and Sarah helped to put my mind at rest, by assuring me that the dogs boarding are generally extremely happy to be in the company of other dogs. Putting my concerns to bed, I decided to make a go of it.

I was now ready to go and excited at the prospect of what lay ahead. I would enjoy working for myself and building up my business empire and meeting new animals and people along the way. Not wishing to put all my eggs in one basket I decided to offer a variety of services:

- Dog walking- which entails pick up, drop off and one hour-long walk.
- Comfort breaks- fifteen to thirty-minute toilet break and play time.
- Dog boarding- dog boards in my home whilst owners are usually on holiday.
- Doggy day-care- looking after a dog for the core hours when the owner is at work.
- Puppy visits- which is much the same as comfort breaks except I get to play with an adorable puppy.
- Cat and small mammal pet sitting.
- House sitting- A requirement to house sit for customers that may have multiple pets and are going away.

Chapter 7

Getting started early 2011

The master plan was to work at my pet sitting enterprise for a period of five years. The intention being that during that time I would earn enough money to pay off my hefty mortgage, which I had now become the sole owner of. This was always going to be an ambitious target. My rationale being; the higher I set the bar, the harder I was likely to work, hence the more money I would earn than if my target had been realistic. Sharing details of my financial aims with Anna, she laughed out loud saying;

"That's a hell of a lot of dog walks."

This was indeed true but I felt confident that by sticking with it and putting the work in; I could achieve my aspirations.

Business was slow in the early days but gradually I began to accrue more clients. New customers came from various sources; the internet website, Carol and word of mouth. To help get things off the ground I got myself some snappy posters and cards printed. With permission I displayed a couple of posters in local pet shops, and left cards with the vets in the vicinity. I was encouraged to find that people were most helpful, enthusiastic even about supporting a new local business. A friend who still worked at the insurance company where I had worked, kindly offered to put a card up on the public notice board. This proved to be quite successful and I gained a few new customers that way; it was good to keep that contact with the old gang. All my avenues were fruitful, albeit in small volumes.

I also acquired new clients from a couple of local well-established dog walkers, Sam and Loz. When out walking with the dogs I regularly bumped into Loz and often found myself sharing the odd moan and groan with her, usually following an altercation I had just experienced with an irresponsible dog owner. By saying all the right words, she always managed to reassure me that I was in the right. Her disarming nature had the effect of making me feel safe and secure; not that I was overly insecure but blowing off a bit of steam in her direction always put my mind at rest.

The couple provided similar services to me and had been doing so for many years. They really knew their craft, proper dog lovers with a great reputation. Between them, they had seven of their own dogs, accumulated by gathering waifs and strays over the years. If one of their customers could sadly no longer care for their dog, the couple usually stepped into the breach. Even with so many pets of their own, somehow, they always seemed to find space for boarders. At the time the pair lived in a modest, three-bedroom semi, which was more like an animal sanctuary than a residential home.

Their place must have been bedlam at meal- times, even the nicest of hounds can be unpleasant when it comes to feeding time at the zoo. Ideally, dogs should be fed in different rooms, but Sam and Loz didn't have the luxury of the space to be able to do that. Initially, it was a mystery to me how they managed to feed the animals without fur flying. Then further on down the line I discovered that the couple owned a dual-purpose caravan which they kept parked up on their drive-way. When the caravan wasn't being used for recreational purposes it doubled up as a doggy canteen in which they fed the dogs, and in sittings.

Whilst out walking, and in the vein of amusing myself in the quieter moments, I imagined the inside of the caravan to be decked out in similar fashion to my old office canteen; Sam and Loz dressed as butchers standing behind a counter displaying prime cuts of meat. There would be sausages hanging up in the background, with the dogs queuing up in an orderly fashion, salivating as they deliberated over which cut of meat they fancied for dinner.

As Sam and Loz were constantly busy, they kindly passed new enquiries in my direction, all of which were gratefully received. Usually, it was a dog boarding enquiry that came my way; probably because this service is not quite as popular with all pet sitters, dog walking is usually more preferable. It makes sense as the typical fees are around £10 for an hour walk, and £17 for an overnight stay. Hence dog walking is comparatively more lucrative for a shorter period of time. Back then, apart from Sam and Loz, there were probably about six other local groups in the same line of business as our-selves.

Meeting with a new customer was similar in many ways to attending an interview. After introducing myself, I explained the services on offer, only too aware that I was being vetted, and quite rightly so. People want to know that they can trust the person who is potentially going to care for their pets, and in most cases have access to their homes. After having lived in the same town for half a century, it was usually the case that I found a connection somewhere along the line with most new clients. I thought it beneficial to try to identify any connections early on in the conversation. Familiarity can sometimes be a reassuring factor, and it also means the customer has the opportunity to obtain a reference from our 'mutual contact' should they so wish.

New customers were required to complete a service contract, which incorporated the terms and conditions. The contract was drawn up by the K9Kresche group, with the intention of capturing all the details of the dog's personality, allowing a clear profile to be built. This enabled me to get to know all the traits of the dogs, ensuring I could care for them properly. The customer also provided details of an emergency contact person, then dated and signed the contract and by doing so, gave their consent for me to look after their pet.

Once the animal was in my care and in the event of an incident due to negligence on my part, I was covered by public liability insurance. Alternatively, if the dog became ill from natural causes or suffered an unavoidable accident, then the onus was on the owner to meet any costs.

Working for myself was great in so many ways but it did mean that I now had to go out there and collect my wages for myself. The days when a nice salary magically appeared in my bank account were long since gone. Asking a customer for payment usually made me feel uncomfortable. But fortunately, most clients paid without being prompted, thus sparing me those awkward moments. Payments were made by various methods: cash, cheque, directly into my bank account or 'returned services', which means swapping services. To elaborate, I board my gardener's dog and she pays me by tending to my garden, no money is exchanged. By the same token; I don't physically pay for my haircuts or beauty treatments. After cash, my favourite currency is undoubtedly curry! One vegan customer frequently visits a divine vegan Indian takeaway restaurant in Preston and pays me with amazing culinary delights. This customer usually texts me to request a dog walk signing off with,

"Curry in the fridge."

But it's not all about the money. Taking payment from customers who need my services in sad circumstances, such as going to a funeral, is something that I can't bring myself to do. Similarly, I don't take money from people who cannot walk their dogs due to illness or any physical issues. If a person is out at work or going on holiday then that's fair enough, but if an old person is unable to continue walking their beloved dog, then that's a sad situation. I usually put such people in touch with the 'Cinnamon Trust', a fantastic charity that provides free dog walking services to the disadvantaged.

As with most things in life we learn from our experiences. In hindsight, I realised that at the start of my pet sitting career I was naive in many ways; especially in terms of the dogs that I offered board and lodgings to. Being keen to help my colleagues, I accepted just about any dog that they put my way without even meeting them or acquiring the usual full dog profile. The reason for this was two-fold, firstly I wanted to oblige and secondly, I needed to get my business financially off the ground. In the home my unusually dominant Retriever insisted on being top dog at all times. If a visiting dog didn't respect her as the alpha female, then it was a recipe for disaster. Taking in un-vetted dogs without having initially introduced them to Brece, turned out to be a massive mistake on my part. I discovered this the hard way...

Brece was eight years of age and at that point had never been involved in any sort of scuffle whatsoever until one fateful day in May 2011 when she blotted her copybook. She was by no means a young dog and way too long in the tooth to start scrapping. The day in question an awful fight erupted between Brece and a colleague's terrier that was boarding with me. It was the first time I had met the dog, and consequently had no idea of its temperament. Both dogs failed to back down over a treat and launched themselves into a full-blown battle. It all happened so quickly, but I suspect that Brece was the instigator.

It's quite shocking to witness and hear a full-on dogfight; the barking, growling, snarling, biting and those scary looking wolf incisors on display, that we so often forget are there. But it's usually not as bad as it sounds 'Its bark's worse than its bite,' as they say. However, it was still a very unpleasant incident making it imperative that the dogs were separated, and quickly. This was by no means going to be an easy task, they were locked in, guns blazing. But with gritted determination, I managed to unlock the pair and quickly dragged Brece off into the lounge, leaving the terrier to calm down in the kitchen. *God knows what the neighbours must have thought.*

Initially neither dog appeared to be harmed, but as usual in these situations I came off worse. By trying to separate them, I suffered a nasty deep gash to my finger which probably needed stitches but I made do with raiding the contents of my first aid kit. After I had patched myself up, I went to check on the pair. The terrier who was far younger than Brece seemed fine. But Brece did not seem quite so fine. In all the panic I had failed to notice that her beautiful fluffy white coat was shockingly splattered in deep red blood. Closer inspection revealed that the blood on her coat was mine, which had spilled out from my injured finger during the fight. It was a relief that she wasn't physically hurt, although mentally she had clearly taken a battering. For quite some time she appeared jittery, with that wild frightened look in her eyes.

The whole ordeal was a massive wake-up call for me. Going forward I realised that I needed to rethink my booking tactics. It had become apparent that I didn't know my dog as well as I thought. She was a completely different animal in the company of other dogs that stepped over her threshold, immediately mutating from a fairly placid dog, to an extremely dominant beast. It was all another stark reminder that a dog is an animal and 98% wolf in sheep's clothing. I had a lot to learn if I was ever going to make it as a pet sitter.

From that day on I realised it was imperative that Brece had to be happy with our canine visitors, so that there was no repeat of the terrible fight. It was, after all, her home and her contentment was paramount. I imagined her to be thinking; 'Oh my God, what's happening? It used to be just the two of us. Why do I now have to share my home with all these random dogs?'

Requiring advice as to whether I was doing the right thing, I decided to seek it from Anna, an avid animal lover who has worked with horses and many of God's other creatures just about all of her life. In doing so she has gained a great understanding of animal behaviour. Respecting her opinion as the wise sage she is, I asked if she thought it was unfair on Brece to continue bringing strange dogs into our home. Anna responded that in her opinion it was not unfair as dogs are pack animals and flourish in the company of other dogs (when they are not scrapping!) After considering her response I concluded that she was indeed right, and besides someone needed to keep the wolf away from the door, and it certainly wasn't going to be Brece. With my financial settlement from work rapidly dwindling, I needed to start earning again. All things considered, I decided to continue with my venture. I was fortunate in one respect as some dogs will not even allow another hound over their doorstep, at least Brece was not quite that territorial. However, her dominant nature needed to be managed, but on reflection this didn't necessarily have to be a negative. All things considered I decided to turn things around and use her forceful temperament to my advantage.

From then on, all prospective new boarders were required to visit Heyhouses for a consultation, during which time the dogs were vetted by both Brece and myself. I made no further allowances for colleagues' dogs and nobody crept in under the radar. I dealt with the owner, whilst Brece dealt with the visiting pooch, demonstrating her role as the alpha female by putting the new dog through its paces. Sometimes she appeared to be giving the guest dog a hard time. But luckily most owners understood the pack hierarchy and did not take offence when their beloved pet was berated by my bossy dog. Applying this process was a sure way of filtering out any dominant, overly defensive, boisterous or anxious dogs, leaving us with just the even-tempered submissive ones. Assuming the visiting dog was happy and comfortable with her dictatorship, then it was a good indication that things would work out. Consequently, I usually agreed to make the booking.

Our joint interviewing practices were thoroughly successful. If it wasn't for her, I possibly wouldn't have detected any negatives in a dog's temperament, until it was perhaps too late. I suppose in a round-about way she was now earning her keep, and she did a good job of it too, she ensured harmony amongst the hounds. The only downside being that she could never quite switch off from her new role as the Alpha female, working at it 24/7, even when not on her own patch. Taking her to friend's houses where dogs resided soon became risky. Naturally she was top dog in her own home but she suddenly appeared to think that her newfound status, extended to all residences. Prior to bringing a pack of dogs into our dwelling, she had been submissive and respectful of any host dog. Her personality switch now meant I had to be careful where I took her;

avoiding places which were home to dominant dogs. For a normally submissive breed, it was surprising just how assertive my Retriever had become, and there was that niggling doubt again; was this how she was in the litter and the other prospective buyers had spotted it, thus swerving her?

Brece and I had another selection criteria and that was that we didn't take in unspayed bitches or unneutered dogs. With regard to the bitches sometimes their seasons can be unpredictable. In addition, I tend to find that they appear to give off pheromones even when not in season, which sometimes has an adverse effect on the rest of the pack. Then the unneutered dogs, as a rule, do not get along with other unneutered dogs, sometimes displaying aggression towards one another, which is a serious hazard. On top of this, the dog will repeatedly 'mark its territory'. They do this by urinating on top of places where other dogs have relieved themselves. This is fine if outside, but not too good when it happens indoors. The last thing anyone wants is for a dog to cock its leg up against a wall or piece of furniture in their own home.

Some owners appear to be noticeably forlorn when they drop off their well-behaved, spayed and neutered dogs at the Heyhouses doggy hotel. It's not so much what they say; but the way they look at their pet. No doubt worrying along the lines that their pet may not get along with the others, or that Brece will continue to give their beloved dog a hard time. These are all natural worries and the sort of feelings I experienced when leaving Brece with Gillian for that first time. But I soon learned that a dog's loyalty can be easily transferred to a new pack leader. As long as the dogs are exercised, fed and given affection, preferably in that order, then they will be quite happy. This is of course assuming the dog doesn't suffer separation anxiety issues, from either their owner or own home.

In stark contrast to the owners, the dogs are excited to be embarking on the dog party, all those dogs and all that fun to be had. Typically, it's not their first visit, after having either boarded before, or visited for the initial consultation. They are happy to be returning and hopefully their furry heads are full of good memories of their previous visit.

As a pet sitter, and specifically as a person required to walk dogs, I now needed a body that was in full working order, especially from a limb perspective. Prior to finding my vocation in life I had used my body sparingly. My mantra being that body parts are like car engine parts; once they have worn out, they need replacing. I had got to the ripe old age of fifty having done little exercise, and indeed never indulged in manual work, but comforted by the fact that I had endured no damage to my limbs or back. *One careful lady owner.*

At this stage I couldn't afford any accidents; any wear and tear would now have a detrimental effect on my livelihood. After having considered taking out personal injury insurance, I thought better of it. The insurance companies wanted a king's ransom for their premium. Frugally I decided against lining their pockets and gambled on the hope that my limbs would not fail me. This left me vulnerable, succumbing to an injury was always a bit of a concern and yet another worry that constantly lingered in the back of my mind, after all at my age I was certainly no spring chicken.

I experienced several reminders of my vulnerability, with one particular incident standing out above the rest. It was an unusually warm Spring day. Brece and I were hanging out in the back garden, she was laid in the middle of the lawn whilst I was performing my daily duty of collecting the archipelago of dog mess from the surrounding lawn. With a nice full bag, I walked to the side of the house to put the waste in the dustbin. Nothing too complicated about this to the naked eye, but to get to the bin involved negotiating a pile of wooden planks, accrued when I upgraded my decking. The previous decking had seen better days, it was starting to splinter and therefore presented a hazard to the dogs. So I invested in replacing it. The old planks were stored in a neat pile with the intention of giving them to Anna, an avid fan of 'old planks of wood,' and not averse to the odd splinter or two.

Naturally, over the passage of time my neat precarious pile had toppled over, leaving the planks spread all over the narrow passageway. Of course, what I should have done was re-stack the wood but that would have been too sensible; instead, I attempted to clamber over the fragile slippery wooden construction. As I was doing so, the thought crossed my mind; 'If I slipped now and broke a foot I would be in a real mess, physically and financially.'

Then right on cue I lost my footing and hurt myself, it was as if I had wished the accident on myself. Hitting the ground like a ton of bricks, I suffered a fair bit of pain to my left foot. Reeling from the shock I could do nothing more than lie on the ground and wait for the pain to abate. This took a considerable amount of time but my main concern was for Brece. She would be beside herself at the fact I was injured. However, I had no need to worry, Brece wasn't in the least bit interested in my situation. She knew what had happened, but chose to ignore me, instead, she ran towards the kitchen door, started scratching at it, attempting to get inside. It appeared that she was trying to get away from me. I imagined her to be thinking; "For God's sake, what are you doing now?"

I couldn't help feeling mildly offended that my dog wasn't in the least bit concerned about my state. As a pack animal, dogs usually instinctively care for the other pack members, she had shown concern for me previously, so why not now? After a good spell of wallowing on the ground I pulled myself up, dusted myself off, then made my way to the kitchen door and opened it for her. With that, she ran straight inside making a beeline for the treat jar. Plonking herself down directly in front of the Holy Grail, she started barking in a particularly dominant manner. It was as if in her mind the whole thing had been an opportunity to get a treat down her gullet, how she computed that, I have no idea. There was no way on earth that this dog was going to be keeping a vigil at my graveside!

Chapter 8

Creature comforts

All my boarders (which was my only source of business at the start) came suitably equipped with their creature comforts. This usually meant that copious amounts of doggy luggage had to be stowed away. It was reassuring that the owners cared so much for their pets and wanted them to be as comfortable as possible in their temporary dwelling. But of course, I needed to make room for all the stuff, something that I hadn't really given too much thought to before I embarked on my business enterprise. The utility room was the ideal storage space and was quickly converted into the doggy locker room with food and excess bedding rammed in there.

Food is the most important accompaniment that the owner needs to provide for their pet's stay. Dogs have varying diets, their stomachs can become upset with a change of food, *God knows how they got on in the wild*. These days many dogs are fed on dried food, a healthier option to wet food, but I can't imagine it's very palatable. I felt sorry for the dogs that arrived with their dehydrated pellets, and usually found myself tempted to mix a little bit of wet food in it just to make it a bit more tasty. Most dogs love their food, it is good that they have healthy appetites and it makes life that bit easier for training and controlling purposes. The flip side being, if out walking with a ravenous dog it may pick up on a scent in the distance and run off in the hope of finding a snack. The greediest breed of dog that I have encountered to date is the Beagle. Lovely as the Beagle is, I find it to be an extremely greedy dog that will devour anything that resembles nourishment of any description. I have known many a Beagle to run off and get lost, the Lytham Beagle who evoked a search party being a prime example.

Looking after a friend's Beagle while she was on holiday proved to be quite an onerous task. At mealtimes I fed Brece first in the kitchen, then 'Seagal' outside in the garden. Once he had wolfed his grub down, he always ran off like a shot to the kitchen back door, where he knew Brece was still munching her dinner on the other side. Taking his position by the back door he would then sit down and relentlessly cry and cry.

The other indication of his insatiable appetite was his habit of plonking himself in the garden by the willow tree, looking up at it whilst whining again. At first, I couldn't fathom out what was wrong with him, why was he interested in the spiralling branches? Then it clicked, he was crying because he couldn't get to the birdseed that was hanging in the tree!

A few owners tell me that their dogs are fussy eaters and consume very little, but this is usually not the case when they are boarding. They see the others devour their dinner and instinctively do the same. Meal-times are a hectic highlight of the day, second to the walk. Most of the dogs get themselves incredibly excited, to ensure no squabbling the 'food possessive' dogs are fed in separate rooms. The minority of slightly more reserved dogs sit quietly, literally licking their lips at the prospect of dinner. The sight of a dog licking its lips in anticipation of food, never fails to bring a smile to my face.

On the odd occasion I have a slightly anxious dog staying with no appetite for food. This is probably because it is away from home and out of its normal routine. As I put the food bowl on the floor, the unsettled dog looks at it with great apprehension, then with eyes full of suspicion, looks at me as if to say;

"I bet you have laced that with arsenic."

Usually by sitting next to such dogs and giving encouragement, the personal reassurance is enough to persuade the reticent dog to eat its dinner. It's such a rewarding feeling to nurture the dogs in this way. I may be no Mother Teresa when it comes to infants, but at least I can look after the odd dog or two.

When Brece has finished her meal, she has an endearing habit of coming over to me to offer her gratitude. But before she does this, her food envy drives her to check out all the other dog's bowls. I suppose it's a bit like going to a restaurant and wishing you had ordered what someone else chose, or better still, there may be some leftovers. Once satisfied that all bowls are empty, she comes into the room where I am sitting, lighting it up with her presence. Plonking herself in front of me she nuzzles my hand as if to say; "Thank you very much, that was scrummy, any chance of some more?" She does this without fail after every single meal, my reward for putting the food on the table.

After a few months of providing board and lodgings to dogs I began to notice that it is essentially the smallest pooches that come equipped with the most luggage. Julie, a lady in her fifties, frequently brought her six-year old King Charles Spaniel, Stodge, to board. An adorable little male dog with a beautiful black, brown and white fluffy coat. In appearance, he reminded me of a St Bernard's puppy, extremely portly and ever so cute.

I found Julie to be an interesting person. She started her working career as a ballerina, then went on to become an interior designer before finally finding her vocation as a minister for the Church of England. It was enthralling to discover what others had done with their lives. Whilst I had been incarcerated in an office for thirty years, people were out there holding down a whole host of diverse occupations. Both elegant and eloquently spoken Julie was certainly the most glamorous minister that I have cast eyes upon. Her well-tailored tight-fitting clothes accentuate her shapely figure, not the typical attire for a minister of the cloth. Neither is her 'never a hair out of place' tinted blond hair. Julie's appearance was nothing short of immaculate. The minister arrived at my door resembling something from the front cover of Vogue, whilst I stand on the door-step looking like I've been dragged through a hedge backwards. I tend to make little effort with my appearance during the day, being caked in mud and doggy DNA is usually the order of the day; besides the dogs don't give a damn what I look like.

Julie didn't strike me as your usual minister, probably due to her appearance but also because she came across as being extremely timid in nature. I could never quite picture her standing in the pulpit and preaching to her flock.

Julie was a prime example of an extremely worried owner who was always sad to leave her little dog behind. On her maiden visit to Heyhouses she was due to travel to Australia with her husband to visit their daughter. She made it abundantly clear that she didn't want to go but felt duty bound, confiding in me that she would have preferred to stay at home with her dog. That first stay Stodge came equipped with a mammoth amount of accoutrements. I suppose I should have realised this would be the case when he arrived at my house for the initial consultation wearing his Louis Vuitton dog collar and matching lead!

The inventory consisted of everything except the kitchen sink: three beds, one for each of my downstairs rooms, fresh bedding, towels, toiletries, two large bags of toys, a banquet of food and copious bottles of water. In fact, there were thirty-six bottles in total! My impatience was beginning to bubble up inside me when I saw the procession of stuff being carried into my kitchen, I was never going to get all that lot in the doggy locker room. *Where the hell was I going to store it all?*

Trying hard not to let my feelings show, I inhaled a large intake of breath, then feeling a bit calmer I asked Julie what all the bottled water was for. In an 'isn't it obvious tone?' she replied;

"In case Stodge doesn't like your water."

It unfolded that sometimes when away from home, Stodge refuses to drink the host's tap water. With that we both looked down at the portly little dog as he waddled over to the communal water bowl, inspected it then gulped the majority of it down in one go.

Surely once Julie realised her dog found my water palatable, she would take the thirty-six bottles away with her, but no, it was not to be. Rather frustratingly she said she preferred to leave the bottles in case he 'went off' my tap water. Sensing how stressed she was and not wishing to upset her any further, I decided not to challenge her on the matter. I resigned myself to agreeing to her wishes, acting as if I was comfortable with the situation. *There have been many times when I have thought I would do well in the local amateur dramatic society*. I just had to find the room somewhere, things were going to be pretty cramped in that doggy locker room. Imagine if all my customers arrived with that amount of stuff! Weirdly the bigger dogs seemed to travel light in comparison.

After Julie left in her continued state of distress, I managed to cram most of her dog's food and spare equipment into the locker room, with the bottles of water taking up two cupboards in the kitchen. I was soon to discover that like the Beagle, Stodge also had a massive penchant for dining. When it came to the appetite stakes, he could give the Beagle a run for his money any day of the week, it was becoming clear how he had acquired his name, and physique. The locker room was Mecca for the stout little dog. He spent most of his time in there, dropping off to sleep in the comfort of knowing that he was laid beside his very own food mountain. There was enough food crammed in there to feed the inmates of Battersea Dogs Home.

Another of Stodge's characteristics was his snoring habit. He was an amazingly heavy snorer; I wondered if he suffered from narcolepsy because as soon as he laid down on the floor, he immediately fell asleep. There was no 'eyes getting heavy' and slowly dozing off; on the contrary, as soon as his head hit the deck, he was out cold. His loud snoring reverberated around the whole of the house. Initially, the volume emanating from his nostrils was startling, but I quickly got used to the noise and even began to find it quite endearing. If it was a person snoring his head off, it would have driven me mad, but because it was a dog, I was accepting, even comforted by it.

Each time Stodge boarded with me his usual routine was to take a drink of my tap water then make his way to his food mountain before passing out. He rarely came into the living room to join the others, unless he felt compelled to tell me it was dinner time. Stodge stayed with me a handful of times and thankfully Julia stopped bringing the bottled water once she learned that her dog had not 'gone off' my tap water.

One visit when dropping off her dog, Julie enlightened me that the main reason she disliked travelling was that she had a phobia of flying. Her mantra being; "If God meant us to fly, he would have given us wings."

Julie was convinced that she was going to be killed in a plane crash. *That poor woman, it really was an ordeal for her to visit her daughter.* In the next breath, she asked me if I would look after Stodge in the event that she was actually killed in a plane crash. Her request caught me off guard, but feeling duty bound, I consented; it wasn't really the sort of thing I felt I could decline. However, a selfish thought crossed my mind; in the circumstances of her tragic death and I did inherit her dog, would he come with a financial settlement? Knowing my luck, it would just be the dog with no support package, but that was not really a conversation that I wanted to get into. As things turned out she outlived Stodge.

Early one evening in June 2011 there was a knock on my door and standing on the doorstep was Julie. As usual she looked smart but even more nervous than I remembered. I invited her in, she spilled into the hall, alone, no Stodge. Her face immediately started to contort into a horrendously mournful expression, bottom lip quivering as she spluttered;

"I have lost Stodge, he has died."

I took her into the kitchen and offered her a seat and the customary cup of tea. Once sat down she went on to explain that Stodge had died following breathing difficulties six months previously, which I suppose sadly went some way to explain his snoring habit. I felt for her, she just couldn't pull herself together. By now the tears were rolling down her cheeks as she lamented over the passing of her little dog. Julie told me that time was doing nothing in helping her come to terms with her dog's death. To make matters worse her husband was beginning to lose patience with her, which added further to her anxieties. I had great empathy for her but there was nothing I could do or say that would make her feel any better. It was all a stark reminder that I too had a similar grief-stricken path mapped out in front of me. Of course, I was very sad to learn of Stodge's passing; he was my first customer's dog to leave this mortal coil. But the smorgasbord of dogs that were coming my way were a great distraction from the sadness.

The dogs came in all shapes and sizes, the range went from miniature Yorkshire terriers to Great Danes. The diversity in the breeds is incredible. How can a Yorkshire terrier be the same animal as a Great Dane, or an Alsatian the same animal as a Pug? And it is man who has created this vast range over thousands of years. Dogs descended from the Grey Wolf some ten thousand years ago. The tamest wolves from a litter were bred, then the tamest from the next litter and so on until eventually a specific breed was produced for man's working needs; then finally the pet came along.

Chapter 9

The Gang - late 2011

The very first regular dog walking job I acquired for myself came in late 2011. Up to this point I had only managed to attract boarders. At the time Wasabi Jones was a 2-year old male golden Springer Spaniel whom I inherited from Carol. She had been walking Wasabi daily for about a 6-month period but as her workload in Blackpool was getting increasingly busier, she found herself struggling to fit him in. Wasabi virtually lived on my door-step so she offered him over to me. Carol assured me that Wasabi was a relaxed dog, well-socialised with other dogs, and that he wouldn't be a problem at all. This led me to believe that as and when my regular walkers started to pick up Wasabi would fit in well amongst the pack and would not present any problems. As Carol knew Wasabi very well, the usual scrutinisation of a new dog for walking would not be necessary, *or so I thought.*

In this country, English Springer Spaniels can be traced as far back as the 1500s but they were only formally recognised by the Kennel Club as a distinct breed in 1902. Before that English Springer Spaniels and Cocker Spaniels came from the same litter. Smaller dogs were used to hunt 'woodcock' and larger Spaniels were used to 'spring' bigger game, hence the names are derived.

I arrange to meet with owner Melissa and of course Wasabi. At the initial meeting I questioned myself as to her dog's breeding; to me he looked more like a small Golden Retriever than a Spaniel. I put the question of heritage to Melissa; she explained that Wasabi had been acquired from travellers, admittedly saying;

"Well, he could be anything really."

She then went on to tell me about his personality hang-ups! It appeared that Wasabi's relaxed attitude towards dogs did not extend to humans. He was about 8 months of age when she purchased him from the travellers, therefore it was difficult to know how he had been treated as a puppy. But I suspect his previous life had been a hard one, which may have affected his demeanour, and not in a positive way. Melissa elaborated that Wasabi's dislike for children, who are frightened of dogs is his main issue. He confirms this by; 'Going for them'. Sadly, this is not an unusual trait in a dog when confronted by a frightened child. I have seen the most placid of dog's behaviour change from submissive to aggressive in the presence of a scared infant. The dichotomy being; the more afraid the child, the more agitated the dog becomes. The dog has detected signs of fear, then goes ahead and snarls or even worse snaps at the infant, thus reinforcing the child's fear of dogs! This makes for a very difficult cycle to break, which is such a shame, firstly because the child is upset, and secondly because that child may not learn to enjoy the benefits that loving a dog can bring.

To my mind the dog is like a mirror, it reflects the same vibes that it senses. If a person or child is emanating positive vibes towards the dog, then it will reflect the same vibes back. But if the vibes are negative the dog will reflect the same negativity back in the form of stress and fear. It always pleases me when out walking with my tribe and we come across an adult with a small child who encourages the child not to be afraid of dogs. This is the right message to give but at the same time, it's a balancing act, there is always that small risk that the dog is not friendly and that the owner may be irresponsible. For information as to why an otherwise non-aggressive dog may show aggression towards a child refer Appendix E.

But that's not all of Wasabi's hang-ups, he also doesn't take to most adults either, incredibly, he doesn't even like Melissa's husband Donald, for God's sake! *I couldn't help thinking that Carol may have been somewhat conservative when sharing Wasabi's characteristics with me.* Melissa explained that when meeting new people his guard usually defaults to 'suspicious fear mode'. As he sat in front of me repeatedly offering his paw, it was hard to imagine he had a bad bone in him. Melissa asked me if I would be comfortable walking Wasabi, despite his personality traits. I pondered for a moment. It was hardly going to be the breeze of a job that I had initially thought. But as I was incredibly keen to get more walkers, I consented. Besides it would be a good way of learning more about animal behaviour, albeit negative.

The first time I went to take Wasabi for his walk he was home alone. I walked into the house expecting him to come running to greet me, but all was quiet. Walking around the home I called his name but there was no sign, he was nowhere to be seen.

The obvious place for an insecure dog to hide is under the owner's bed, a search of Melissa's bedroom was called for. No luck with the first double bedroom but a quick check under the second double bed, revealed Wasabi's hideout. Clearly afraid the little fellow was extremely reluctant to come out, vulnerable perhaps as Melissa, his pack leader was not around to protect him. Encouragement was required. Things were not going too well, at one point it was looking as though I was going to have to throw the towel in, but with perseverance he came out from his secure retreat.

After a shaky start he was completely accepting of me and we had no further issues. I know you shouldn't have favourites, but I can't help having mine and Wasabi is definitely one of them. Probably because I have gained his trust and he is now secure in my company, an extremely rewarding feeling. As long as we stay clear of children and strange men, things go pretty smoothly on our walks.

My second daily regular customer to join the gang was Hendrix. Hendrix is the most beautiful Field Spaniel I have ever cast my eyes upon, both inside and out. Field Spaniels are a sturdy medium-sized dog originally developed to retrieve game from land and water. In the century, the Spaniel was redeveloped into a longer legged dog more suitable for working in the field. This dog then became known as the Field Spaniel. They still make excellent hunting dogs but these days are used more as show dogs and especially as pets as they love people and make for a loyal family friend.

Hendrix is a very handsome fellow indeed. His immaculate dark shiny brown coat peters out towards a long swishy, waggy tail which acts as a barometer of his mood, a happiness propeller; the faster it propels the happier he is. Long sturdy legs reach down to wide paws groomed in the usual feathers fashion which comically resemble chicken's feet. Between his floppy Spaniel ears sit his beautiful almost artificial looking amber coloured eyes, it's as if they are made from glass and reminiscent of a teddy bear's eyes. To complete the ensemble, he has a slight dusting of white on the tip of his nose, almost as if he has been caught with his snout in the icing sugar.

Hendrix joined our merry band as a two-month old puppy, whereupon Wasabi welcomed him into the fold and immediately took him under his wing. Wasabi showed the little pup patience and tolerance which is not the typical behaviour of an older dog to display towards a puppy as normally older dogs are irritated by the youngsters. The two of them quickly became the best of buddies, my dynamic duo. Hendrix boards with me from time to time, and I also have the pleasure of walking him each morning Monday to Friday.

Tanya and Rob Bolton are his proud owners, a married couple in their late forties and parents to a teenage daughter, Holly. Apart from owning a home in St Anne's the couple also own a town-house in Thailand where they frequently holiday, leaving Hendrix to board with me. Rob is employed as a builder and regularly works away from home which means I don't see a great deal of him. It is the lady of the house that I tend to deal with when it comes to all matters of the family pet.

Besides having a dog the family also own a Maine Coon cat called Sylvester. Sylvester is a six-year old, long-haired, black and white in colour and the first of his species that I had ever had the pleasure of meeting. Maine Coons are the biggest domestic cats in the world, probably the size of a medium dog. Sylvester also acted more like most dogs than a cat, friendly and amiable towards strangers.

The friendly cat is endowed with a set of massive ears, the tips of which are covered in gravity-defying vertical fur, he makes for a gorgeous fascinating creature. As an outdoor cat he is free to come and go as he pleases. Initially this came as a surprise to me as Maine Coons are a very expensive breed of cat and in my experience expensive cats are usually confined to the safety of the house. Such cats are not typically streetwise and don't always fend well for themselves in the big wide world.

I used to feel sorry for house cats, but now I see the logic in keeping them inside. Although the cats are confined, at least they are safe and sound. We wouldn't let a dog out to roam the streets yet we subject our

71

cats to such dangers. The French seem to have solved the problem though. As a frequent visitor to rural France in the past, it always amused me to see people out walking with their cats on a leash. But it wasn't as daft as it first appeared. The French had the right idea, and the cat had the best of both worlds. Seeing a poster displaying details of a beloved missing cat, just never happened en France.

At 6ft, Tanya is well-built and wears her dark brown hair in a long bob. Secretarial style glasses frame her twinkly friendly eyes. With her above average height for a female, sparkly eyes and Cheshire Cat smiley face she puts me in mind of a friendly giant. Tanya partly fills her time as a self-employed Reiki practitioner but she has many more strings to her bow. She is also a practising naturopath providing a bespoke service to her clients by combining both her naturopath knowledge and her Reiki skills. When Tanya was in her early forties she suffered and recovered from both skin cancer and breast cancer. Thankfully she is now in remission and getting on with her life. She is just one of my many female customers over the age of 50 who has been affected by breast cancer.

The good thing, if there is a good thing, is that all the ladies are now in remission and in good health. Breast Cancer seems to be such a common occurrence these days. My surviving customers talk about their illness openly and candidly, almost as if it was a bout of flu they endured. A far cry from the days of my youth when the 'Cancer' word was whispered quietly and in corners. Hearing of such positive results gives me a small sense of satisfaction that I did my little stint at the Cancer Research shop, despite the dissatisfaction I endured at the time.

After her harsh wake-up call Tanya turned her life around in terms of what she put into her body and her mind. She decided to become both a teetotal vegan and a practising Buddhist. Buddhism is where she finds her peace and solace. As if that wasn't enough to keep her occupied, she also works mornings at the local YMCA where she teaches Yoga classes. If Tanya had any more strings to her bow, she could quite easily start up her own orchestra.

Although the family live on a busy road; when I enter their home an unusual peaceful calmness always wafted over me, almost as if I had walked into a haven or a retreat. Buddha statues scatter the rooms and pleasant fragrant aromas drift through the air, creating an oasis of tranquillity. I visit many houses to see to pets, but Tanya's is the only home where I experience such a peacefulness. She reliably informed me that all the calmness emanates from the meditations she practices, which in turn create the calming energy about her home.

As a puppy Hendrix was relatively well-behaved on the walks. Joining the pack at such an early age meant he was well socialised with other dogs which enabled him to learn his manners quickly. Brece did everything she could to help him in that department. And of course, he was fortunate to have Wasabi by his side as his mentor. But in the confines of his own home, the gorgeous young bear was quite a handful, prone to regular bouts of household destruction and not on a small scale. In the utility room, which formed part of an extension to the house lays his den, his safe place. It was cosy in there with everything he needed, food, water, bed, lots of toys and balls for him to play with. Collecting him for his daily walk in the early days he was always to be found confined to the utility room. This room has two doors, one leading to a second living room, and a further door that opened out onto a beautiful back garden.

Although never left home alone for more than the recommended three hours this was plenty of time for the little bear to practice his housekeeping and joinery skills. Each time I collected him I was greeted with varying levels of destruction. Being a Springer, he was able to 'spring' himself up onto the worktops, clearing them of any clutter that he thought should be removed. He was also more than capable of opening the cupboards and rummaging through the contents therein. When he got bored of these antics, he started to eat the woodwork. Over a period of time, he managed to chew all the skirting boards and architraves of his den. Tanya and Rob saw little point in replacing the wooden features until such time that his munching habits abated. Without doubt, his most destructive incident happened on the day that he found the secret room...

Entering the utility room in the usual fashion one morning I was caught off guard to see Wasabi wallowing amongst piles and piles of paperwork. This time he had surpassed himself. I couldn't understand where all the paper had come from, that was until I spotted a third door in his den which I had never noticed before. Unfortunately, the secret door had accidentally been left open.

Feeling curious as to what lay behind the secret door, I peered inside to discover that the secret room was, in fact, an office, or had been, before Hendrix got his chicken paws on it. The small room was furnished with a desk, chair, computer, and shelves secured to the walls. Hendrix had managed to clear all the shelves and desktops of any clutter, trashing the whole place in the process.

The tidy up operation was clearly going to take a considerable amount of time, something which was in short supply on that morning. But I couldn't leave the place as it was, so I proceeded to have a quick spruce up. In the middle of all the debris the object of Hendrix's focus revealed itself; the remnants a chocolate bar wrapper. The chocolate had long since vanished, and there was no way of telling how much he had eaten which was a worry as chocolate is poisonous to dogs. Closer inspection of the wrapper revealed that it had been a milk chocolate bar and therefore relatively low in cocoa, presenting less of a problem than dark chocolate. As Hendrix is a fairly large robust dog I wasn't overly concerned. If it had been a small toy dog that had munched its way through the chocolate, then that would have been more of a concern.

Wading through the debris another piece of shredded paper caught my eye. Bending down to pick it up, I could just make out that the paper was partially emblazoned with the 'Easy Jet' logo. A closer look revealed that the paper had once been three return flight tickets to Thailand!

I picked up the larger pieces of paper from the floor and left the remnants on the side for the family to salvage what they could, the minute scraps remained on the floor. After our walk I sent Tanya a text to pre-warn her what was in store for her when she returned from Yoga. It was bound to be a bit of a shock for her, but as with most things the destruction and carnage looked worse than it was. And thanks to the wonders of modern technology Tanya was able to reprint a fresh set of tickets.

In the fullness of time Hendrix matured and thankfully grew out of his destructive ways, at which time Tanya promoted him by giving him the keys to the rest of the house. From then on it seemed strange picking him up and not finding him in his den. Instead, he was to be found skulking on the stairs, where he appeared unsettled and slightly anxious with his new-found freedom. I'm not sure why this was, perhaps it was because he now had more space to guard, and was potentially exposed to more new strange sounds. Personally, I think he preferred the security of his den, over having the run of the house, in much the same way that a young dog finds security in its own cage.

A new morning routine was to evolve. Although Hendrix clearly knew I had arrived, he always remained lolloping on the stairs, the Mountain goes to Mohamed. But before I put him on his lead affection is required, which I am more than happy to provide. I embrace him and share my thoughts with him as to what a handsome devil he is, he likes this.

Whilst out walking it's such a joy to watch him charging around the dunes, leaping, bounding around, doing his 'Springer' thing. His long sturdy legs enable him to make long and high jumps. With the skill and dexterity of a baby kangaroo he launches himself from one dune to the next. Being a young dog, he has copious amounts of energy and enjoys his walks with incredible enthusiasm. He plays the whole time and gets on like a house on fire with every single dog that crosses his path, especially dogs of the same breed that share his enthusiasm for play. If any negativity comes his way, he shrugs it off in his affable submissive manner, never harbouring any bad feelings or reflecting any animosity towards any dog.

In play Hendrix usually takes another dog off away from the pack to go exploring, but I don't worry because I know he will always come back. From the word 'Go,' he had great recall, I hardly had to do any work at all in that area. Utilising his excellent recall skills, he returns bringing his playmate alongside him back to the fold. He is a great asset at keeping the rest of the pack together. It's as if he watches out for the other dogs and appears concerned if one of his buddies has dropped off the radar for a short time. The wandering dog is usually sniffing some amazing scent if I am lucky, or rolling in fox poo if I am not quite so lucky. In the same way I would tell him to go and find a ball, I shout to him, 'Where is Molly? Go and find Molly," he is off like a shot in search of the straggler. Invariably he finds the dog then barks with excitement alerting my attention to the dog's whereabouts. The straggler dog does what is expected and happily accompanies Hendrix back to the fold. He is my shepherd, herding the group together and also the joker in the pack, playing with all and sundry, a key member of our group, and one that I love with a passion.

I refer to Hendrix and Wasabi as my dynamic duo, the two of them are best buddies, they absolutely adore being in each other's company. It is such a joy to watch them in their play, their happiness is incredibly infectious. On the dunes, they play chase, and hide and seek. But Hendrix's favourite trick is ambushing his mate. Running ahead of the pack he takes cover lying in wait until Wasabi catches up. Whilst Wasabi is looking for his buddy, Hendrix then strategically picks his moment and pounces on him. Hendrix has his combat manoeuvres off to a fine art and always manages to startle his buddy by catching him off guard.

Amongst all his positive attributes there is one slight negative, which happens when we come to the end of every single walk. Not wanting his fun to come to an end, Hendrix jumps up on top of a dune taking the higher ground, he refuses point blank to move off it and get into the car, all the while looking at me with his indomitable stare.

When I see that look in his eyes I know I am going to have a job getting him into the car. In the past, it was relatively easy to coax him down off his castle with the aid of treats. But being a smart little fellow he quickly learned that if he took the treat, I would truss him up. He wasn't going to fall into that trap again. Instead he sits alone on his dune looking at me defiantly through his teddy bear glass eyes, refusing the treats. As the treats clearly weren't working, I moved on to random sticks that were lying around. Again, the sticks worked for a while, but they too had a lifespan. It didn't take long for him to realise the treats had been exchanged for sticks.

Once the sticks failed, I moved on to his beloved ball. Diligently dropping it near to me, in the hope that while he was trying to catch the ball, I could catch him. Again, this worked initially but not for long, in the end he had become immune to my entire repertoire of deceptions, more creativity on my part was required. I suppose his reluctance to get in the car is quite amusing, but when short of time or on a hot day with dogs slowly baking in the car, the humorous side of the situation eludes me.

It was the end of one of our morning walks, Hendrix was being his usual stubborn self, sat on a dune and refusing point black to get into to the car. I doubt a fillet steak would have persuaded him. To make matters worse, he suddenly caught sight of a man with a ball launch who was at the far end of the car park and worryingly, close to a busy road. On a mission, he surged towards the irresistible sight in front of his eyes. Panicking at this point, the awful scenario of him running out into the road flashed through my head. I needed a new trick up my sleeve to stop him running towards the road, and it had to work. There was absolutely no point in drawing on any of my old tricks, they weren't going to cut the mustard, an original fool proof plan was called for. Then suddenly and instinctively, without a second thought I flung myself onto the ground, and started flailing around, making mock painful yelling noises. I surprised myself.

Lying on the ground still yelling, I prayed Hendrix's pack instinct would kick in and that his concern would outweigh his desire for the ball. From the corner of my eye, I could see that he had stopped dead in his tracks, he was standing stationary, clearly in two minds as to what he should do, ball or me? I kept still, motionless, it was imperative to keep up the charade, if he saw me move, he may think I was okay, then resume his quest to get to the ball. But he's a clever little chap, would he be fooled by my ruse? Thankfully he was, his curiosity got the better of him. Still rigid and lying on the ground I could see that he was skulking back towards me, head bent and sniffing the ground. He approached me and gently started to sniff my face, with that I quickly sat up, grabbed him by the collar, and managed to leash him. Thank God my desperate trick worked. It was a great relief but also acutely embarrassing once I realised that my little drama had attracted the attention of a couple of onlookers, who were presumably wondering what the hell I was doing and asked me if I was okay. I refer to this as my 'last resort' stunt and prefer not to have to draw on it unless in dire straits, it's my least favourite of all tricks.

Gradually, I learned that the best and least embarrassing way to catch Hendrix is to pretend we were going back on the beach for another walk. He likes this idea, so off we go on our faux walk. After a couple of minutes when his guard is down, I then have a chance to catch him and rein the little ragamuffin back in. Heading back to the car I feel relieved, but also slightly mean that I have tricked him, robbing him of further fun.

Rather annoyingly Hendrix decided to teach his older buddy the 'There's no way I'm getting back in that car' routine, adding weight to the argument that 'IT IS possible to teach an old dog new tricks.' I now have to contend with the two of them looking down at me from the top of a dune, or a pile of dirt. Luckily Wasabi's resolve isn't quite as polished as the young scamp's. With the aid of a few treats, it is relatively easy to get Wasabi back into the car, leaving his stubborn buddy to sit it out alone.

Like Wasabi, Hendrix is also afraid of men. If he sees a lone man whilst walking, his temperament usually defaults to suspicious mode. Becoming anxious, he then typically starts barking at the man. Interestingly, if we see a man that is either with a woman or another dog, he remains relaxed. The woman or dog seem to negate any suspicion he harbours towards the man, yet the man's attributes remain the same when in company, or alone. It's always a bit embarrassing when he starts his barking routine and no doubt slightly intimidating for the lone man. It's even worse if Wasabi is with me as the two of them gang up, but thankfully most men are understanding and don't take too much offence. When he has one of his episodes, I call him back, and he comes away without hesitation; making our apologies we continue with the walk. It's not just my dynamic duo that are prone to this sort of behaviour, many dogs are wary of men. For information on why dogs are afraid of men refer appendix F.

Boarding with me on a regular basis, and as long as we don't have too many men popping round, Hendrix makes for a low maintenance dog to care for. He doesn't bother with Brece and she rarely bothers with him. That is until he starts to play hard with a playmate. At such times 'the fun police' intervenes. When things are getting a bit boisterous and too much fun is being had, she will go over to them, barking loudly as if to say;

"Right come on you two, settle down now before one of you gets hurt." Just as parents do to their young rowdy children. The dogs get the message, look at her, look at each other and then settle down.

Like the majority of pets, Hendrix is absolutely adored by his family. As a child, I recall people saying that they preferred animals to people, I used to think to myself; 'Yes, animals are lovely, but it can't be right to say such a thing.' But now I know it to be true, at least of some people, the Bolton family being no exception. Recently they returned from a 3-week trip to Thailand, as requested I dropped Hendrix off at their house. Ahead of my arrival the entire family must have been looking out of their front room window, waiting in anticipation for the return of their beloved Hendrix. Before I had even pulled up properly, Rob ran outside his house and stood on the pavement, waiting for me to finish my parking manoeuvre. I wished he wasn't watching me, his scrutiny was bound to make me do some appalling parking.

Once parked up *in a fashion*, the floppy-eared rascal and I got out of my car. On seeing his dog after the long separation Rob was beside himself, physically displaying his love towards his dog, he couldn't take his eyes off him, so warming to witness. In close succession Tanya came running out of the house, the same thing, just pure joy and excitement to see her dog. Next, and continuing the relay, daughter Holly followed suit.

By this time the whole family were on the pavement of the busy road, the happiness exhibited was just off the scale. Standing watching the happy scene, it dawned on me that we love our dogs unconditionally in the same way a parent loves their child. But in my opinion love for a partner is not quite the same, sooner or later conditions usually sneak in. I'm sure that if Rob or Tanya for that matter, had been away for 3 weeks, the reception from their spouse would be nothing like the reception they bestowed on their dog. The spouse probably wouldn't even get up out of the chair, it would be a case of;

"Oh, you're back then?'

Chapter 10

Mr. Rochester and Brad - late 2011

My third member to join my daily gang was Mr. Rochester, commonly known as Rocky, a beautiful white and orange English Pointer. Although the colour is referred to as 'orange', the tone is actually more of a lovely warm light brown. He possesses the breed characteristics: long head with large floppy silky ears, medium-sized elegant slender body and tall gangly legs which undoubtedly contribute to his clumsiness. My grandmother renowned for her large repertoire of colloquialisms, would have described him as; "A great big lummox."

Pointers have been bred for several years to 'point' out birds and small game. When they scent game, they stand tall and still, almost statuesque, with one foot raised off the ground, pointing hunters in the direction of the game. It's quite an awesome sight to see a Pointer doing what it was bred for. As they sniff the air in a majestic manner, an eerie calmness seems to come over them and they become fixated. The breed puts me in mind of the sort of dog that accompanies the lord of the manner around his country estate, usually in pairs. The Pointer has many great qualities; it is amiable, sensitive, kind, affectionate, extremely active and able to work all day long in the field, never appearing to tire.

Rocky's owner, Brad, contacted me via my website. He needed someone to walk his dog during the week while he was out at work. It was a Friday evening and as arranged I went around to the address given to meet the man and his dog. I was looking forward to meeting a new customer and the opportunity to peruse the interior of another new house.

Brad, his dog and home did not disappoint. It was about 7 pm when I arrived at a massive Victorian brick semi-detached house on the promenade directly opposite the beach. Walking up the driveway, I wondered what Brad would be like. I had not actually spoken to him at that point, so consequently I had no idea of his age, or what to expect. Standing on the doorstep I rang the bell. A minute later the door opened to reveal a well-dressed handsome man standing at about 6ft 1, probably in his early thirties. He was wearing a smart tightly tailored blue suit and brown leather brogues; with his rakish looks he cut a fine figure of a man.

It struck me as strange that he should be so well-dressed in the comfort of his home. The first thing I do when I get home is to slip into something more comfortable, trackie bottoms or better still a snug dressing gown, and my trusty sheepskin slippers. Brad clearly has higher standards than me. As he invited me into a living room, he introduced himself and his girlfriend, Amy, who was sitting on a winged armchair. On seeing me she stood up to greet me. I would hazard a guess that she was in her late twenties, with a crown of thick long shiny blonde lustrous hair that wouldn't have looked out of place on the set of a shampoo advert. Both attractive and elegant in appearance she had an ethereal air about her. The pair made for a very attractive couple indeed.

Brad's house had recently been renovated to an exceptionally high standard. In my capacity as a dog walker, I get to frequent some amazing homes. At this point, I had only been in the hall and front living room, but from what I had seen of the couple's abode, it was clearly the most impressive house I had visited to date. Glancing around the living room I focused on the splendid decorations, the room had a very grand feel to it, opulence oozed from the walls. Positioned in front of the enormous window sat a large turquoise chaise-longue, patterned with a mock Georgian tapestry featuring the gentry on horseback accompanied by their hounds. Exquisite green heavy flock curtains framed the white sash windows. A massive square glass coffee table positioned on top of a white marble floor, sat in front of an enormous white baroque alabaster fire surround with open fire. The walls were covered with luscious Matthew Williamson Bird of Paradise wall-paper which surprisingly did not clash with the surrounding bold fabrics. Hanging from the centre of an elaborately decorative white plastered ceiling, hung a huge frosted glass chandelier, which must have been a nightmare to clean. Several large ceramic lamps placed on occasional tables provided ambient lighting which brought the whole ensemble together. The style was traditional and classical which surprised me as I would have expected something more contemporary from a young couple.

Brad then introduced me to the bundle of fun that is Rocky, who was also handsome, in a canine sort of way. At the time Master Rocky was a boisterous, 5-month old adorable young, un-neutered very strong pup. Being the owner of a large hotel in St. Anne's, Brad explained that he spent a lot of time at work managing the business, consequently, he needed a hand with Rocky. It was clear that Rocky was a handful and that this wasn't going to be an easy job but I liked both Brad and his dog, so I agreed to take on the challenge of walking Rocky. My duties were to commence the following Monday. But that wasn't all. Whilst still at the consultation the couple mentioned that they were going away at the weekend, taking Rocky with them but leaving their two Abyssinian cats at home, Branston and Pickle. Brad asked if I would look after the cats in their absence, to which I was more than happy to oblige.

In my experience a cat does not usually greet people with the same unbridled enthusiasm as a dog does (Maine Coons excluded), they tend to shy away from strangers. But not all of them; a minority of cats are more like dogs in terms of handing out greetings and affection. But in general, I need to work harder at gaining a cat's trust as opposed to a dog's. Once gained it is a thoroughly rewarding feeling, a sort of privilege. Abyssinians are a rare breed of cat; with their small long narrow faces, large yellow eyes, slender bodies, and long swishy tails they resemble little Avatars.

At this point there was no sign of the cats. Brad informed me that they had been inside the house just before I arrived but must have dashed out once they realised they had company. This led me to believe that these cats would be the predictable shy type.

Yes, I would enjoy swanning around their beautiful home whilst tending to their cats. Before leaving, Amy said she would show me the set up for the avatars and beckoned me to go with her. Following her into the hall, she opened a door, switched on a light and we descended some steep steps. Although she didn't announce the fact it was obvious that the door led to the cellar. Whilst walking down the stairs I couldn't help wondering why we were going down into the cellar.

At the bottom of the stairs we arrived at the bowels of the house and all became clear as she explained that the cats were kept there when the couple were away. Informing me that the avatars had a habit of bringing mice into the house and Amy didn't want that to happen when they were not around. Apparently, she didn't mind if the mice inhabited the cellar, but there was no way she wanted them running around their home. I fully understood where she was coming from, but at the same time I couldn't help but empathise for the little avatars being relegated to the cellar. It was bound to be damp and miserable down there. Also, selfishly, I was also somewhat disappointed for myself. It now appeared that I too was to be relegated to the cellar to tend to the cats, my delusions of grandeur were short lived.

The cellar was a labyrinth of rooms. Looking around I began to realise that it was actually quite a good set up down there, home to the boiler, consequently, it was warm and cosy. The cats had their beds down there plus lots of toys and activities for them to play with. Besides, cats aren't bothered if the walls are decorated in 'Farrell and Ball' or simply whitewashed. There was a sofa down there that had seen better days, and a battered winged armchair that wouldn't have looked out of place in the taxi rank office on Coronation Street.

Amy proceeded to show me the ropes, as she did so I inquisitively wondered to myself if the couple enjoyed a happy relationship. They appeared to, and they certainly had all the trappings to help them along their way.

My impression of Amy was that her personality did not match her appearance. I expected her to be confident, self-assured and assertive but she displayed none of those attributes. As usual, I had jumped to conclusions and judged the book by its cover. Down in that cellar, she came across as almost humble, with a tendency to finish her sentences with the word "Sorry,' almost self-deprecating. As someone considerably younger than myself perhaps she felt uncomfortable in telling me, as an older person, what she wanted me to do.

As luck would have it, it was time for the cats to be fed; Amy treated me to a live, somewhat complicated, dress rehearsal. Donning a pair of pink rubber gloves, she started to prepare the cat's dinner. Firstly, she thoroughly scrubbed two bowls, this took a considerable amount of time. Then she filled the pristine bowls with a sandwich consisting of 'Kitty Cat' biscuits; a sachet of wet food on top, then a further sprinkling of a top-notch dried food retailed as 'Cat Caviar' to finish. The 'Cat Caviar' was extremely pungent and Amy made no bones in telling me that is was extremely expensive and must be used sparingly. Then she apologised and gave me a nervous smile. It seemed odd that she should mention the cost of the cat caviar, I had assumed that money would be no object to the apparently affluent couple.

The cats suddenly appeared from nowhere seemingly attracted by the extravagant caviar. Both males, Branston white in colour and pickle a lovely warm shade of mink. Although clearly reluctant to share their cellar with me, they put their reservations to one side in favour of dinner. Amy placed the bowls on the flag stone floor. At the same time, she shared a story with me about a time when her 60-year old mother was looking after her cats and managed to get herself locked in the cellar for a period of three hours. Apparently, the cellar door had jammed and she was unable to release it. Adding to her predicament she had left her phone upstairs in the kitchen. Shouting for help, eventually a neighbour came to her rescue and managed to help her clamber out through a window that was slightly ajar. After the unfortunate incident, and not unsurprisingly, her mother refrained from feeding the cats ever again.

Amy kindly went to great pains to assure me that this wouldn't happen to me, as she now had a backup plan in place; there was an external door in the cellar which opened onto some steps leading up to the outside garden. The plan was that she would leave a key to this door inside the cellar, which would be my escape route in the event that the internal door jammed again. I was to gain access to the house by the front door, then go down to the cellar to tend to the cats. I couldn't help thinking that I was bound to feel apprehensive descending the steps alone for the first time. Most new jobs made me feel uneasy as it was, this was certainly not going to be an exception. The unfortunate incident with her mother would undoubtedly play on my mind. I just knew that all my time spent in that cellar would be spent worrying about getting locked in, with the additional possibility of mice jumping out at me.

I visited the cats on the Saturday, there was no sign of them, *or the mice, thank God!* I performed my duties then left without seeing hide nor hair of them. Sunday was a different story, they greeted me at the bottom of the cellar stairs and seemed pleased to see me. Happily intertwining themselves in between my ankles doing their cat thing, purring away no doubt in anticipation of cat caviar. After feeding them, I sat on the battered sofa and watched them dining. When finished they came and sat next to me, one on each side, both showing a great deal of affection towards me. Branston repeatedly pushing his head against my hand, forcing me to stroke him, whilst Pickle gently pummelled his paws against my lap. A feeling of relaxation crept over me, I felt so comfortable that I found myself becoming horizontal on the sofa. With my eyes closed the pair of them clambered all over me, purring away, it felt almost therapeutic, even the thought of mice didn't worry me.

Monday morning, it was back to Brad's to commence my doggy duties. The arrangement was to collect Rocky, walk him, then drop him back at his house. I hadn't offered Brad the half day package as, to be honest, I didn't think I could cope with Master Rocky for a full five hours a day. As expected, Rocky was hard work, definitely the most energetic dog that I had come across to date, the complete opposite of the therapeutic avatars.

He was both incredibly strong and completely untrained, not the best combination in a dog.

Our encounters followed a pattern, pulling up outside the majestic house in my battered dog mobile was the trigger that sent Rocky into overdrive. As soon as I opened the front door, he came tearing over to me from any corner of the house with a force to be reckoned with. Picking up speed as he neared me, I braced myself for the inevitable impact. Rocky had little awareness of etiquette or personal space, but even he was beginning to learn that he couldn't just keep crashing into people. Slamming on the brakes just before he reached me, he skidded along the parquet floor like something out of a Hanna Barbara sketch. I soon learned to avert the inevitable collision by quickly stepping aside. Coming to an abrupt halt his entire body would slam up against a wall and end up in a heap on the floor. Then in Bambiesque fashion, he gathered his gangly legs together, regained his balance, and got up on all fours again.

Next stage in the ritual was the continual jumping up at me. It was as if he was on a perpetual trampoline, and it carried on for the entire time I spent inside the house. Although picking up Rocky was always complete chaos, I could always be assured of a most tumultuous physical greeting from him; but not without escaping some innocent bruising on my arms as he demonstrated his abundance of affection and excitement.

Whilst continually bounding up and down in yo-yo fashion I somehow had to try and grapple with this super strong dog and leash him, at the same time trying to avoid physical impact with him. It was his head that I had to watch out for, it was as hard as a nut. Impact meant pain for me, but not for him, if we locked heads, he wouldn't feel a thing. Nothing seemed to phase Rocky, pleasure, and excitement was his anaesthetic, his opiate. After a few minutes of strenuous effort, I eventually managed to truss him up, but I never came off unscathed; scratches on my fingers and jarred joints all adding to my battle scars.

Each morning I never quite knew what state the Victorian mansion would be in. It was usually in disarray both upstairs and downstairs: shredded newspapers, magazines, cushions all strewn about the rooms, and that was just for starters. Rocky wasn't properly house trained either, which meant dog mess was usually lying about the house: just carnage.

Picking up Rocky was an arduous task and that was just the prelude to the walk. Putting the leash on him did not abate his excitement, in fact, it exacerbated it, as he knew he was one step closer to his walk and freedom. Once trussed up we made our way to the front door. Trying to lock it behind me whilst keeping hold of the uncontrollable animal was an incredibly difficult task, but with gritted determination, I just about managed it. Outside the house, door successfully locked he then hoicked me all the way down the drive to where his chariot awaited. He pulled with such force that I literally thought that my arms would be wrenched out of their sockets. It took every ounce of strength in my body to hang onto that dog. If he managed to escape from his lead, it was a given that he would run onto the busy road, that would be it, we were dicing with death.

By now I had managed to get him leashed, out of the house, locked the door, before being whisked all the way down the driveway. *God! I must have been completely mad in those early days*. All I had to do now was get him in the boot of the car; this part was a breeze. He was more than happy to jump into the dog-mobile, he knew next stop was the beach. Whilst I sat in the driver's seat I usually took a couple of minutes to compose myself. After checking out my new cuts, bruises and jarred joints I was ready to drive off to our destination. It was always a stressful journey. Having Rocky in the boot of my car was like having a wild Gazelle travelling with us. He remained on his perpetual trampoline but added a touch of strident hollering and squealing to help us along on our way. Once finally at our destination, the beast was unleashed. This was what he had been waiting for: now his fun could begin.

Hurling himself out of the boot, he charged off to do his own thing. There was no way I could keep him on the lead, anything I did to try to hang on to him was ineffectual, as was berating him. With no choice in the matter, I just had to let him go and wait with the other dogs by the sea wall while he charged around.

My wandering minstrel was now free and on a mission to cover as much ground as physically possible in an hour. He ran far out to sea, making it difficult for me to keep track of him. Calling him back was useless, his recall was dubious, well non-existent. I watched him as he disappeared into a black dot on the horizon and hoped he would stop before he got to the Isle of Man. The black dot eventually vanished. Even though Brad had assured me that Rocky always came back, this moment was always a worry. By this time we had usually attracted unwanted attention from others passing by. I imagined the onlookers to be thinking; "How the hell is she going to get that dog back? Let's just hang around and see what happens." I always wished they would go on their way, their attentions just exacerbated matters for me. I kept my eyes peeled on the horizon, until the black dot reappeared and started to get bigger. After about fifteen minutes of having his fill of tearing around the landscape, much to my relief and the entertainment of his audience, he finally made his way back. Without appearing to look for me he always seemed to know the precise spot where he had left us.

Once we were reunited, he was incredibly happy to see me again, loyally jumping up again as if it was the first time he had seen me that day.

Now that he had let off some steam, we were then able to start the walk. It was an hour of Nirvana for him, but an hour was just not enough exercise for a working dog such as Rocky.

Walking Rocky was a bittersweet experience. On the one hand, I was always scared stiff that he wouldn't come back to me. But then it was so lovely to watch him running around enjoying his freedom, *when he was in sight*. Observing a Pointer run is an awesome sight, with their long gangly legs they move with an elegant gallop, in a similar way to a stallion. An Olympian of a dog.

All things considered and taking account of how out of control he was, we didn't seem to get into too many scrapes with other dogs or indeed their owners. I would have expected the odd;

"You should have that dog on a lead."

Fortunately, this never happened. Other people and dog walkers alike all seemed to be fond of Rocky, he really was a spectacle to be admired. In fact, we only ever had one altercation and that was when a Golden Retriever had a bit of a go at him. Rocky was being his usual pest, wanting to play, but play was not on the agenda for the Retriever. Presumably Rocky thought the dog was Brece and was excited to see her, sadly it was a case of mistaken identity as she was at home at the time. The Retriever was rapidly becoming irritated at Rocky's invitation to play and eventually snapped at him. Nothing serious, just a warning.

Although Rocky wasn't physically hurt in any way, he seemed to be emotionally wounded. It was as though he couldn't understand why the other dog had been so unfriendly towards him, he would never be so unpleasant towards another dog. He had such a pitiful confused look on his face, it was all so alien to him. Not for long though, he was soon off on his next adventure.

After our chaotic walks, I dropped him back off at home. Although relieved to be doing so, the relief was always tinged with a touch of sadness. He never wanted to return as it meant being left again. Once back in his prison he immediately ran to the lounge window and jumped up on the turquoise chaise longue in the front window, blending in with the hounds of the fabric. But Rocky was one sad hound, I could feel him watching me with his lovely big brown eyes boring into me as I walked down the path towards my car. This tore at my heartstrings. I imagined him to be thinking;

"You can't seriously be leaving me here all alone when I could be out having so much fun, can you?"

After about 3 months of walking Rocky most days, and with arms that were six inches longer than when I started, Brad decided to move-house and downsize. His destination was another house in Lytham not far from the Victorian mansion. During the actual move, unsurprisingly, things were a bit hectic for Brad, and I hadn't managed to get a new house key off him. For my maiden visit to his new home, I was to use a spare key left in the garden behind the barbeque and enter the house via the orangery. However, 'best-laid plans of mice and men', things went horribly wrong. When I got to his new house, the key was not where it was supposed to be, which meant I couldn't gain access.

The moment Rocky knew I had arrived he naturally assumed he was going for his walk, I could hear him barking and whimpering with excitement, he was on high alert and raring to go. I gave Brad a quick call to explain the situation. Brad was confused and couldn't understand why the key was not where he had left it. He was due to go into a meeting at the time, therefore unable to come home to assist. Much to Rocky's dismay, there was nothing else for it, but to leave him at home. All day I intermittently worried about Rocky, I hoped he would be okay and not causing too much destruction. Brad called me that evening and put me out of my misery. On his return from work, he was greeted by Rocky's latest carnage. Inwardly, I think we both expected a level of destruction but not quite on the scale that Rocky had managed to achieve.

The stressed dog had ripped all but one of the wooden blinds down from the windows of the orangery. Not content with that he then proceeded to shred them to bits, rendering them completely destroyed. To give Brad his due he did not seem overly annoyed at the situation, although he did manage to slip into conversation that the blinds were very expensive ones. I think he realised that it wasn't anyone's fault and it certainly wasn't Rocky's. Later it transpired that Amy, who was now his ex-girlfriend, had been round to pick up some of her stuff. She had taken the key, let herself into the house, but had forgotten to put it back. I was surprised to learn that the couple had parted ways and saddened that what I assumed to be a happy relationship was short lived.

Against my better judgement and in a moment of madness I agreed to offer Master Rocky a weekend's board and lodgings. Let's just say that I deeply regretted my decision, it was the weekend from Hell! Brad had contacted me to say that following his split with Amy he needed to get away for a few days but was having trouble finding someone to look after his dog- *no surprise there*. It was looking like kennels were the only option but he wasn't comfortable with the idea and neither was I. A lot of dogs are fine in kennels. I know plenty that even love going to the kennels, but Rocky was certainly not the type of dog that would settle in a confined space, alone. Duty-bound I reluctantly agreed to board the crazy dog.

It was Friday lunchtime when Rocky checked in to the doggy hotel, check out was Monday lunchtime; surely, I could cope for just three days.

First thing I did was to take him out for a long walk on the beach with a couple of other energetic dogs. After two hours we returned, I felt sure he must be tired after all the exercise. But it was not to be, once home, Rocky was still on high alert, bounding around everywhere. I expected him to soon tire, perhaps it was delayed fatigue, he was bound to crash out eventually, but no, it never happened. It appeared that it was impossible to tire him, the more exercise he got, the fitter he became, requiring more and more.

To be honest, I just couldn't cope, it was a hell of an ordeal. Unlike the other dogs in my care, he was constantly on the go, never settling, a maelstrom of unbridled energy. He trashed the place in front of my eyes, ripping pictures off the walls, knocking objects off the coffee table and shredding any soft furnishings that crossed his path, my very own wrecking ball. It was as if the excitement of being with so many other dogs was just too much for him to handle. Besides annoying me, he continually annoyed all the other dogs, wanting to play with them twenty-four-seven. He was incompatible with every single one of them, none of them shared his enthusiasm for play, at least not on the scale he demanded. Brece was particularly displeased, repeatedly trying to put him in his place but it was water off a duck's back. Most young dogs learned when put through their paces by her Royal Highness, but not Rocky, I don't think he would have ever got the message. She would look at me, simmering, with an indignant look in her eyes as if to say; "This dog is just not going to get it, it's really not going to work out."

It wasn't as if he could be kept in a different room away from the others, to give them some respite, as I was astonished to discover he had a remarkable talent for opening closed doors! He managed this by jumping up at the door: putting a front paw on the handle, pushing it down, keeping the handle in the down position and finally walking backward on his hind legs, until such point the lock released and the door opened.

The whole process took a couple of minutes, but his tenacity always paid off. Using his skills and intelligence he managed to open all the doors of my house, naturally severely scratching the paintwork in the process. This made it impossible to keep him separated from the others. Sometimes in the past I had thought of him as a dumb dog, but in the fullness of time I realised he wasn't dumb at all, in fact, he was a highly intelligent dog. His bad behaviour was not a reflection of his lack of intelligence, just lack of training and exercise.

This was going to be one long weekend. There were times when I screamed at him in despair as he continually irritated all and sundry. One particular occasion he was winding Brece up a treat, barging into her, barking and relentlessly wanting to play. Tensions were brewing, I scolded him, even tried to drag him away from her but all in vain, he kept going back to barge into her again and again. *God, it was frustrating.* I knew Rocky wouldn't have gone for Brece, but she was about to lose it with him. Teeth bared, top lip quivering; she was now past the growling stage. I knew the signs. Sensing a scrap in the offing I had to pull something out of the bag to protect Rocky from Brece. Out of desperation I acted in a way that I had never done before or since; I smacked Rocky on his snout. The quick smack startled him, and immediately stopped him from winding Brece up, sort of like rewiring his brain. He looked at me in disbelief as if to say;

"I don't get it, what happened then? Sorry, I will try to behave, but I just find it so difficult."

It was the same look in his eyes that he directed at the Retriever that had previously snapped at him, but he didn't hold it against me. I felt bad

96

about my actions, but at the same time justified. If I hadn't intervened Rocky would have come off a lot worse than he did.

On the extremely rare occasion when he did settle, he jumped on the couch next to me and lolloped all over me, giving me his paw in the most affectionate manner imaginable. But even those moments weren't relaxing. It was too risky to even have a drink, as he appeared to have absolutely no control over his gangly legs and would typically knock any drink out of my hand. Monday lunch time couldn't come soon enough.

In the passage of time, I learned to mentally charge such strong, energetic, out of control dogs as Rocky with an ASBO (Anti-Social Behaviour Order). Going forward I avoided taking on new ASBOs like the plague. Poor Rocky, none of his bad behaviour was his fault. Pointers are working dogs and should be in a field all day not cooped up in a house for the most part. There was no doubt that Brad loved his dog, but he really wasn't doing the right thing by him. In buying a working dog that required copious amounts of exercise which he wasn't in a position to provide, he had failed to do his homework.

Although Rocky was incredibly hard work, I was immensely fond of him. It's a peculiar state of affairs, just because a dog is difficult to manage and drives me mad, it doesn't seem to put me off them. I love them the same as the others, if not more. His larger than life behaviour was all part of his huge personality which made a massive impression on me, both good and bad.

Despite him being a complete pain in the neck my family and friends also loved him. Probably because he was so incredibly loving and affectionate without a bad bone in his body. I never once saw him show any sign of irritation towards any other dog, maybe that was because he was the one doing all the irritating. Exuding pure innocence, joy and affection, he displayed all the Pointer characteristics in abundance, an amiable, sensitive, kind, Whirling Dervish of energy.

Finally, Brad realised that something had to be done about his dog's uncontrollable behaviour before someone got hurt. After finally doing some research, he decided to send his crazy dog off to a training school, a sort of doggy boot camp which was based in Yorkshire. I hadn't realised that such places existed until Brad enlightened me. Rocky was to stay there for a 6-week period.

The plan was that Rocky would go away as an out of control menace then return as a fully trained well-behaved dog. The 6-week period passed, I was looking forward to the prospect of seeing Master Rocky, thinking how great it would be to be able to walk him in a controlled fashion. On his return from boot camp, I went to collect him on a Monday morning for his usual walk. Feeling excited, I opened the front door. But things hadn't quite gone quite according to plan. As he came hurtling towards me with the force of a baby bull, my antennae detected there had been no improvement in his behaviour. He was exactly the same and back on his perpetual trampoline.

It appeared that Master Rocky was untrainable. Although that's not strictly true. Rocky was unnerved first time he saw a dead sheep on the beach, *I didn't feel too great either*, but as always, the dogs had noticed the remains well before me. Rocky displayed great reticence as he slowly crept towards the carcass, inching forward then backwards again, as if the thing might come back to life. He had never seen the like. Brece who was much more comfortable with the situation, ran up to it, then body slammed herself on top of it, no problem. A quick roll then she got up, glancing over to her apprentice as if to say,

"That's how it's done, son".

Rocky soon got the gist of things, following suit he hurled himself on top of the rotting carcass, leaving me with two foul smelling dogs to get back into the dog-mobile. Brece had successfully managed to train the young Pointer to roll on dead animals

Besides being weirdly fond of Rocky I was also fond of Brad. I found him to be a friendly jovial person, open, perhaps a tad too open at times. I was to learn that being a dog walker was not just about walking people's dogs and all that that entails; it was also about listening to the owner's problems, worries and concerns. A few customers tend to confide in me, talking their problems through. I don't flatter myself by assuming people think I am a good listener. I think in general people trust their dog walkers with their pets, so there is already a relationship in place, built on trust. When it comes to problems, I think people like to speak to someone who is not involved in the heart of the matter, a pair of impartial ears perhaps. Maybe the dog walker fits that bill, I was happy to lend an ear.

When in Brad's company he talked openly about his relationship problems with Amy. He obviously still loved her but for whatever reason, they had parted ways. Each time we met he brought me up to speed on the latest events. I patiently listened to recent developments and tried to lift his spirits by thinking of positive things to say to him. It got to the stage where Brad would ask to join me on the walks to have a chat. This meant him taking time away from the hotel to do just that. Of course, I didn't have a problem with this, he was good company and it was always nice to have human companionship on the walks. But at the same time, it did feel a bit strange talking to a person from the opposite sex about relationship problems.

It was good that he was talking though, so many men don't tend to talk about their problems, preferring to bottle things up and retreat to their man cave. It did, however, mean that Brad was paying me to walk Rocky when in fact he was walking his dog himself, with me in tow. Perhaps I was now being paid for the counselling and not the walking.

Brad started to rely on me in all manner of things. At the un-Godly hour of 3 am one Friday night my sleep was interrupted by the sound of my phone ringing, Brad's name displayed on the screen. Answering his call, it was apparent that Brad was the worse for wear, after having been on a stag party all evening. The reason for the call was that he had mislaid his keys and had managed to lock himself out of his house. Not being too drunk to realise that I had a spare set he proceeded to phone me, and asked if he could call round to collect them. *For God's sake!* This was the last thing I wanted to happen in the middle of the night; a nice looking, younger, drunk man coming around to see me in all my glory, but what could I do? Of course, I had to say yes, I could hardly see him locked out of his house all night. I quickly tried to make myself presentable. Brad arrived 30 minutes later in his drunken stupor and apologised profusely. Handing over his key I told him that it wasn't a problem, although that was not strictly true, I felt uncomfortable about the irregular situation. It's not a typical occurrence for a customer to turn up at my house at 3 am, but then Brad was not your typical customer. We had an unusual sort of relationship; I suppose it was turning into more of a friendship than a professional relationship.

For the second time since meeting Brad he was on the move yet again, he was now going to rent a house in Ansdell. I'm not sure why he moved around so much, perhaps he just kept getting itchy feet. The latest move was not without its problems either. Due to some sort of complication with the lease it meant that he was going to be homeless for a 3-week period. That's when the next irregular incident happened; we were out on a walk together, yet again Brad paying me to walk Rocky, when he asked if he could move in with me for the 3-week duration!

His request took me completely by surprise; this was something else that I did not particularly want to happen. Naturally, I expect to get asked to board dogs, that's my job but I am not in the habit of boarding the owners too. It wasn't a habit that I wanted to get into either! I definitely didn't want a customer sharing my house and I certainly couldn't cope with Rocky around twenty-four-seven. On the spot I had to think quickly. Coming up with a white lie, I told him that a friend who had recently split up with her husband, was about to move in with me, meaning my spare room was going to be in use. He seemed accepting of my response and thank God that was the end of that. Somehow against my better judgement Rocky kept his place with the gang, life was never dull with the crazy Pointer around.

Chapter 11

Laura's Ark

A large chunk of every day is taken up driving around town, collecting and dropping off the dogs. Sometimes, and again in the vein of amusing myself, I like to refer to my car as the Ark, a vessel for transporting the dogs, two by two.

Driving isn't really my bag, but a necessity for ferrying my furry cargo from A to B. I lack confidence, possibly because I was a late learner and an untalented one at that. I particularly dislike motorway driving and going to places for the first time. Learning to drive was a nerve-racking experience for me.

My friends on the other hand appeared to enjoy their driving lessons, they even looked forward to them, but not me, I dreaded them. I felt incredibly vulnerable behind that wheel as if in charge of some sort of deadly weapon, that could easily go out of control at the drop of a hat and run someone over. Drawing on my female intuition I sensed that my instructor, Gerry, didn't think much of my driving skills either. It wasn't so much what he said but the way he looked at me whenever I made a blunder, of which there were many. At such times he would hold his glare for far longer than necessary, thus making me feel even more incompetent. He did, however, compliment me on my emergency stops, which was something I suppose.

After an embarrassingly large number of lessons (thirty plus), Gerry finally thought I may be ready for the test and put me forward. The big day arrived, I felt extremely apprehensive to say the least. Fortunately, there was the usual safety net of the double lesson ahead of the exam, and God knows I needed all the help I could get. Perhaps a two-hour lesson could transform me from a blundering idiot to a competent driver, stranger things have happened, but realistically it was doubtful. During my final lesson I drove to the test centre with Gerry by my side in his immaculately clean car. Gerry's car was always pristine, and always smelt brand new as though he had just picked it up from the showroom. On the journey things seemed to be going OK when suddenly Gerry slammed on the brakes, sharply saying;

"I didn't think you were going to slow down, did you not notice the roundabout."

I quickly looked at him just in time to see all colour drain from his face; he was clearly concerned.

He was right though, I hadn't noticed it. The roundabout is a massive junction, they don't come much bigger, but somehow, I had failed to spot it. I could only put this down to nerves, he held his laser beam stare for a particularly long time on that occasion. Our emergency stop had clearly upset a fellow driver to the rear of us, as the indignant driver drove past, he wound his window down shouting; "You idiot, you are never going to pass your test."

This was not a good omen. Coming to my defence Gerry gave the agitated driver a rude hand gesture. Things were not boding well for a pass; I don't think it was possible to have felt any more nervous than I did on that day. With absolutely no confidence in my own ability, how could I expect an examiner to consider me competent?

We just about made it to the test centre in one piece. After a long spell in the waiting room, my examiner finally materialised. In typical fashion, he was a gravitas of a man, surly, middle-aged with more than an air of arrogance about him. He did nothing to put me at ease, quite the contrary. Feeling nervous about a whole host of things on that day, I worried that I would fall at the first hurdle and even fail the eyesight test. Prior to embarking on my driving lessons and not being in possession of twenty/twenty vision, I decided to get myself a pair of spectacles to assist me. My sight was borderline, and my optician told me that I didn't actually need glasses, as my eyesight was satisfactory. But I decided to err on the side of caution and invest in a pair, they could only be an asset.

What possessed me I don't know, but I got myself a set of glasses with nice big blue frames which wouldn't have looked out of place on Dame Edna Everage. Wearing the glasses always made me feel uncomfortable and I don't think they helped with my sight in the slightest. In fact, I think they hindered my vision, rather than enhancing it. The large frames inhibited my peripheral vision to a large degree. But thinking it was the right thing to do; I persevered and wore the ludicrous spectacles for the test.

In complete silence, the examiner and I made our way back to my instructor's car to embark on the nerve wracking experience of the test. As we did so he pointed out a vehicle that was quite a distance from us. Finally breaking the stony silence, he asked me to read the registration plate, which I did to the best of my ability, and waited nervously for his response;

"Wrong, go ten ft. closer." He was almost robotic in his diction. Getting closer to the vehicle entailed climbing up a muddy embankment. Wearing white canvas boots, the order of the day, I made my way up the muddy knoll. My heels began to sink into the soft earth beneath me and my once white canvas boots quickly became ensconced in thick black mud. When at a distance that I assumed was approximately ten ft. closer I read the number plate aloud for a second time. The examiner slung me a look of disdain and said nothing. At that point I didn't know if I had been successful in my second attempt or not, we proceeded to the car and the ordeal continued.

After completing the terrifying experience of the test and feeling less than confident, the examiner told me to pull up to the side of the road. Once stationary he went through numerous tasks that I had executed incorrectly. A long list ensued, without knowing if it was the correct protocol, I defended myself on a few points. Remaining rigid in my seat I looked down at my mucky boots, most of the mud had now dried and fallen off in clumps which lay on the mat. Gerry would not be best pleased with the mess, it would do nothing for our relationship, I was sure of it. The atmosphere was tense as I waited to hear the worse, but I was shocked when he surprisingly said the unexpected positive three words;

"You have passed."

"Are you sure?" I was astonished.

"Yes, but don't make me change my mind."

My examiner was clearly becoming more impatient with me by the second. I kept quiet from that moment on. But it was hard to contain myself, I passed first time! Success doesn't happen to me, but that day it did, it was a special new feeling to me. But I couldn't expect the examiner to celebrate in my euphoria, perhaps my instructor would be a better bet. I drove back to the test centre in a silent atmosphere charged with my excitement. Getting out of the car the examiner and I walked back into the waiting room whereupon we were immediately greeted by Gerry who quizzically asked;

"Well, how did it go?"

"I passed."

I was elated to be saying those words. And there was that laser beam glare again, this time tinged with bemusement. Gerry took a few seconds to come up with anything then said; "It's strange, the ones you think are going to pass, fail, and the ones you think are going to fail, pass." I must admit I too was incredibly surprised. To this day I still don't know how I managed it. First thing I did when I got home was to chuck my Dame Edna specs in the bin. *I won't be needing those again!*

In contrast to some of my friends, males in particular, I was never particularly impressed by the status symbol of owning a flash car. Some people seem to dote on their vehicles, especially when they have just bought a brand spanking new car. Being invited to go and see a friend's new car always filled me with a sense of awkwardness. It was an expensive inanimate object that was bound to depreciate in value, where was the excitement in that? But if it had been a brand spanking new puppy that they were wanting to show off; then that would be a different matter.

In the early days of my pet sitting career, I was the proud owner of a blue Volkswagen Polo. My Polo stood me in good stead, it was reliable and fairly sturdy for a small car. I thought long and hard about exchanging my Polo for a van and advertising the name of my business on the side of it. A van with built-in cages for the dogs was certainly the safer option. But I didn't particularly like the idea of confining the hounds in cages. I know it's more secure than having them free range, but caging the dogs was something that made me feel uncomfortable. Also, some dogs dislike being in an enclosed van, they prefer to see out. In fact, what they like most of all is to have their heads sticking out of a car window, tongues dangling while they take in the views. After much deliberation; I decided to continue using the Polo for the transportation of my pet cargo and against advertising on my car. I'm not exactly sure why I didn't want to advertise, obviously, it would have brought more business my way, but I opted for anonymity over an increase in trade. Later I was glad I had made that choice; in Blackpool things between competitive dog walkers had become somewhat fractious. Rival dog walkers started 'naming and shaming' competitors by taking photos of other's vans, then publishing the evidence on social media exposing them for various reasons. Allegations such as dogs being left too long in a particular van, dog walkers not exercising the dogs long enough were commonplace.

Although not particularly fond of driving, I began to grow partial to bobbing around my local vicinity, ferrying the dogs in the Ark. I usually knew where I was going, and it didn't involve motorway driving. For the most part my mood was relaxed, I enjoyed listening to the radio, whilst observing people going about their everyday lives. The exception being when setting off first thing in the morning and hearing an unexplained noise from the interior of my car. The uncertainty as to what the noise was usually triggered my paranoia and I got the awful sinking feeling that I had forgotten to drop a dog off the previous day, and it had been in my car all night, suffering in silence. This particular blunder had never actually happened to me but this fact did not stop me from being haunted by the possibility that it could.

Planning my route each day, I aimed for the quickest and therefore most cost-effective journeys. My customers all live in the Lytham St Anne's area and are situated in close proximity. Some customers even live on the same road which is rather convenient. After being in the office for the core hours of the day for a period of thirty years it was great to get out and about during the day. I was free, liberated and beginning to discover that the town was a hive of activity to which I had previously been oblivious.

Observing certain vehicles on a regular basis, numerous things struck me;

Firstly, the large number of council workers going about their work: cleaning the roads, weed spraying, refuse collecting, tending to the town's gardens, repairing potholes *in a fashion*, cleaning the beach and such like.

Secondly: private service workers, cleaners, gardeners, window cleaners, rival pet sitters and mobile dog groomers, all employed by people working full time who are not able to tend to these duties themselves.

Lastly: the public and private health services, NHS District Nurses busy in their duties, they certainly have their work cut out tending to the town's infirmed. Ambulances, private and public alike, transporting people to and from hospital. Pharmacy vehicles, delivering medication to the sick, all working tirelessly.

As a child on hearing the sound of the ambulance sirens, I had always assumed that there was a lot of local road traffic accidents. It wasn't until I became a pet sitter that I realised it wasn't the case. Whilst driving around I started to notice the ambulances parked up outside the many care homes and retirement apartments. Usually it was the case that the ambulances were taking an ageing person to hospital attempting to keep them going that bit longer.

I also started to notice specific cars recognisable by their registration plates, almost in the same way a person is recognised by their face. In an almost voyeuristic manner, I began to observe where the drivers lived and visited, pondering as to what sort of people they were and what sort of lives they led. I also became aware of the vast amount of personalised number plates that were out there (designer faces), something that I have never quite understood. One registration plate in particular springs to the forefront of my mind. The owner of a local hotel was the proud owner of a red Lamborghini. Although not impressed with sports cars, with the Lamborghini's low to the ground design and futuristic headlights, even I could tell it was an impressive piece of machinery. To the front and back of the vehicle the number plates proudly sported the letters LOVER1! *Why would you do that?* It's always been alien to me as to why some people want everyone to know who they are, what car they are driving, where they are going or where they have been. In addition, they pay a lot of money for the privilege. Obviously, there are a lot of people that don't share my preference for anonymity.

Another thing that I became conscious of was the fairly large number of schools in the town. Getting myself stuck in the 3.30 pm school traffic was a regular occurrence. At this time of day 'lollypop' people become ubiquitous, suddenly appearing at junctions and traffic lights. Getting caught off guard by a lollipop person jumping out when the traffic lights are on green, is always something that catches me unawares. Still, at least I get to draw on my emergency stop skills!

Then there are the cyclists, a constant worry to me when I am driving about. Firstly, I am not too sure about men in Lycra, and secondly, I struggle with the correct road etiquette when approaching cyclists. Even when I think I have got it right, by giving them space and patience, somehow, I usually manage to cause offence; they let me know this by giving me 'The Finger' sign. *When did the two finger 'V' sign get replaced by the solitary finger, and how did everyone know when to start trending it?* In my opinion, cyclists seem to antagonise drivers and vice-versa. I know I find it irritating when they ride two abreast.

Many of the things I do to ensure the dogs are safe in the car, are obvious. Such as, counting how many mutts get out for the walk and making sure that the same number get back in. At the same time ensuring no paws or tails are caught in the way when closing the door. This can be quite challenging as all dogs could be in a safe position, then I make the decision to shut the door at which point a dog may have decided to move a body part into a dangerous place. Thankfully no harm has ever come to my dogs in this manner, but vigilance is always required, especially with the younger dogs that are not typically great with their commands.

A less obvious task is getting the dogs into the car in the right order. Any territorial dogs need to go into the car last otherwise they will snap at a dog invading their space. By the same token, a dog may be nervous of getting into the car if there is already an unwelcoming dog in situ. The nervous dog will pick up on the body language of the dominant dog and become intimidated and not want to get in. All hounds must get into my Ark in the correct order.

Once the dogs are safely in, we can then head off to our destination. I don't tend to secure the dogs unless we have a rather active dog or a restless puppy on board. The dogs usually sit calmly even though they are perhaps a tad cramped. Seven dogs in a Polo can be a bit of a tight squeeze, but I don't think it matters assuming they keep still. To be honest I think they enjoy the close contact with one another, in the same way they did as pups when they comfortably laid on top of each other showing no sign of irritation or discomfort.

Whilst driving along, my canine friends watch me intently, never taking their beady eyes off me. Looking up at the rear-view mirror I see their reflection, they sit quietly staring at the back of my head, shoulder to shoulder resembling beautiful furry skittles. Even though they can't see my face they watch the back of my head for any change in my behaviour or body language. At any one time, there can be as many as fourteen cute doggy eyes watching my every move.

When waiting at a junction or traffic lights, I turn around to see them in the flesh, topping up on my endorphins. Their good behaviour impresses me no end, but I think the thing that impresses me the most is that a couple of them like to use the arm rests. I have a hilarious boxer and a Cockerpoo who seem to instinctively understand what they are intended for.

Still at the helm, if I happen to display signs of irritation by perhaps raising my voice at a fellow driver, the dogs become startled and confused, they look at me as if they to say;

"What is wrong, what is the problem?"

My raised voice appears to make them anxious. Because of the effect my impatience has on the dogs I have gradually learned not to raise my voice when driving, or at least not as much as I used to. Perhaps the dogs were teaching me to be a better driver!

Although my doggy journeys go relatively smoothly, they are not without incident. It was a routine day when I pulled up outside Tilly's house to take her for her habitual morning walk. Getting out of the Ark I left three dogs inside, whilst I went to collect Miss Tilly, a lovely black and white Cavapoo. It wasn't until we were walking back towards the car when I witnessed it gently rolling down the road that I realised Forrest Drive was on a gentle gradient. I must have picked her up hundreds of times and this fact had always eluded me. Yes, like a complete idiot, I had left the handbrake off. The Ark complete with three dogs, (one of which was now sat in the driver's seat), was slowly manoeuvring itself backward towards the centre of the road.

To complete the scene an oncoming Range Rover driven by a middle-aged woman was slowly approaching the rogue Ark. With no idea how the hell to deal with the situation I stood motionless on the precipice of disaster, mouth wide open while the scene unfolded. The driver of the Range Rover paused, presumably waiting to see which way the dog was going to take the Ark. It was a blessing that there was no traffic to the rear of my car. Continuing to slowly roll backwards, the not so careful lady driver decided to intrepidly pass on the right-hand side of the Ark. It crossed my mind that she was taking a huge risk. There was no certainty that my car was going to stay on the same course, or indeed not pick up speed. Fortunately, she managed to successfully overtake the Ark, which by some fluke had stayed on its course. The woman drove off into the distance and the Ark continued to slowly meander, backwards down the centre of Forrest Drive. As soon as the coast was clear I quickly pulled myself together and ran towards my car, jumped in it, pushed my furry co-driver out of my seat and finally put the handbrake on. I thanked my lucky stars that no harm was done, but it was a traumatic couple of minutes. Surprisingly the dogs had all remained calm, all par for the course!

You would think I had learned from that ordeal but, no, I did the same thing a few months later, except on that occasion the situation was even worse. It was at the exact same place. I got out of the car and yet again forgot to put the handbrake on, then I went to collect Tilly. This time the traffic was much heavier. Leaving the house, I was just in time to witness the Ark slowly rolling backwards, holding up the traffic, this time in both directions. It's hard to describe exactly what was going through my head as I watched my car careering down the road for a second time. I suppose

112

it was a combination of shock and disbelief, probably more disbelief than anything else, I had made the awful blunder, yet again. Once the image had registered in my brain, I had to do something, and quickly.

It had become apparent that the Ark was now picking up speed and heading towards a taxi that had stopped dead in its tracks. The taxi driver was unable to reverse as traffic had now backed up behind it. Sprinting like the clappers and perspiring profusely I managed to catch up with my car, quickly opened the door, hurled myself over the driver's seat (which was vacant this time), grabbed the handbrake, and finally yanked it upwards into the 'On' position. Just in time to avert a collision. Turning around I sheepishly looked at the driver of the taxi and mimed an apology towards him. He appeared remarkably calm and gave me a wry smile as he slowly drove past, no doubt thinking to himself; "What an idiot."

I was way too embarrassed to make eye contact with any of the other drivers, hoping above hope that none of them recognised me. Yet again, I had survived another debacle and was fortunate to get off so lightly and unscathed. Naturally, the whole handbrake situation was beginning to make me feel somewhat paranoid. What was wrong with me, why couldn't I manage to put a handbrake on? Other people seem to carry out the simple act automatically but not I. It just didn't come naturally to me. Trying to address the problem I got myself into a routine where I had a word with myself before getting out of the car. Mentally chanting;

"Is the handbrake on? Is the handbrake on?"

Concentration and mindfulness was called for. Sometimes even when I had got it right and actually remembered to put the handbrake on, the unnerving sensation that the car was still in motion swept over me. Paranoia was getting the better of me, my mind was playing tricks, I was probably mentally scarred by now.

I make excuses for myself but it's a puzzle to me as to why there isn't a warning beep on all manual cars when the engine is off, yet the handbrake is still off. Cars are designed to 'beep' if the lights are left on, but to my mind, a lot more collateral damage can be caused by leaving the handbrake off. I know this because several years ago one Sunday morning my sister Anna's Freelander knocked a lamppost over in a similar fashion. Parking up outside a friend's house, after failing to put the handbrake on she got out of her car. A man passing by asked if she was the owner of the Freelander to which she sheepishly replied; "Yes."

He went on to inform her that her car was rolling down the hill. With that she turned around just in time to see her vehicle crashing into a lamppost. The lamppost immediately crumpled in front of her eyes. A woman came rushing out of the house situated directly behind the desecrated lamppost, yelling;

"What are you going to do about this mess? You can't leave it like that! There are live wires exposed and I have children in my house!" The woman was angry, not holding back.

"I don't know what to do, I have never knocked a lamppost down before."

By this time Anna was upset and worried. The passer by kept a low profile. Eventually, Anna had the presence of mind to call the police who arrived an hour later and cornered off said lamppost. Anna was naturally upset by the whole ordeal but took comfort from the fact that things could have turned out so much worse. The housing estate was open plan with no garden walls or fencing. Had the lamppost not been situated where it was, her car would have undoubtedly rolled into the woman's house. Anna was thankful for small mercies, but not best pleased when she received a letter from the council invoicing her for the hefty sum of a thousand pounds.

Apparently this is the going rate for replacing a lamppost knocked down on a Sunday. Going forward it's automatic cars all the way now for Anna and me. We clearly have some sort of missing gene in our family!

Chapter 12

Maintenance of the ark

At times the interior of my car, 'the Ark' is like a gallery of eclectic doggy art: impressionist work on the windows created when the little darlings nuzzle their snouts up against the glass, a collage of sand paw prints pepper the flooring, and then there is always a splattering of dog hair draped across the upholstery for good measure. What was the point of keeping on top of cleaning it when at least twice a day it's going to get covered in sand and fur? Whilst I keep on top of my housework, keeping the Ark clean was always going to be a battle and one which I was never going to win; I quickly learned to concede defeat. But it is not always filthy, I like to get it valeted about once a week by a professional cleaner, thereby ensuring there is no harmful bacteria lurking. My cleaner certainly has his work cut out.

On occasions, and not surprisingly, there has been the odd bit of drama played out within the confines of the Ark, that required an industrial cleaning operation. One such incident stands out above the rest; it involved Rocky, and Jess an unsprayed young Weimaraner, another dog that I had inherited from Carol. During a phone call Carol informed me that although she was due to board Jess, she had found herself in a position where she had more dogs than she could manage- cue me. Consequently, I naively agreed to take Jess off her hands and that was without ever having met the dog before, but at the time Carol was desperate and I wanted to help her out. The fact that Jess was unspayed was a concern to me especially as Rocky was still intact. Although Brad had said that he was going to get Rocky castrated, he had not got round to getting it done. Personally I think he found the whole notion off putting. However, Carol had been assured by the owner that the fact Jess was unspayed would not be a problem, as she was nowhere near her next season. *A recipe for disaster if ever there was one!*

Jess checked in. From the word go she was extremely hard work, all the negatives of bad dog behaviour rolled into one; strong, extremely boisterous, out of control and not responding to any commands. Brece was not in the least bit amused. Jess is the type of dog that would never pass her vetting process had she not slipped under the radar. It was regrettable that I had ever agreed to look after the crazy Weimaraner; I couldn't help thinking that somehow, I had been stitched up like a kipper!

To set the scene it was a warm day, late 2011, unusually warm for the time of year. I had herded the dogs into the Ark ready for our morning walk. Brece jumped into her usual position of the front foot-well, then I opened the back door and Jess jumped in, rapidly followed by Rocky who seemed very keen to be in Jess's company. After which, I got myself into the driving position. Before I had even put the keys into the ignition a fracas broke out behind me, a hell of a scuffle had erupted. Quickly turning around, I caught sight of Rocky trying to hump Jess in a most determined manner; utter disaster in the confines of the Ark!

Jess must have come into her season, or about to, which meant that the owner had either misled Carol or just got the timings wrong, and indeed timings can go awry. The thought of Jess's condition made me feel queasy, especially when the recollection of her standing on top of my dining table like some sort of mountain goat, popped into my head, *gross*. The whining and wailing from Jess grew louder, she was clearly in distress. There was no way I could have them 'locking', the thought of a litter of mini Rocky's on the planet did not bear thinking about. It certainly wasn't going to be an easy job to separate the pair, a serious task lay ahead of me. Still sat in the driver's seat I contemplated on how to resolve the situation.

I peered down at Brece in the front foot-well, hoping for some sort of inspiration. On this occasion, she failed to come up with the goods, but she did come up with something else. Looking up at me with her big doleful eyes she produced a massive rasping burp, then proceeded to vomit across the interior of the car. In true Jackson Pollock style, the sick splattered all over the passenger seat, the floor and inside the usual nooks and crevices of a car. To make matters worse the vomit was not your usual consistency. It was thick, greyish in colour and extremely pungent, as if she had hauled it up from her bowels.

This was all I needed, but I couldn't allow myself to be side-tracked by Brece's tummy upset, my priority at that moment was to get Rocky off Jess. Jumping out of the car I opened the back door and was relieved to see that the odd couple had not yet consummated their marriage, but it was not for the want of trying on Rocky's part.

With the door ajar, Jess saw her opportunity to escape and charged out of the vehicle before I had chance to grab her. At breakneck speed she ran off down the centre of the road, obviously not too enamoured with Rocky as a potential suitor. Thank God there was no traffic about. In rapid succession I chased after her. Of course, there was no way I was going to catch up with her, she was running with the speed of a Greyhound. Then a spot of good luck came my way; Sean, my friendly postman happened to be walking along the pavement halfway down the road and ahead of Jess;

"Sean, catch that dog please, she's okay she won't hurt you."

I was frantic by this time. Without considering the risk to himself, Sean gallantly charged into the middle of the road and managed to catch Jess by the collar. *Definitely beyond the call of duty.* My marvellous postman managed to keep hold of her until I reached him and relieved him of his extra duties.

Prior to being someone entrusted to look after people's pets, I hadn't given too much thought to the role of the postman. But now I look at Her Majesty's servants in a different light. They have quite a lot on their plates; often having to run the gauntlet of being chased off properties by protective dogs, good in a crisis and always happy and affable when going about their duties, even in torrential rain. I now have a new-found respect for our friend the postman.

Thank God no harm had come to Jess, but it was another close shave. After that scary episode I made a conscious decision not to accept any unvetted boarders from any of my colleagues, under any circumstances, no matter how desperate they were.

For obvious reasons I rarely allow human passengers inside the Ark. I feel mortally embarrassed if anyone asks me for a lift unless of course the Ark has been recently valeted. Otherwise, the only passengers allowed inside are drunks, who wouldn't notice the Eau de doggy, or people suffering from a cold who have temporarily lost their sense of smell. Anyone else is refused entry.

Naturally the Ark needs to undergo services and the occasional repairs. During such times I am kindly granted the use of a courtesy car. Keeping the loaned car clean for the interim period is yet another endurance task I undertake, *even I realise it is not acceptable to return a courtesy car covered in doggy DNA.* The Ark was booked in early one Monday morning for the annual MOT, the garage owner kindly bestowed me with the usual courtesy car. The arrangement being that I would drop it back the following morning after the MOT and any minor repairs on my car had been completed. Driving away in a lovely spruce Kia Sportage, I couldn't help wondering if the garage owner would have granted me the car had he realised my profession. I thought it prudent to keep such information to myself.

It was a normal working day, so crucial that I made every effort to keep the Kia clean. For protection I covered the seats with purposely designed waterproof sheets. Next thing was to decide on the venue for the morning walk. If there was any chance of keeping the car clean it was imperative that the dogs remained as clean as possible. This meant the destination was key, it had to be somewhere safe but void of mud or sand, which greatly limited my options. Picking up my compliment of seven dogs, I set off for the walk, still unsure as to where to take my mob. Then I remembered an enclosed non-muddy, non-sandy field in the next village just north of Lytham. Not one of my regular haunts because of the distance but worth going the extra mile in an attempt to keep my pack of marauding dogs unsoiled.

However, I had not taken into consideration one of my newer crew members 'Mckenzie Monster', nicknamed for obvious reasons. Mckenzie is a one-year old male water obsessed Golden Retriever, lovely but incredibly strong and as daft as a brush. Arriving at the non-muddy, non-sandy field I released the beasts; the usual suspects, Brece, Wasabi, Hendrix, Rocky a couple of boarders and of course Mckenzie. As expected, they all excitedly scrambled straight towards the field. But it didn't take long to realise that my plan was not foolproof. After a quick circuit of the field, Mckenzie Monster led his battalion through a brand-new hole that had recently appeared in a fence which opened onto what can only be described as a quagmire! A Retriever does not care if the water is clean or muddy, it's of no relevance to the dog, all that matters is that it is water. After much glee and gay abandonment, Mckenzie and his battalion emerged from the quagmire, covered in black filthy sludge. My heart sank at the spectacle before my eyes. I was now looking at seven filthy stinking dogs who had to be transported in the loaned car, *just great*. I did, however, take some solace in the fact that I had taken measures to cover the seats with the waterproof sheeting.

After a stressful hour we made our way back to the car, once there I got the mucky pups back inside then set off. On the return journey it slowly dawned on me that although I had taken precautions to protect the upholstery, I had done nothing to protect the rest of the car interior, but there wasn't much I could do about it now.

Whilst still driving the sound of a dog crying profusely interrupted my thoughts. I quickly glanced around and was greeted by the sight of a big squirming mass wriggling beneath the plastic sheeting. It didn't take long to realise that the mass belonged to Mckenzie Monster, obvious by the size and the big white fluffy tail wafting vigorously from underneath the waterproof sheeting. Mckenzie frantically tried to release himself. After much squirming and wriggling he finally succeeded, smearing the upholstery with the pungent residue of the quagmire in the process. *This was all I needed*. Normally Mckenzie would be the last dog to be dropped off, but after a quick change of plan I took him home ahead of the others and was relieved to be doing so.

Alas, that was not the end of the day's saga. Worryingly, I had a poorly dog on my hands, Nelson a 4-year-old cocker spaniel who was boarding with me. Since arriving at my house two days previously he had been drinking and urinating excessively, not a good sign. That evening on returning home after my hectic day, I made myself a cup of tea and took a few minutes to relax, putting my car valeting problems to one side. After the excitement of the walk Nelson seemed fine, but then he became slightly agitated and wanted to go out into the garden. The two of us went outside, I watched him as he emptied his bladder and bowels, then I checked his poo. This is something that I tend to do as a matter of course, a sort of doggy health check and not some weird fetish. The examination did not go well, I was alarmed to find that his waste was marbled with blood, and it wasn't just a bit, there was a lot of it. He clearly required urgent medical attention, wasting no time I made an emergency appointment for him. We headed off to the vets, courtesy of the filthy Kia Sportage.

That evening I was due to pick up another dog, Susie, who was due to stay with me for five days. Killing two birds with one stone I decided to collect Susie en-route to the vets, together with her food, bed, and toys. I arrived at the vets, got out of the courtesy car leaving Susie secured in the back, with her food safely out of temptation's way on the front seat. Nelson and I made our way to the surgery.

On our approach, it soon became apparent that Nelson was not a big vet fan. There were a few tell-tale signs, stopping dead in his tracks, and whining profusely were a few indications. Seeing and dealing with 'Vet Fear' in a dog is commonplace to me, but Nelson's fear was off the scale, he wasn't just afraid but terrified. After a bit of a struggle I managed to get him into the building, once inside his whining racked up a few more notches. We stood in front of the frosty receptionist, a middle-aged lady with auburn hair and wearing glasses. Nelson howled the place down. It soon became apparent that our doggy theatre was attracting a lot of glances from other pet owners who were patiently and quietly waiting their turn. Some people appeared to be understanding of the drama we were presenting, but then others, not so. The receptionist being in the latter group, she could hardly bear to look up at us. In a noticeably irritated tone and still avoiding eye contact she managed;

"What's the name please?"

I gave Nelson's details, then she told us to take a chair, pointing to the seat furthest away from the reception desk, we duly took our orders and sat down. Looking around that waiting room there were probably four other owners with their dogs of varying shapes and sizes. All dogs sat quietly even though they were in the presence of a couple of cats who were safely secured in their carriers besides their owners. It always surprises me how cats and dogs seem to be able to tolerate each other when in the oppressive atmosphere of the vet waiting room. It's not as if the animals don't know they are sat alongside their arch enemies, yet they sit silently, dogs calm, and cats not hissing; outside on the streets it would have been a completely different story.

Thankfully breaking the tense atmosphere, a male vet in his forties popped his head round the door of a consultation room and called out Nelson's name. Nelson and I skulked off and followed the vet into the consultation room. As we did so I felt the relief lift from the shoulders of the congregation of that waiting room.

"What seems to be the matter?"

I explained Nelson's symptoms and was glad that the ordeal was coming to an end. But my sense of comfort was short lived. On being examined by the vet and without as much as a warning growl or snarl, Nelson took it upon himself to bite the vet's hand. *I hoped he was up to date with his tetanus jabs.* The vet appeared to take things in his stride and thankfully the puncture did not draw blood. I suppose this sort of behaviour is par for the course for a Veterinary Practitioner. Sensibly and as a precaution, he then muzzled the anxious dog and continued with the examination. After a few minutes, the vet diagnosed Colitis, a condition which is basically an inflammation of the bowel and can be treated with antibiotics, and a change of diet. Rich sustenance is not advisable.

But this was not the whole picture, I explained the situation with regards to Nelson's urinary habits. The vet responded by saying he needed a urine sample from Nelson in order to check his kidney functionality. Previously during the examination, he had detected that Nelson's kidneys appeared to be enlarged, which can sometimes be an indication of kidney disease. At this point my heart sank; what if he did have a kidney disease, how was I going to tell the owners? When was I going to tell them? Should it be whilst they were on holiday or on their return? Was this my job, the vet's job or the emergency contact's job? I just didn't have any of the answers or know what to do for the best. In the meantime, getting a water sample from Nelson was my next focus.

Leaving the examination room, we headed back to reception to settle the bill. By this time a small queue had gathered at the desk. Although Nelson's ordeal was almost over this fact did not appear to appease him, not in the slightest, his screeching was at fever pitch. Feeling acutely embarrassed about the noise levels coming from the little fellow I decided to put him in the car to relieve him of his anguish and spare everyone's eardrums, especially the delicate ears of the receptionist. I rushed in order to get back inside as soon as possible to settle the bill, just in case the frosty receptionist thought I was leaving without paying. Once at the car and erring on the side of caution I decided to keep Nelson and Susie separated. They had not previously been left alone and therefore there was no telling how they would get along with each other. I couldn't afford any more disasters that day so I put Nelson in the front of the car, whilst Susie remained secure in the back.

With that, I made my way back to reception to resume my place in the queue, settled the bill, then returned to the car. I felt glad that the ordeal was almost over, all that was to be done now was to get the water sample from the distraught dog, then clean the Kia up ahead of exchanging cars at the garage the following morning. Opening the car door, my sense of relief was quickly negated by the sight of Nelson happily munching his way through Susie's RICH food! In all the commotion I had completely forgotten her food was still on the dashboard!

That evening we all settled in for the night, but it wasn't exactly a 'Silent Night'. At times I thought Nelson was going to go into orbit, explode even, such was the volume of flatulence passing through his bowels. *God knows what effect all this had on his colitis.* There was a happy ending though, I successfully managed to collect a water sample from Nelson and presented it to the vet early the next morning. The vet tested it there and then and, thankfully, Nelson was only suffering from a urinary tract infection and not the more serious condition of kidney disease. After a quick spruce up of the courtesy car at the valeting place, I returned the car to the garage with no one any the wiser.

Being a pet-sitter was starting to feel like taking part in a daily marathon game of chess; sometimes I made a bad move that led to serious consequences, sometimes I didn't see a threatening move coming my way, then other times circumstances were completely out of my control. The hand of fate moved me around that board like a vulnerable pawn; all the while desperately trying to avoid checkmate.

Chapter 13

Location, Location, Location

The location for the daily walks is extremely important, it must be safe, well away from traffic and suitable for all the individual quirks of my eclectic bunch. Some of the dogs gravitate towards water, or worse still, traffic; these things need to be taken into consideration when planning the venue. I am fortunate living where I do as there are a few great safe places to walk a large troupe of dogs.

In the past, I have covered for Carol who continually walked her dogs in the extensive grounds of a large hotel in Blackpool. Finding the same walk a bit tedious I asked her if there was anywhere else safe in Blackpool to walk the dogs, it was a surprise to me when she said that there wasn't. Of course, there is a massive beach at Blackpool, but no off-road parking close by, meaning it is too risky to let a herd of excitable dogs out of a car parked on a busy road. There are a few recreational parks in Blackpool, but again they are not secure enough to let dogs off lead, leaving the hotel grounds as the only suitable venue. I felt blessed that I didn't run a dog walking business in the resort of Blackpool.

The places I usually prefer to walk my dogs are Fairhaven Sand Dunes, St Anne's Beach, and Lytham Hall.

Fairhaven Sand Dunes are situated north of Lytham beach. The dunes are covered in coarse star grass and stretch about two miles towards St.

Anne's beach. In days gone by this part of the dunes was yet another golf course. Now the land has returned to its rough state, but it is still possible to make out areas that previously served as the greens. The dogs, typically Wasabi and Hendrix have great fun running up and down the undulating mounds, taking different routes whilst they happily play chase amongst themselves.

The only disadvantage of this walk is the mud residue left by the tidal estuary which is pocketed in the long grass that covers the shoreline. The mud, locally known as cockle mud, is created when sediment from the salty water of the Irish Sea mixes with the fresh-water sediment of the River Ribble. It is particularly obnoxious in its consistency: thick, slimy, oily and always accompanied by a strong odour of fermenting fish. With the texture of crude oil, once it gets on the dogs it is extremely difficult to clean off. Washing a dog covered in cockle mud is futile; as soon as the mud is diluted it just spreads even further, ending up with more sludge than at the start.

I've tried to clean cockle mud off many a dog before and have always failed miserably. During the cleaning process, the dog naturally shakes to dry itself, which in turn splatters the remnants of mud all over the walls, and I mean all over.

In hot weather, the dogs cannot resist the allure of the sea to cool themselves down and off they go charging into the mud. Molly and Max, another two water/mud obsessed Golden Retrievers are frequent bathers in the mud baths. Max takes the lead, I swear he says to Molly;

"Come on, let's go for a wallow."

The two of them are off like a shot. Not content with just a paddle Max is partial to a good old roll, it's as if he is compelled to baste the whole of his body in the fermenting sludge. The two emerge from their mud spa resembling a pair of hippos, leaving me to negotiate the clean-up operation. I have learned from experience that it's best to try to avoid this area of the dunes in hot weather.

From the vantage point of the high ground of the dunes, I enjoy looking out towards the estuary and observing the abundance of birdlife in the distance. But I don't have to be stood on high ground to appreciate the phenomenon of the migrating birds. Ahead of winter, the estuary is a popular attraction for birds from various parts of the world. They arrive in their gaggling hoards; the noise can be quite deafening and not something that goes unnoticed. As a child, I failed to appreciate the amazing spectacle that is bird migration even though it virtually occurred on my doorstep. Now older, the phenomenon amazes me, things that I took for granted as a child and showed no interest in are now fascinating to me. In springtime, the birds migrate back to where they were born to breed, and the local community is once again treated to the awesome sight of hordes of birds leaving our shores to return to their breeding grounds. For information on the birds migrating to the Ribble Estuary refer appendix G.

On occasions a very rare bird will land at the dunes, attracting birdwatchers from far afield. They arrive in their droves wearing the correct attire and sporting fantastic photographic equipment that the paparazzi would be envious of. In fact, when I first caught sight of a group of birdwatchers with their cameras and gigantic lenses, I thought they WERE the paparazzi. Expecting to bump into some celebrities on the dunes, I was slightly disappointed to find only twitchers.

My first encounter with a mass of twitchers happened during October 2011, Halloween morning to be precise. As I walked down my garden path to set off for the morning walk, the weather felt mild for the time of year. The sun was low in the sky and shining through a light mist, making for a beautiful orange warm glow. Autumn was in full swing, the orange and gold leaves of the trees were falling to the ground in bucket loads. An occasional pumpkin on a neighbour's doorstep added to the orange ambience. Trundling through the crisp leaves the gang and I made our way towards the car. After shoe-horning them inside we headed off to our destination for that morning, the sand dunes.

As we spilled out of the car, we found ourselves right in the middle of a large clan of birdwatchers. It was a surprise to see them, and I think they were both surprised and disappointed to clap eyes on me and my unruly pack, which included Rocky, who could only be a hindrance to them. But surprisingly Rocky wasn't any trouble at all; I had completely forgotten about his 'pointer' breeding. As soon he jumped out of the car he became eerily calm, stood still and began to 'point' in the direction of what I assumed was the attraction. Rocky's behaviour impressed me no end, and I was even more proud when a couple of twitchers remarked on what a beautiful dog he was.

It appeared that the star attraction was a Desert Wheatear, an extremely rare bird which had found itself off course. There was great excitement about the place as the bird which should have been in the Sahara Desert had found itself on Fairhaven Dunes. Catching a few glimpses of the cute little thing, I could see it was sandy in colour and not much bigger than a sparrow.

The hordes of twitchers stood around watching and filming the bird; they appeared to have been doing so for several hours. With their collapsible chairs, and packed lunches they were well and truly settled in. Catching more glimpses of the little bird I couldn't help but feel sorry for the poor thing, it was lost and in an unsuitable climate. It confused me as to why people weren't trying to give the bird nourishment after its long journey. But I knew not to interfere and quickly got the dogs out of the way before they blotted their copy book. Last thing I needed was an angry mob of twitchers on my hands.

Just north of St Anne's pier lies North Beach, arguably the safest and cleanest place to walk a pack of dogs. A car park sits conveniently off road and directly by the beach, making for a safe place to let the dogs out without risk of them running onto the road. Situated close to the mouth of the estuary, the sandbanks which stretch for miles before meeting the Irish Sea are only submerged at high and spring tides, both of which massively reduce the area available for walking. At such times the beach can get congested: dog walkers, horse riders, kite flyers and suchlike all sharing the greatly reduced shore area. But for most of the day the tide is out and there are miles of clean golden sand, ideal for walking a herd of dogs. It is an 'off lead' beach which makes it possible to have the pack unleashed, running around in all different directions, but still in sight.

Anything that is not typical tends to stick out like a sore thumb such as the time when I saw a myriad of black images in the far distance at the foot of the dunes. It was not a usual sight and difficult to determine exactly what the images were from where I was stood. The dogs and I were finishing the walk and heading back to the car park in the direction of the apparition. As we got closer the images became bigger and naturally, the closer we got the bigger they became. Eventually, when almost upon the vision all became apparent. Before my eyes were hundreds of male orthodox Jews in full attire, walking along the dunes, chanting in what I can only surmise was Hebrew. It was as if the men were on some sort of pilgrimage, but where from and where to? They were heading in the direction of Blackpool, hardly the 'Wailing Wall'. It was quite an astonishing sight, the dogs thought so too. In typical fashion, some of them started to bark at the procession. For some time, I stood rooted to the spot watching them go on their way into the distance until they faded yet again into little black dots, before vanishing altogether. Making my way back to my car I was expecting to see hordes of coaches parked up, the pilgrims must have arrived in some sort of transportation, but the car park was completely empty. It was a mystery to me as to how they had found themselves at the beach, another one of those instances that, frustratingly, I knew I would never get to the bottom of.

In days gone by, donkeys gathered by the pier. In my youth my siblings and I enjoyed the occasional donkey ride at weekends, that was until my riding accident when I was thrown off the back of a rogue donkey. Sometimes when the tide is in and the wind is blowing off the Irish Sea that pleasant slightly fishy, yet fresh breeze fills the air. As children we could often smell the aroma from our back garden. When the breeze wafted up our nostrils, we associated the smell with the donkeys imagining them to be congregated on the beach. Shouting excitedly to each other; "I can smell the donkeys!"

These days that fresh sea breeze smell does not seem to be as prevalent as it was in my youth. Whether this is down to some sort of climate change effect, I don't know, but what I do know is that on the rare occasions when walking and the sea breeze hits my nostrils, I experience a lovely nostalgic feeling hurtling me straight back to my childhood; I think to myself; "I can smell the donkeys."

I am proud of the North Beach, walking on it just about every day I metaphorically started referring to it as 'My beach'. The landscape of the beach remains consistent, apart from the number of people and the sea either being in or out. Sometimes the tide goes out leaving cappuccino honeycomb sea foam and more often than not, washed up debris. The council do a great job of keeping it clean, at high tides it is cleaned every day. All sorts of stuff gets washed up: the usual plastic bottles (*those poor turtles),* driftwood, seaweed, shoes, glass bottles, dead birds, and the occasional grisly dead seal or sheep. The list is endless but the most disturbing of all debris and something that certainly does stand out, is undoubtedly HUMAN REMAINS. Finding a dead body on the beach is not a regular occurrence but it does happen from time to time. Rather horrifically it happened to Sam.

Whilst taking an early morning walk with her pack Sam noticed that a large object had washed up on the shore. Her dogs went scurrying over to do their dog job and investigate matters. Sam followed assuming that she was looking at the remains of a sheep, all the while trying to call her dogs back to avoid a multiple dog rolling on dead sheep debacle. All the while Sam was getting closer to the object, the dogs determinedly ignored her commands. At about a distance of twenty feet, the shock kicked in when she realised she was looking at the remains of a human body! She looked away in horror, at the same time, a man from the coastguard services suddenly arrived on the scene. Sam exchanged a few words of despair with him, then dragged the dogs away from the poor soul. She then went on her not so merry way, feeling somewhat shaken up after the gruesome discovery.

Not being an early riser myself, walking on the beach at the crack of dawn is something that I rarely do. This ensures that I am not going to be another unsuspecting dog walker who makes yet another gruesome find. The only time I am on the beach early morning is on a hot summer's day when it's too warm to walk the dogs in the heat of the day. Even then I don't get there at an unearthly hour, thereby ensuring that I am not the first person on the beach. If anything awful was to be washed up, the early bird discovers it and not the lazy toad!

Although the council make a valiant effort to keep the beach clean; they certainly have their work cut out, especially in periods of heavy rain and high tides. In these conditions, an additional problem arises whereby copious amounts of sheep manure washes ashore. It is no secret that the manure emanates from sheep that graze on the salt marshes situated at the mouth of the Ribble Estuary. The presence of sediment in these areas has helped the development of salt marshes, where salt-tolerant plants are able to grow.

The sheep graze on the vegetation which is said to produce high-quality lamb. As the tides come in and go out, the sheep manure is swept out into the estuary eventually getting washed up on 'My beach'. It's not a pleasant sight and obviously not a great tourist attraction. I'm not sure why this problem has not been addressed. The local council are always looking to increase the number of visitors to the area, perhaps addressing the 'sheep manure' problem would help in their quest. At high and spring tides the problem persists to this day.

About half a mile north of the coastguard station, the sand is excavated on a daily basis. JCBs and trucks drive far away from the shoreline to dig up tons and tons of sand which is then brought back to the dunes area and dumped into tanker trucks. The sand is then taken to Southport where it is washed and sold as building sand to be used in the construction industry. This process has been going on for many a year, it's a wonder that there is any sand left, but there still seems to be plenty to go around. The only risk here is that a dog could get in the way of one of the trucks, but the drivers are vigilant and to my knowledge there has never been a truck-on-dog incident.

The dunes and the beach are great places to walk the dogs but my favourite of all local places is Lytham Hall. Steeped in history the hall is situated approximately one mile inland from the coast. Lytham Hall is a grand Georgian mansion previously owned by the Clifton dynasty. For the early history of Lytham Hall refer appendix H.

In the 1970s, the Clifton family sold their estate to the insurance company which I was previously employed by. The company invested over two million pounds on the restoration of the hall. At those times the building was used for filing, storage, and the grounds for corporate events and the occasional open days.

The hall was the venue where my colleagues and I sat part of our Business Analyst exams. The actual examination room itself was ostentatiously furnished with beautiful antique Waring and Gillow furniture and walls adorned with massive oil paintings, not your usual classroom environment. The oppressive paintings were a huge distraction to me and I found it difficult to concentrate on the exam, but my colleagues didn't appear to be distracted in the same way as I was. Personally, I struggled to answer questions on 'Profit and loss accounts' whilst Sister Ursula, looked down on me, holding a human skull in her hand. God knows how but I just about scraped through my exam with a pass, no thanks to Sister Ursula.

The insurance company eventually sold the hall to the local town trust who in turn sold it on to the North West Heritage Trust. During this transitional period some of the building once again fell into disrepair, but the sound parts were still used for events, weddings and tours. Nowadays the grounds of the hall are open daily for the public to walk around, free of charge (except Sundays). In summer months, some of the grounds are used to stage open-air films and plays. Now under a great new management team and with the aid of public money and lottery funding, the restoration work continues and the hall is once again returning to its former glory.

The building is set in acres of tranquil gardens adorned with lily, fishing ponds, and acres of woodland. The grounds are relatively well maintained, thanks to an army of volunteers who devote their time to the upkeep of the estate. A sanguine bunch of folk; chatty, friendly and obviously in a good place in their lives, all making for a lovely ambiance and peaceful walk. In stark contrast to the beach, the landscape of the hall changes dramatically with the seasons.

The flora starts to burst into life in late January when the first snowdrops start to sprout. Winter loosens it's grip and in March clusters of daffodils spring to life. The stunning bluebells and blossom trees flower in April. Then later in the year around May to June time, we are treated to the stellar display of the magnificent rhododendrons. These spectacular flowers come in a variety of colours but only purples ones populate the grounds of the hall, making for a fantastic stylish contrast against the green background of the trees and shrubs. These bushes have matured and continually flourished over the centuries into impressive trees which seem to bloom for months on end.

Summertime, the lily ponds burst into colour as the beautiful pink lilies salute the sun during the day before closing at dusk. But without a shadow of a doubt, my favourite of all the seasons is Autumn. The pigment changes of the magnificent oak trees turn the leaves to the beautiful rustic colours that we associate with autumn, red, yellow, gold and brown. Standing mesmerised in my reverie I watch the leaves slowly flutter off the branches, spiralling to the ground to rest on the impressionist golden carpet. When walking around the grounds there is always something to feast the eye on, whatever the season and whatever the weather.

However, it is not a suitable place to walk a pack of hounds, mainly due to the risk of the dogs diving into the lily pond. I usually only treat myself to a visit when I have one or two sedate dogs that are not water or mud obsessed. Also, due to seasonal ground roosting birds there are times when dogs are not allowed off lead. It always surprises me just how underused the grounds are, although I am quietly pleased that they aren't busier. It's such a pleasure to have the place virtually to myself. Roaming around the grounds I continue in my reverie imagining how it must have been to have lived in such a grand place, back in the day. The bark of a dog giving chase to a squirrel breaks my delusion and I suddenly remember I am a humble dog walker, and not the Lady of the Manor.

Chapter 14

'Logging On'

I have to confess that before starting my pet sitting business, I didn't particularly enjoy walking Brece; I saw it more as a chore than a pleasure. Probably because back then I was working full time and as such I didn't have much spare time for walking. But now being financially rewarded to walk dogs is a great motivation; I now have the time, the inclination and what's more I love it. Sometimes I don't want the walks to come to an end, picking up my stride and enjoying the release of my endorphins as long as I can.

Most of the dogs much prefer a walk over food. I know this to be true as I put it to the test once with five dogs that were boarding with me. Placing a plate of sausages on the floor beside the front door, the excitement amongst the dogs quickly kicked in, food and, or the gateway to Nirvana, which would it be? Opening the door, it didn't take long to get my answer. With the speed of hypersonic missiles, all five completely ignored the succulent sausages, charged straight past the food and excitedly made their way to the front gate. Once at the gate they stood looking and barking in the direction of my car. Unlike Pavlov's dog, my dogs drooled over the vehicle as opposed to the food. Brece, being a greedy gannet, had a different take on things, she hesitated, probably thinking to herself;

'Umm food or walk?' Perhaps if I gobble the food down quickly enough, I can catch up with the others, and still go for a walk.' Which is exactly what she did. In record time my greedy dog devoured all the sausages, then caught up with the rest of the gang at the front gate.

Our friend the dog is an opportunist, even if he has just been on a walk and I am about to take my next batch of furry friends out, the previously walked dogs still go crazy at the prospect of another walk. The dog does not think in a logical manner; 'Hang on, I've just been on a walk so it's not likely that I will be going out again anytime soon.' Instead, it thinks; 'Great, a walk.' The dog lives for the moment never dwelling on the past. The expression on the faces of the excluded dogs always makes me feel incredibly guilty, even though they have all been well exercised. They stare at me, eyes burning into mine, as if to say;

'You can't seriously be leaving us lot behind, can you?' All of them contenders for gold medals in making me feel mean. The walks are without a doubt the highlight of the day for the mutts, they are all carefully matched to ensure harmony amongst the group. It's better to take young dogs out together, then older dogs separately, grouping them in accordance with their verve. I pull up to the destination for the walk with the sound of hollering and barking ringing in my ears, the gang know the dog party is only seconds away. After checking the coast is clear I open the car doors allowing them to hurl themselves out with great gusto, even tumbling over each other as they scramble to get going. Once they are free, they tear around the place, euphoric to be finally embarking on their great and happy adventure. The walks typically follow a pattern:

First activity, logging on; As social animals dogs are extremely interested in sniffing all scents left by other dogs, as if they are logging on to 'doggy social media'. A dog can detect a lot of information by sniffing another dog's scent: such as the gender, if it has been spayed or neutered, or if the scent belonged to a bitch in heat. The sniffing is at its most intense at the beginning of the walk but usually continues intermittently throughout the duration. The dogs mark their territory as they trot along by putting their scent down on top of scent, thus making their scent the strongest. It's usually the males who do this, but sometimes the bitches will do it too, especially the dominant ones.

Secondly, toilet activities; The subject of dog mess is not exactly a charming topic but it's an important one and plays a large part in the role of a dog walker. I need to be aware of the dog's toilet habits in order to inform the owners of any irregularities. Abnormalities are often an indication of the health of the dog, as it was with Nelson when he had managed to catch himself a urinary infection. Also, any poo that has not been picked up is understandably a cause of great irritation to others and makes for a highly emotive topic.

At the beginning of the walk, besides all the sniffing, the dogs relieve themselves. Some of the dogs have been at home for about 3 hours and consequently bursting for a toilet break. It's convenient that most of the dogs take their time to sniff at the beginning of the walk as it means I get a chance to clean up the waste without the pack dispersing too far.

In my new role I was to develop many skills; eyes in the back of my head being the most useful. Picking up one lot of mess whilst another dog is relieving itself out of view, is a common occurrence. The whole poo station area is carefully checked before we move on. At times I don't so much need poo bags but poo carrier bags. Naturally, there will have been an occasion when I have missed some waste. Compensating for this, I pick up the erroneous mess that other dog owners have overlooked. This doesn't bother me in the slightest, I am proud of our local areas and want to keep them as clean as possible, as do most other dog walkers these days.

Similar to the dog that can switch off to the sound of some noises, I now appear to be able to switch off to the smell of dog poo. That special fragrance now goes unnoticed which is rather handy in my line of business. At one point, I feared my sense of smell was failing me, but it was not the case. I smell other scents perfectly well; perhaps I have rather fortunately just become desensitised to the odour. Yet another skill I appear to have developed is; successfully picking poo in high winds without it blowing back out of the bag. This requires a certain amount of dexterity as there is a high risk that some of it may end up on my hand, *not ideal*. Enough now about poo!

Like the other dogs, Brece is also partial to exercising her nostrils, but the activities that she gets the most pleasure from are body-slamming and rolling on the ground. As soon as she gets on the beach, she is excited and demonstrates her happiness by launching into her body-slamming routine. The trigger being her bucking bronco impersonation, which involves prancing along the beach with her back end repeatedly rising up in the air. The bucking continues for about a minute, then stooping down, she swipes one side of her face on the sand rubbing it back and forth. This seems to be the prelude as to which side of her body she is going to slam down. She then hurls her shoulders on the ground with a thud (same side as her face), her back end follows suit, with an even louder thud. When the whole of her body is in contact with the ground, she can then commence her rolling ritual; writhing and wriggling around in bliss, relieving herself of all those itches.

Thirdly, the walk itself; As well as being top dog indoors, Brece is also top dog outside the house. When her rolling routine is complete, she can then commence her walk. My flagship dog trots along ahead, the others following behind, except for Rocky who has usually galloped out to sea. The walk is now underway. Whilst Brece rules with an iron fist in the home, outside she is protective of her pack. If a rogue dog comes into her group, appearing to be intimidating towards one of her members, she goes over to intervene and sort the matter out. She does this by continually barking at the intruder until it goes on its merry way. There is never aggression on her part, just dominance and sheer determination. She is telling the intruder; 'Back off and don't mess with my pack.' She behaves this way even if it is Rocky who is under threat. Despite the fact that she could not bear having him in the house when he boarded with us for the weekend from hell, she did not seem to hold this against him. I would have expected her to be thinking along the lines of 'Go on mate, you can have a go at that one.' But no, she is still fiercely protective over Rocky as she is with all the dogs in her pack. It warms the cockles of my heart when I see her look out for the others in this manner.

The dogs are happy to follow in her wake at their own pace, except for Rocky of course. Some belting from side to side, some trotting whilst sniffing all those exciting smells, with the occasional distracted mutt trailing behind. Most dogs tend to stay within the pack as they have great fun freely running around and socialising together. It is such a joy to watch them enjoying themselves so. The younger dogs such as Wasabi and Hendrix love to play chase. Between them they decide who is going to be the runner and who is going to be the chaser. Usually, a dog will pick up a stick if I am lucky, or some sort of dead bird part if not so lucky. This is the catalyst to start the chase, the dogs tear after the dog with the bounty.

Professional dog walkers have varying styles of walking a group of dogs. Some walkers tend to stay in a small area, throwing balls for the dogs. They get good exercise in this manner, and it's probably a safer option than allowing them to disperse over a large area, they stay close by, therefore there is less risk of any of them going astray. I, however, like to make things a bit more difficult for myself. My preferred method is to go for an hour walk, covering a large area with most of the dogs 'off lead'. It's great for the dogs to run around in all directions, playing freely with their mates. This means that keeping a close eye on the dogs is imperative, especially focusing a third eye on any slightly nervous ones. By continually counting I have my full complement of dogs every minute, I can be sure that if a dog has been distracted and left the pack, then it can't be too far away.

With a new dog, even if the owner has said it's OK to let it off lead, I test the dog's recall before doing so. It may have great recall for the owner, but this may not necessarily extend to another person, especially with the new distractions around. The litmus test is a simple case of calling the dog's name, while it's still on lead. If the dog responds and looks me in the eye, then I usually have control of the dog. When trying to train Brece as a pup, I knew no eye contact, no chance! If a dog's eye contact is poor it means it is distracted and will not respond to me, and so more work is required. Once eye contact is good then I can be certain that the dog will come back to me; well as certain as I can be. It's never 100% possible to predict what any dog is going to do; its behaviour can be affected by so many different external factors.

To help gain a dog's attention I find treats work wonders; the dogs love a little snack on a walk and it's a great way of gaining their attention. When collecting a dog from its home, sometimes I take a handful of dried pellets from its own bowl, to use as treats. The dog was not interested in his food when it was in its bowl, but now it has turned into a treat, then that's a different matter. The other dogs want the treat, said dog sees this and suddenly becomes interested, now wanting to eat his own food; he behaves as the pack behaves.

Of course, it is fine for the dogs to play and tear around with each other, play fight even. However, if the play starts to get too boisterous, things need to be calmed down. If the dogs get too excited sometimes, they can go into a different zone, this new zone is sometimes a difficult place to bring them back from. They don't tend to listen to me if things have tipped past that point of no return; why would they? Play is much more fun. The excitement takes over and what started as a playful fight may turn into a spot of aggression.

Naturally I get talking to other walkers, just polite banter but being out two or three times a day sometimes the banter can get a bit tedious and repetitive. I am plagued by five sets of dialogue from fellow walkers. The first being;

"SOMEONE IS GOING TO NEED A BATH WHEN THEY GET HOME."

Usually directed at Brece -my mucky flagship dog after she has immersed herself in sullied waters. The second being;

"BY HECK, YOU'VE GOT YOUR WORK CUT OUT THERE."

This is an accurate observation to make, but I often wonder if the orator of the comment had any idea how often these words have reached my ears. Of course, people are only being amicable and friendly, but it does become a bit tiresome at times. Depending on what sort of mood I am in, I politely reply with a forced smile nailed to my face;

"Ha, Ha yes I have."

But if I am not feeling too great, perhaps a fraction stressed with a doggy situation, I ignore them. This probably seems rude, but it is more important to keep my eye on the ball as opposed to making idle chat.

As I go about my daily walks it often strikes me just how interested dog owners are in each other's dogs, probably even more so than they are with one another's children. When dogs come across other members of their species, they usually run up to each other, a quick sniff around each other's nether regions is the only introduction needed. Whilst the dogs are introducing themselves the owners stand around watching the dogs perform their rituals. With nothing better to do the humans typically strike up a conversation. Usually, about the dogs, the banter commences;

What's your dog called, how old is it?"

Dog walking is an incredibly social activity, I speak to people from all walks of life, those conversations would never have been struck up if it wasn't for the incredibly social nature of the dogs.

A walker soon gets to know the names of all the regular dogs on a walk, however, it takes a lot longer to get to know the owner's names. The owners are always referred to as 'Diesel's Mum,' or 'Diesel's Dad,' depending on what the dog is called of course. It's acceptable to say to someone;

"What's your dog called?" But it doesn't seem appropriate to ask;

"What are you called?" Hence it takes a lot longer to find out the name of the owners. The third repetitive dialogue that I endure when walking, relates to the weather. People will invariably comment on our climate;

"GRAND DAY ISN'T IT?"

"WHAT HAVE YOU DONE TO THE WEATHER?"

"IT DOESN'T KNOW WHAT TO DO WITH ITSELF."

We do it all the time, a way of being polite towards one another, and a means of potentially starting a conversation, part of our quintessential culture. The weather, either good or bad has a massive influence on the role of a dog walker, I have been out in all sorts of weather, storms even. But in the event of extremely inclement weather and strong winds I've learned that it's not safe to take a herd of dogs out. The main problem being that the dogs can't hear me calling them. The wind can carry a voice off in a different direction to the one intended, greatly increasing the risk of losing a dog. The getting wet side of things doesn't bother me too much and the thought of going home and getting dried off is always a comforting one. That said I don't particularly enjoy getting soaked through to the skin and having a lot of wet dogs and towels around the house can be a bit of a dampener, not the best aroma, *one smell that I yet have to become desensitised to!*

Sometimes it appears it's raining the proverbial 'Cats and Dogs' but it's rare that it rains incessantly, all day long. There is usually a break at some point. We have a local saying; 'Rain at 7, gone by 11.' This nugget of wisdom emanates from the Blackpool donkey owners and I tend to find it's largely true and usually more accurate than the met office. I would say that 90% of the time if it rains early morning it will be dry, or dryish by 11.00 am. Which is handy as that's when I start my walks, by which time it's usually dry and any DEAD BODIES have been cleared up! If, however, it is raining just after 11.00 am I still go for a walk, that is assuming it's not blowing a gale force wind. Quite often I am the only dog walker on the beach, the others have more sense.

The walks generally go without a hitch, the exception being meeting up with another dog walker who may have as many dogs as me, if not more. When this happens the two groups charge towards each other for the meet and greet and perhaps a spot of play. Now combined together in one super pack things can get somewhat confusing when keeping tabs on my dogs, especially if there are dogs of the same breed amongst the other pack. It's an easy mistake to count one of the other pack members thinking it's one of mine. Now, I know it's safer to try and steer clear of large packs of dogs. Another lesson learned.

Chapter 15

Living with the pack

With business continuing to grow I set about getting myself a better structure to my daily routine. A typical day would involve collecting my cuddly creatures for half-day care at approximately 11.00 am, walking them, after which bringing them back to my house. Then a second walk in the afternoon before taking them home for about 4.00 pm. This ensures the animals are happy after having enjoyed exercise and company for the best part of the day. It also means that they are home in time to greet their owners on their return from work. Then there are the full-time boarders, any cat visits or other small mammal visits are carried out before 11.00 am or after 4.00 pm. The occasional blissful puppy visits are squeezed in at lunchtime. I have to pinch myself sometimes as I would happily pay someone to let me play with their puppy, yet here I am being paid for the privilege!

Each day the guest list varies. Some people need daily dog care, whilst others only require cover for one or two days per week. Customers communicate their requirements through different media: it could be a telephone call, text, WhatsApp, messenger, email or just mentioning it when they see me. Being flexible is a prerequisite of the job; I also need to be able to deal with last minute bookings and cancellations. Therefore, it is crucial that I keep on top of my diary, something that I struggle with from time to time; as was the case when I completely forgot that Polly, a beautiful Springer Spaniel was staying with me for the day.

It was 11.10 am, I had gathered my crew for the habitual morning walk then I got the call from Casper's owner, Deb. Instinctively I knew something was wrong. Her preferred method of communication was text, so for her to call me was a strong indication that something wasn't quite right. Normally when she required doggy day-care, she dropped her dog off at around 10.45 am in time for the morning walk. It didn't take a genius to work out that I had set off for my walk and forgotten to include her pet on my list for the day. In trepidation I answered her phone call; She spoke sternly;

"LAURA, I am sat outside your house waiting for you and I have been doing so for some considerable amount of time."

I knew I was in trouble the moment she used my name; people only take time to pronounce my name if I am in trouble, being a pain in the neck, or they are patronising me. Deb was perfectly entitled to use her prickly tone on me, all I could do was apologise and get back home as quickly as possible. Grovelling to her I offered my apologies;

"I am so sorry, Deb, I will be with you in ten minutes"

Swiftly making an about turn after only having picked up half of my crew I drove back home and parked up on the opposite side of the road to Deb's car. I was conscious that she was watching me pull up and felt slightly fearful as to how she would respond to my incompetence. She was bound to be annoyed and who could blame her. We got out of our cars simultaneously: skulking towards her, head bowed, I acted and felt like a guilty puppy. At a few metres from her she blurted towards me;

"What happened, did you just completely forget that you were having Polly today?" She was abrupt and her tone remained stern.

Gathering my thoughts; I deliberated as to how to respond to her fair question, should I make up some fantastic excuse or just come clean?

Going for the latter I candidly replied; "Yes." I felt bad that I may have messed up her plans, and all because I had forgotten to put the booking in my diary. Deb looked at me, now in silence. After a few seconds and in a tone that was much softer, she beckoned me; "Come here."

Continuing my guilty puppy role, I walked towards her, then rather surprisingly she gave me a great big hug, telling me not to worry and words to the effect that these things happen. Her kind gesture lifted my spirits, and my guilt floated away thanks to her gracious manner. People can be so nice.

In addition to initially being rubbish at maintaining my diary I am also rather untalented at keeping tabs on my customers' dog leads. In the past my attitude towards safeguarding dog accessories was best described as cavalier, much to the annoyance of a couple of my clients. There were many times when I accidentally returned a pet with the wrong leash. When I made my apologies, some people were relaxed about my carelessness, replying along the lines of;

"I'm not surprised you get the leads mixed up with the number of dogs that you walk."

Then others were not quite so relaxed and wanted their own leads back. One customer, in particular, was meticulous about such matters and often complained if she had been given the wrong leads for her three cocker spaniels. Once when tackled about the situation, I found myself saying out loud;

"Well at least you've got the right dogs, haven't you?"

Of course, I wasn't quite so flippant with all my customers, just the ones that I thought would let me get away with it. Gradually I learned to make atonement and be more careful with the leads, after all the owners were entitled to get the RIGHT DOG AND RIGHT LEAD BACK. A weekly routine ensued whereby I held an amnesty and made sure each dog was returned with its own lead. What I really should do is take a leaf out of Sam and Loz's book. They have their own stash of leads and never use, or consequently lose, a customer's lead. This is something I always intend to do but never get around to it. If only I could be more like Sam and Loz, *my role models.*

My new pet sitter role was turning out to be far more enjoyable than I had ever imagined. Every Monday morning with a heart full of joy I would set off on my rounds to pick up my cuddly mates. Walking up the garden paths, my grin stretches across my face at the thought of the unbridled affection that is about to come my way. Home alone, once the dogs realise freedom is on the horizon, they positively burst with excitement.

The feeling is mutual, although I manage to contain myself in comparison. For the most part, working at the insurance company had been an enjoyable experience but I lacked the same enthusiasm that I now have for my new career. Looking back, I never once thought to myself on a Monday morning; 'I can't wait to see my friends Trish and Lisa.' Although extremely fond of my work colleagues, going into the office on a Monday morning was always tinged with a sense of gloom, which overshadowed any positive feelings that may have been hovering. I consider myself extremely fortunate that the Monday morning blues are now a long and distant memory.

Although my work was far more enjoyable than I had ever envisaged it was also far more difficult. The flip side of all the joy and affection is the enormous responsibility that I take on when looking after my customer's precious pets, who in most cases are more like family members and not just animals. Invariably I walk about seven hounds at a time. This entails collecting the mutts on time, safeguarding the customer's dog and house key, walking the dogs and ensuring that a dog in my care does not upset another dog.

By now I had been providing my pet sitting services for about a year and my niece Sally had been seeing her boyfriend Luke, for about the same period of time. Then in Winter 2011 following the natural course of a relationship she set up home with Luke, meaning I was now left to live with the dogs and only dogs. I suppose to a lot of people living with a completely different species seems strange; even I think it's a fraction odd at times. After Sally left, I took in the occasional lodger to help with the mortgage but always preferred the company of a pack of dogs marauding around my home over a human being. I find the mess dogs can make, the noise and the occasional scuffle far less irritating than a relative stranger rummaging through my cupboards. It's not that I don't enjoy human company, I do, it's just that in the long-term dwelling with humans has never really worked for me; family excluded.

Living amongst a pack of dogs is not the chaotic environment that people may assume it to be. Within the confines of the house for the majority of the day, the animals are settled or asleep, they get along well with each other and are happy to be in the pack. Of course, there are hectic times, the most hectic being when a visitor arrives, things can get a bit vocal, otherwise, it's a peaceful and happy environment in which to dwell. To achieve a level of harmony amongst the dogs it helps if there is a hierarchical system in place. Brece is only too happy to continue in her role as the alpha-female and the visiting dogs respect her position. She has already filtered out any that wouldn't succumb at the consultation.

All the dogs have their own individual personality but in time their personalities can change. In the past, I have had a few dogs boarding who were initially timid, never saying boo to a goose. Such dogs appeared to be okay at the consultation but once left and without their owner they can feel slightly insecure. Then, as they get used to the others and know that they are safe; their confidence increases. It's rewarding to see a dog develop a healthy level of self-esteem. But sometimes the scales can tip too far; a previously timid dog may try to make its way up the ladder and dominate a new member of the group. Casper, is one such dog.

As a youngster he was trained to the gun but failed. I assume he had a hard life before being matched with his new devoted owners. Initially, when he came to stay, he was incredibly nervous, hiding away upstairs, and keeping out of the way of the others. As he began to feel more secure his confidence increased. Initially this was encouraging behaviour but his confidence continued to increase and at an alarming rate, to the point where on a few occasions he saw fit to challenge Brece's leadership. Things had to be nipped in the bud. At such times, I had to be forceful with him, luckily, he backed down, and the canine coup was averted. If he hadn't submitted, he wouldn't have been able to stay again. For Brece's sake and for the stability of the pack, I can't allow another dog to undermine her position.

A dog's behaviour can also change in other ways. I have witnessed quite a few instances where a dog has changed its habits, leaving me to disagree with the saying 'You can't teach an old dog new tricks.' The changes, however, are not always for the better! As was the case when Hendrix taught his buddy Wasabi, how to refuse to get back into the car after a walk. Brece is another example. In the past she was relatively relaxed when the postman arrived to deliver the mail, that was until my sister Anna and her four Jack Russells came to stay with us a couple of years ago. Terriers are extremely protective of their territory and commonly give all postmen a hard time. The little feisty dogs see the letters coming into the house as an invasion and must do everything in their power to protect the property. After a few days of watching the terriers' behaviour, Brece developed the same stance, and also decided to go crazy as soon as she heard the postman coming up the drive. Copying the little terriers, she echoed their terrible racket, jumped up at the door and gouged her claws into the paintwork. After the Terriers had long since gone she continued to exercise her new found vocal talents. It got to the point that I decided to put a letterbox on my front gate, hopefully making things a bit easier for Sean: my patient affable postman, my paintwork, and my long-suffering neighbours.

Brece exercises her authority with our canine guests in all manner of ways, determinedly keeping them in check, but she is particularly forceful with boisterous puppies. When it comes to the youngsters, she operates a strict totalitarian regime demonstrating absolutely no patience whatsoever for their verve and playful behaviour.

Initially, I found her forcefulness to be harsh, but in the fullness of time, I began to realise that her dominance with the pups was actually a great asset to me. As the young rascal goes about its day causing the usual puppy havoc; it invariably fails to respond to my commands and completely ignores me. But there is someone that the pups do respond to and that is Brece. At times of chaos, the 'fun police' quickly arrive on the scene, assesses the situation, intervenes then swiftly resolves the matter. She reprimands the little tyke by barking forcefully at it, the berated pup quickly responds by stopping whatever it was doing. This system works as puppies are not familiar with the sound of a person's voice, but they are used to their mother's bark. Brece is replicating their mother, and the puppy knows better than to ignore its mother's orders.

At times Brece will even bark at a pup when I am in a different room and unaware of what is going on. For example, if the little bandit is trying to jump up on the table to swipe something off it, as she knows she is not allowed to behave in such a manner, then the puppy shouldn't either. As I walk into the room; I watch her performing her matriarchal role. Standing over the pup she barks in a most determined manner until the rascal gets down from the table. Again, sometimes this looks a bit harsh, but the puppies accept her authority, they learn their manners this way.

For these reasons introducing a pup into a pack is a positive thing, for both the puppy and owner. The pup will become well socialised with other dogs from an early age, and assuming it has been spayed or neutered, the owner should have no problems with their pet in terms of interaction with others. Its behaviour will also come on in leaps and bounds, thus making training for the owner that bit easier.

In addition to her committed work with puppies Brece also continues to dominate the adult dogs, reinforcing her position as top dog, and demonstrating her status in many ways. A typical trigger is the communal water bowl; returning from a walk she insists on being the first to quench her thirst. If another dog gets to the watering hole before her, she forcefully barks at the cheeky mutt until it gets out of her way. The dog takes its orders, steps back from the bowl then patiently waits for her to finish. When she's had enough, the parched dog is then permitted to resume drinking. The same applies to a dog who may have a toy or another object that she wishes to purloin. Going over to the animal she performs her barking ritual until it gives up the toy or whatever it may be that she thinks would be better off with her.

Besides respecting her, the other dogs are also wary of her. Sometimes I hear a dog barking in another room, a sort of 'help me' bark; quiet and intermittent. Usually, it's the case that Brece is lying in a doorway and the dog is too scared to go past her, in case it disturbs her. The dog continues its 'help me' bark until I come to the rescue. In the early days, I used to feel sorry for the reticent pet, but soon learned that the dog did not take offence, and it's a great thing to have that sort of respect within the pack. I encourage it to a certain extent but always nip things in the bud if she becomes too much of a dictator and begins to bully a dog. Similarly, when I leave the house for a short period of time, as I walk down the drive, I always hear her make a couple of loud barks. Her way of saying;

"Right you lot, I'm in charge now, so watch out."

Within the pack I find myself showing nepotism to Brece. I am extremely fond of all the dogs that cross my threshold but love mine with a passion; my 'Best in Show'. In order to make sure that she doesn't feel as though she is being pushed out in any way, I treat her slightly differently to the others. Instinctively ensuring she gets preferential treatment by giving her food ahead of the others. As luck would have it, this is the correct thing to do as it reinforces her position as top dog, and the others are content in the security that they know their place within the pack.

Having a pack of dogs living with me did not seem to deter visitors. My friend Nathan visited on a regular basis and was in the habit of bringing rotting animal parts round (in the form of bones) for the dogs to chew on. The grizzly bones were usually massive and varied between knuckle, shoulder, and shin. Although it was a very kind gesture on his part, it did mean that I had to pick my distribution times carefully. If anything was going to bring out the primeval fighting instincts in a pack of dogs, throwing a big juicy bone into the mix would do the trick. Tending to politely accept the bones I stowed them away in the doggy locker room.

Occasionally I 'Threw the odd Dog a Bone', taking great care as to which dogs were around and never leaving them unsupervised.

Brece sometimes shares her toys with the others, but bones are a different kettle of fish, unless of course, it is with her cousin Jake. Jake is a male Collie cross who belongs to my brother Dave and is the only mutt permitted to visit that she does not feel compelled to dominate. Quite the reverse, she seems to look up to him, acting differently in his presence. She becomes almost giddy, and follows him everywhere, not dissimilar to a lovesick teenage girl with a crush on a boy. *I swear she flirts with him.*

On one of Jake's visits, I noticed the hoard of bones was racking up, the locker room was beginning to resemble a desecrated graveyard. So, I decided to give the pair a bone as a treat. They had shared bones before, making me confident they would share amicably again. Looking back, I certainly had enough bones hanging around to give them one each, but I preferred them to share. Having one rotting animal part gracing my floors was more than enough.

At the same time I had Molly and Max, the mud wallowing Retrievers boarding with me. M and M were like an old married couple in some ways, the difference being they were amicable, and always content in one another's company! Although not siblings they shared the same owners. Dogs that come to board in pairs, usually settle very quickly as they have each other for companionship. M and M's owners owned a second house in Italy, where they frequently visited for holidays, leaving M and M to holiday with me.

The Retrievers quickly became a welcome part of the furniture at the doggy hotel. At about 10 years of age, Max makes for a much bigger dog than Molly. His beautiful amber eyes seem to stare into your soul; continually questioning when he will get his next meal. In contrast, Molly has lovely brown eyes, a much softer face and slightly darker fur, which is extremely fluffy and soft to the touch. Being a couple of years younger than her mate she is slightly more agile and makes for a very curvaceous spritely dog. As she bounces along on her walks, tail contentedly wafting in the air she put me in mind of a canine version of Marilyn Monroe, beautiful, blonde and very shapely.

The pair were inseparable companions, like two furry bookends. They eat together never snatching one another's food, happily spending twenty-four hours a day together, often playing with each other but never squabbling. Max usually instigates play by nonchalantly strolling over to Molly and gently biting her on the mouth. Molly picks up the gauntlet and by the same token gently returns the compliment by biting him back on his chops. An amicable play-fight ensues, a joy to watch. When they aren't playing, dozing, eating or walking they watch each other like hawks; instinctively keeping a close eye on one another, in case their mate is doing or has heard something that they need to know about. But they are rascals when it comes to soft furnishings, their soft mouths are partial to shredding anything that is soft. This means I need to be careful not to leave any cushions, slippers or toys lying around.

Molly and Max happily share their toys with each other, but that's not all their share, they also take turns sitting next to me on the two-seater couch. If a space becomes available Max seizes his opportunity and rather chauvinistically jumps up to enjoy his privileged position. But he doesn't stay long, after about fifteen minutes he always climbs down.

At first, I thought this was because he was hot, preferring the cooler comfort of the wooden floor. But observing their little routines, in time I came to realise that this wasn't the case. Each time he got down from the sofa he was making way for Molly, who immediately took measures to take her place next to me. Max wasn't hot at all, obvious signs such as panting were not visible, he was finally showing his gentlemanly side by sharing the prized position.

In contrast to Max, Molly never jumps up on the couch without being invited. Instead, being incredibly well-mannered she walks towards the sofa swishing her fluffy tail through the air with an expectant look in her bright brown eyes. At which point I give her encouragement to jump up next to me. Most people discourage pets jumping up on the furniture, but anything goes at the Heyhouses doggy hotel. Laying on the couch is a big deal for the dogs, and besides I enjoy having the big furry things sat close by. After all it's no hardship to throw the covers in the washing machine on a regular basis.

I have yet to come across any other mammals who are as naturally sharing as a pair of Golden Retrievers. It's not as if they are taught to share things with their siblings in the same way children are, they do it instinctively. I've spent hour upon hour observing M and M admiring their close connection, sometimes wishing that my own relationships were half as harmonious as the bond that the humble dog shares with his soul mate.

Meanwhile, back to the plains of the Serengeti Brece and Jake were laid on the wooden floor of the lounge, amicably sharing a massive knuckle bone. The pair patiently took turns with the bone while M and M patiently watched on, gnawing on Dentastics in way of consolation. Things were going well until Jake decided to move the goal post by hogging the bone for himself, which in turn began to agitate Brece. She knew full well it was her go but didn't seem to know how to manage the situation. With any other dog it wouldn't have been a problem, she would have barked incessantly, but she never did this with Jake, preferring to show him her softer more feminine side. Instead, she restlessly paced up and down the lounge making little ineffectual yelping noises. Of course, he completely ignored her and continued gnawing his way through the knuckle bone. A better plan was called for. Then suddenly, she demonstrated some rather creative thinking; she jumped up, barked loudly and ran outside into the back garden.

When this sort of thing happens, it triggers a chain reaction in the others. They think something is happening, and they need to investigate matters and more importantly protect the property from potential intruders. Jake, Molly and Max closely followed her, leaving the bone unattended. This was her chance. Once all the dogs were outside in the garden, she made an immediate U-turn, ran straight back into the house, and stealthily claimed the coveted bone for herself. This left the others in the garden, perplexed as to what was going on. She had orchestrated the whole scene just to get the bone off Jake. From that moment on I looked at her with a new-found respect, she was far more intelligent and cunning than I had ever given her credit for.

During the core hours of the day sometimes there can be as many as ten dogs around the place, at times things can get a bit noisy. Some dogs are more protective than others and will bark at people passing the front window, whilst others let the pedestrian walk by in peace. But just about all of them make a racket when people arrive at the door. Then I have 'Doug the Pug' who is on air traffic control. He covers the skies protecting us from potential air attacks from planes or drones. I can rest assured that we are secure on all fronts. Doug also goes particularly crazy when he hears the noise of sirens emanating from police cars or ambulances, of which there is always an abundance. Not being a fan of the sound of barking myself, and for my sake and the sake of my neighbours; I try to keep the vocal acrobatics to a minimum. There are a lot of furry nominees for the 'Vocal Oscar' but Doug is the hands-on winner every time.

Keeping Heyhouses clean and tidy is very challenging at times, trying to do chores around the place is often fraught with difficulties. When I am on the move some of the dogs remain settled but the majority will be in hot pursuit. With about twenty little legs following me everywhere I go, things can get a tad congested at times. Spaniels, especially, appear to know where I am going before I do myself, and typically get there before me. They possess a remarkable talent for grafting themselves to my heels, swerving in and out of my steps, literally getting under my feet. They are no doubt anticipating that at some point there will be a Mecca stop, the treat jar. If by chance I do stop off at Mecca they sit there, ears pricked up, eyes full of hope boring into mine as if to say;

"Look how beautiful I am, don't I deserve a tasty treat?" I always succumb. The instant the treat is devoured, they continue their stare as if the previous five seconds never happened. In an almost hypnotic state, they are saying the exact same thing again, 'Look how beautiful I am, don't I deserve a treat?" I suspect most dogs would continue in this loop, until all the treats had been gobbled up.

Once my chores are completed, or I have given up on them, I settle down, as do the dogs. The exception to this rule being when a dog disappears from the group, and things become eerily quiet. It's usually the case that said dog is rummaging somewhere and definitely up to no good. The adventurous mutt has typically sniffed out the treats in my coat pocket, eaten them and made numerous holes in the process. Several of my coats have perished in such a fashion.

It wasn't just my work and home life that had dramatically changed course, but my social life too; looking after customer's pets meant things had taken a bit of a nose-dive in that department. I was still able to go out, but never for more than a couple of hours. Although I knew Brece was fairly happy being by herself it wasn't right to leave customer's dogs for too long, especially when being paid good money to keep them company. Having to go home early on a night out was never a chore, in fact, most of the time it was a welcome excuse to get back to my lovely buddies.

Chapter 16

Nights in with the pack

After a hectic day, I enjoy relaxing, and languishing on the couch with my furry buddies. The day-care dogs have gone home, and I am left with Brece and any boarders; it's evening and time to relax in front of the TV. Most of the dogs like to snuggle up next to me on the couch, then settle themselves in and prepare for a nap. At this point sometimes Brece is of the opinion that another dog may be sitting too close to me. Letting her jealousy get the better of her she comes over to the intruder barking as if to say; "Oi, get out of the way, that's my place." The encroaching dog sheepishly gets off the couch to make way for the alpha female. On occasions, when things are getting a bit crowded on the couch and there is no room left, a dog has been known to jump up and perch on my shoulder. This seems to be a particular trait of one of my Cockapoos, Snoop, part dog and part Velcro, my very own furry parrot.

Once the hounds have settled, a Mexican wave of contented sighs swirls around the room, the dogs exhale in succession before drifting into their evening slumber. Once asleep if an unsuspected noise wakes a dog, it immediately looks at me to check my reaction. If it sees that I am calm and relaxed, it knows there is no threat and can therefore settle down to resume its nap. Dogs see the person who is caring for them as their leader and take their direction from them. The leader's presence gives the dog confidence and a sense of security. It has been proven that the dog's heart rate is lower, when in the company of their owner or carer.

Similarly, when the hounds are napping, and they happen to wake naturally without a disturbance, they also look directly at me. It's always the first thing they do, it's as if they made a mental note of my position before their nap. They have remembered my position then automatically check I am still there. Once they see I haven't moved, again they contentedly return to their slumber. The pack leader is still watching over them, which gives them reassurance that everything is fine, it really is quite endearing.

It never ceases to amaze me just how much time a dog spends sleeping. They can be with me in the lounge all evening dozing and when I go to bed, they sleep all night too. Perhaps even enjoying the odd nap during the day, in between walks and meals. Never appearing to get too much rest, and if nothing else is going on, they switch off at the drop of a hat; as if conserving their batteries. On average people sleep 8 hours a day, except for hormonal teenagers who are endowed with an abundance of sleep hormones, enabling them to sleep the clock round. But even teenagers can't hold a light to canines when it comes to the dozing stakes. Most mature dogs in my experience can be dormant up to about sixteen hours a day, sometimes even more, especially older dogs. At times I think how great it would be if people had the same talent of switching off and going to sleep if there is nothing better on the agenda. Perhaps relieving boredom which may, in turn, lead to alcohol and drug-related problems. Being a mad dog woman, these are the sort of thoughts that go through my head whilst I sit watching over my slumbering friends.

Another regular thought that filters through my muddled head is my theory that dogs unknowingly follow many of the Buddhist beliefs. Buddhists believe that we should live in the 'here and now' enjoying the moment, which is exactly what a dog tends to do. The dog does not bear a grudge against another that may have snapped at him the day before (although he may learn not to make the same mistake again). By the same token, he doesn't lie awake worrying about the present or the future. As soon as the dog lies down, it switches off and almost immediately falls asleep without its mind ticking over and mithering about things, as people often tend to.

In addition the Buddhists don't want for material possessions and neither does the dog. Exercise, food and affection is all that is required to make him content. Observing the dogs' behaviour, I notice further comparisons to the Buddhist, such as respect, compassion and companionship. The dog offers all these qualities to his fellow pack members, making for a contented life. Looking at the dog, then at a person, I know which one I think is the happier, *we could learn a lot from our pets.*

At bedtime after I have finished all my thinking, I ascend the stairs shutting the dog gate behind me and leaving my buddies downstairs. Upstairs is out of bounds for most, but there is always an exception to the rule. On occasions, I allow the odd dog to stay on my bed, that is, of course, if Brece approves. My special privileges are usually granted to a worried or insecure dog who may be feeling slightly anxious on its first night away from home. At such times Brece seems to understand the situation and has no objection as the privileged animal trots past the gate and up the stairs. She looks at me as if to say; 'Alright, just this once.'

One such dog that is granted regular special permissions is Snoop, my Velcro parrot, who boards with me from time to time. In my experience

Cockapoos are particularly excitable creatures that require a lot of attention. Sensing he would be more settled sleeping on my bed, I allow him the honour. He happily scuttles off upstairs after me, leaving the others at the bottom of the stairs. Thankfully Snoop is a dedicated sleeper, I don't hear a peep out of him all night, just how I like it. If things were different, I'm not sure he would be granted his privileges. In the mornings my eyes slowly open to be greeted by his furry face closely positioned about an inch away from mine. He has been watching me quietly, waiting for me to wake, without moving a muscle until I do, then he goes crazy.

Mornings bring great excitement to the house. Snoop and I make our way to the top of the stairs looking down on the remaining excitable dogs in the cheap seats. Resembling some sort of ageing Hollywood movie-star I traipse down the stairs to receive my applause. My doggy fans greet me with the usual enthusiastic rhapsody; all tails wagging and yelping with glee. Some even jumping up and down, probably more at the prospect of breakfast than seeing me.

Picking up on the excitement and not being one to take a back seat Snoop easily becomes the most excitable of the lot of them, whimpering and hollering the whole time. He runs around me with his tail going ten to the dozen. I swear that if his tail moved with any more veracity, he would become airborne; back end first, before crashing down to the floor, like a helicopter crash landing. He wants his place in the front seats and will do whatever it takes to get it, seemingly oblivious to the fact that he has been in my company all night. It's as if he hasn't seen me in an age; again, he is a dog living in the moment.

Molly and Max are also typically happy and excited at the sight of me flouncing down the stars in my morning glory. Finding a toy in celebration, they play tug of war with each other, tails wagging profusely, exuding happiness. But if I happen to turn around and go back upstairs for something, they drop the toy as if it was a lead balloon, and their mood plummets. They look at me with such a sad expression on their faces which fills me with guilt. I dash upstairs then rush down as quickly as possible, so that they can resume their play.

When a dog's visit comes to an end, the owners return to pick up their pet. A few dogs seem to know their owner's arrival is imminent. Uncharacteristically, they become restless; some will sit by the front door. When a dog does this, I think to myself; 'Why is Snoop sitting by the door?' Then it dawns on me, his owner is due within the hour, the dog reminds me! Perhaps another example of the dog's ESP skills.

It's great to hear all about the owner's holiday, where they have been, and what they have done. But the highlight of the occasion is witnessing the joy and happiness exuding from both owner and pet, as they are reunited. Sometimes the owner brings the whole family along, as they are all longing to see their pet. The reunion is a time of great enthusiasm for family, their pet, and the remaining mutts. As the dogs bay for attention this level of excitement can occasionally lead to a bit of a tussle. In an attempt to avoid any scuffles; I put the remaining dogs in another room away from the chaos brewing at the front door. Brece however, is permitted to stay for the meet and greet. She insists on being on the front line at all times and needs to see what is going on and be a part of it; it's another privilege that she is granted. Naturally, she assumes it's all about her, in fact, she seems to think that every single person that comes to the house, has come to see her. Once the penny drops and she realises the visitor has arrived to see their own pet, and not her, her pride is wounded. She thinks to herself;

"I need to pull something out of the bag here, I'm not getting any attention or love here."

So, she resumes the position of 'Teddy,' by sitting up on her back legs, front paws in the air in the knowledge that her little stunt will please the crowds; invariably her pose provokes an; "Aww, look how gorgeous you are." Someone usually gets hold of her paws, enabling her to stay in position without losing balance, all the while she laps up the attention.

Once all greetings and possessions have been exchanged, the visiting dog eventually leaves returning to the bosom of its family where it should be happy and settled, as if it has never been away. This is usually the case; however, at times I suspect that the occasional dog might even be happier in the boarding environment, than in their own home. When staying at Heyhouses they are back in the pack and they love it, especially dogs of a similar age and vigour, as they have playmates to hang out with all day long. This was indeed the case for my dynamic duo Hendrix and Wasabi.

As coincidence would have it the pair boarded with me for a two week period. Playing together all day long, they craved one another's company, two peas in a pod. In this instance, I had a slight concern that the twosome may not be quite so happy once separated and back in their own homes. Unfortunately, my worries were founded. Once home the animals pined dreadfully for each other. Both owners reported stories of their pet moping about the place and enduring loss of appetite. To my mind it was similar to separating siblings as puppies. It was sad to hear the updates, but in time the dogs adjusted back into their home life. The good thing is that they still get to see each other on the weekly walks, picking up where they left off.

Chapter 17

Dog days- 2012

Summer 2012 arrived. With the warmer weather came the promise of even more enjoyable walks with the dogs. But not long into the summer I realised this wasn't quite the case.

"BY HECK, YOU'VE GOT A GREAT JOB THIS TIME OF YEAR, HAVEN'T YOU?"

In all honesty, the answer to that question was;

"No, not really," but I usually responded with a forced smile on my face along the lines of;

"Ha Ha! Yes, you're right, I have."

We say things we don't mean all the time, in the same way when someone greets us by asking how we are? We politely reply;

"I'm fine thanks," even though we may be at death's door and not fine at all.

People often assume that walking dogs in the summer is a doddle. I thought this myself, then quickly learned it's actually anything but a doddle. On reflection I probably prefer inclement weather to clement, as the saying goes in the outdoor fraternity; 'There is no such thing as bad weather, just bad clothing.'

Undoubtedly, I enjoy summer walks on the beach but only when the place isn't festooned with day visitors. In my experience, the better the weather, the more people, hence the more problems when walking a troupe of dogs. The good weather attracts people to the beaches in their droves, they come well equipped with their children, deck chairs, wind breakers, buckets, spades and picnics all in preparation for an enjoyable day at the seaside.

During the months of May to September dogs are understandably banned from the area surrounding the Pier and the amusement arcades. This restriction means holidaymakers can be left to enjoy their picnics without the worry of a pack of dogs trying to grab their butties or even worse, peeing on their panniers. Thankfully the council make a fair compromise to dog walkers by allowing dogs off lead all year round on North Beach, which is about a mile away from the Pier and amusements.

It's always mortally embarrassing when one of my dogs decides to cock its leg up against a picnic hamper, not that it's a regular occurrence but it has happened from time to time. Without a shadow of a doubt the worst peeing incident that happened on my watch was when walking with Casper. We were on North beach and about thirty minutes into the walk, when without warning, Casper ran towards a sand dune in the distance, leaving me and the others to run after him. As we got closer it appeared that it wasn't a picnic that had caught his attention, but a little boy with a Down's Syndrome condition.

The boy was sat motionless and alone looking towards a woman close by who was sculpting impressive looking sandcastles together with a young girl. I assumed the woman to be the little boy's mother. Ignoring the pair, Casper ran straight passed them and headed towards the lone boy. Casper then introduced himself by sniffing the boy's leg, with increased enthusiasm he went around the back of the child for a further inspection. I was getting worried at this point as Casper then started sniffing the child's back, tail wagging furiously. Alarm bells went off in my head, fearing the worst I screamed at him to come away. Naturally, the boy's mother looked up to see what was going on. At that exact moment Casper decided to cock his leg up against the child's back and wantonly emptied his bladder. Both the child's mother and I were horrified, I don't think the little boy was too enamoured either, he ran towards his mother, in floods of tears. God it was awful, I still cringe now when I think about the unfortunate episode.

Some people are fine if a dog is attracted by the aroma of a tasty morsel wafting from their picnic hamper, and don't mind if the dog goes in for a closer sniff. But others aren't best pleased at being disturbed by a pack of wolves and can understandably get upset. Then there are those who are genuinely afraid of dogs; it can't be nice for these people to have to endure dogs running up to them. The last thing I want to do is cause distress to someone when they are trying to have a fun day out, even if they are on the dogs allowed beach.

If only the council could clarify matters and direct people who are not comfortable with dogs, to the Pier beach. Because of the confusion, walking on North Beach in summer is fraught with difficulties. Once on the beach the dogs are extremely excited to be out on their great adventure, and what an extra bonus to potentially grab the odd butty along the way. Brece is one of the worst offenders of picnic sabotage. Once she gets the waft of food up her nostrils, she quickly morphs into the canine version of Yogi Bear, there is no holding her back. The trick is to get all the dogs out to sea and away from the holidaymakers as quickly as possible.

One hot day I had managed to do just that without incident. After about half an hour of fun the gang and I turned around and headed back to the car park, the dogs were happy, and fortunately, we had managed not to upset anyone. However, my luck was short-lived. The sight of a new set of happy campers plonked right by the beach exit, tucking into their al fresco meal, caught me off guard. Although Brece was tired after her walk, the whiff of food in the air revitalised her. With ears pricked up, nose sniffing the air and tail wagging vigorously, she zoned in on the aroma of a few tempting scraps. Her recall is good on most occasions, but there's no competition between a command from me and the prospect of a delicious morsel. I called her several times, each call getting louder and increasingly more desperate, but my cries fell on deaf ears. She was on a mission, wafting her big fluffy tail as if to say;

'If you think I am turning down the opportunity of a tasty butty, then you can think again.'

She was off, I didn't have a cat in hell's chance of getting her back on the lead. It was obvious what was going to happen and I failed to catch her in time before her jaw inevitably turned into a Venus fly trap and swiped an entire butty right out of an unsuspecting day tripper's hand. This really wasn't what I needed; I was hot, bothered and extremely frustrated. Why did people want to consume their picnics in such close proximity to dogs? And secondly, why did they set up stall right by the beach entrance? With all the will in the world, it's impossible to keep dogs away from picnickers that choose to camp by the narrow entrance.

The beach covers a vast area with miles and miles of dunes, which are usually sparsely populated, even in the height of summer. Surely the higher ground of the dunes or a beach where dogs are banned, would be a much better setting to enjoy a picnic in peace and quiet. I couldn't hide my agitation at the sight of Brece munching the man's lunch, but on this occasion, my frustration was directed at the man as opposed to my greedy dog. In a flash of anger, and without thinking I blurted out;

"Why do you people plonk yourselves right by the beach entrance to have your picnics?"

The unsuspecting holidaymaker was caught off guard, he looked up at me with an astonished look on his face;

"Oh, I'm sorry." He was genuinely apologetic, which in turn made me feel guilty. On reflection I felt embarrassed about my outburst, I should have apologised for Brece's behaviour, but I didn't.

Attempting to clarify matters for both local dog walkers and visitors alike, I decided to contact the council to see if anything could be done to alleviate the confusion. To my mind a simple sign on North Beach car park to the effect;

'Dogs allowed off lead,' would do the trick.

The council is talented at putting up signs, so surely, they would assist in this matter. But it was not to be, a polite female representative from the council told me that I was not going to get my new sign. The reason being that new Personal Space Protection Orders (PSPOs) were due to be enforced the following year. The woman spoke as if it was obvious what a PSPO was, but it wasn't obvious to me. After a bit more delving, I was to learn that PSPOs are proposed new powers permitting dog wardens to distribute increased fixed penalties in association with dog offences. Currently, dog wardens, of which there are two in the area, are only authorised to distribute a fine for failure to pick up dog mess. The new orders will extend the warden's powers enabling them to issue fixed penalties for 'dogs off lead' in 'on lead' areas. If the proposals were to be implemented, new signage would be required. Therefore, there would be no new signs in the interim, at least until a final decision had been made. Frustratingly my battles with the picnickers were to continue for the time being.

Yet another downside of hot weather is the transportation of the dogs. Having dogs in a car in hot weather is certainly not ideal. They cannot be left for too long and definitely not without all the windows open, and plenty of water for them to drink. Even stopping off on my rounds to pick up another dog in the heat can be tricky. It means finding a parking place in the shade which of course isn't always that easy. People are really on the ball these days when it comes to dogs being left in vehicles in hot weather, and quite rightly so. In summer the temperature inside a car is more than double that of outside. On top of this the dog is stuck wearing a nice furry coat, hat, and gloves. To make matters worse, the dogs are only able to cool down by panting or sweating from their paws. In such conditions, a dog can suffer brain damage or even die from heatstroke in just fifteen minutes.

Apart from running the gauntlet of angry picnickers, unsafe conditions for the dogs, infuriating day visitors, another cross we have to bear is full frontal nudity! The hotter the weather, the fewer clothes people are likely to be wearing.

It was a balmy hot summer's day in July 2012, late afternoon, the sun unforgiving. We had been enjoying a bout of high pressure for a couple of weeks. It was so hot that people were walking about with their bottles of water attempting to avoid dehydration. But the true barometer of the heat was the sight of the ubiquitous elderly ladies who only appear to venture outdoors when the temperature reaches the high twenties. This particular afternoon they were out in their droves, dressed in bold floral cotton dresses and aided by their walking sticks. That afternoon we had been treated to a light shower, the first one in weeks. The air was filled with that damp musty smell created when rain disturbs the soil after a long dry spell. As we set off for our walk, I was enjoying the dusty smell the rain had created. Arriving at the beach as usual I walked far out to sea with my entourage, well away from the holidaymakers.

The ebb and flow of the tide had left large craters, leaving the beach to resemble the surface of the moon. Some of the craters were filled with sea water creating mini lakes, ideal paddling pools for the dogs to enjoy jumping into, to cool off. In the distance, I saw an old man walking towards us. I would hazard a guess that he was in his early eighties and carrying a large amount of visceral fat around his midriff. With skinny limbs protruding from his stout torso he had taken on the spider look; what's more, and rather shockingly he appeared to be naked! As we got closer it transpired that Spiderman was not entirely naked but donning a gold shiny thong! He must have strutted his stuff quite some length of time to get so far out to sea. Besides having a detrimental effect on me, the sight of the almost naked man, also had a negative effect on the dogs. They started barking profusely, whilst literally running circles around him, *it was all rather embarrassing.*

I have seen some sights in my time on that beach, even coming across a man sunbathing and wearing nothing but sunscreen. The naked man emphatically tried to convince me that 'My Beach' is a nudist beach when I know full well it isn't. This was not a pretty sight either and I think the dogs were of the same ilk as me; again, some of them started barking at the nudist.

If a dog comes across an unfamiliar sight, or for the want of a better expression, one it has not been 'exposed to' before, it can lead to confusion and the dog reacts by anxiously barking. It is for this reason that dogs need to be familiarised with as many different sights and experiences as possible whilst they are young, nudists not being one of them! Perhaps we are prudes, but the dogs and I prefer the winter season when people are respectfully clothed.

The more people, the more dogs and the more tennis BALLS. A ball may seem like an innocuous object but in my experience a tennis ball can turn out to be far more trouble than it's worth. Balls can trigger rivalry amongst the dogs, which can sometimes lead to a spot of bother. Another downside is that the dogs desperately require the balls to be thrown for them, and I throw like a girl. For these reasons I don't tend to take balls on the walks any more. However, if my ball-deprived dogs, especially collies and spaniels, get a whiff of another dog's ball they are off like a shot, swiping it from its owner, no problem.

Most owners are possessive over balls and usually want their own tennis ball back, a substitute is not acceptable. Retrieving another dog's ball from one of my lot can be extremely tiresome, but it must be done and on a regular basis, especially with Hendrix on board. This was exactly the case when Hendrix swiped a ball that belonged to a sluggish chocolate brown Labrador when we were on the beach one afternoon. I set about my repertoire of cunning tricks to try to separate Hendrix from the Labrador's ball.

The owner of the Labrador and ball was a rather portly male day visitor, I say day visitor as I had never seen him on the beach before and he spoke with a strong East Lancs. accent. The man was naked from the waist up. From the waist down he was wearing, Union Jack shorts, brown sandals and the obligatory white socks pulled up to the shin. *Still I suppose I had to be grateful, at least he was wearing shorts.* I spent a good five minutes trying to get the ball off Hendrix while the man in sandals and socks watched me struggle in silence. The sluggish Labrador was getting more anxious by the second and looking forward to being reunited with his ball.

It was down to me to get the ball and the Labrador knew it. Remaining by my side he looked up at me the whole time with his bright eyes full of great expectation. Eventually, my tenacity paid off, Hendrix relinquished the ball, and I stupidly stood there holding it in my hand.

At this point the Labrador was beside himself such was his excitement at being teamed up with his ball again. Suddenly without warning the Lab jumped up to retrieve the ball from my hand. I was surprised at how agile the rotund dog was, and also upset when I realised that it had accidentally punctured my thumb and drawn blood. The portly day visitor appeared to be oblivious to my injury although I don't know how as the blood was clearly visible and I was behaving as if I had been mortally wounded. At this point he shouted out in my direction; "Eeee will 'ave your hand off.'

This was good to know but I couldn't help thinking if the man had shared this nugget of information earlier, I would have immediately dropped the ball thus saving myself an injury. By this time my dander was up, my thumb was hurting and bleeding quite heavily. My main concern being that an infection may be heading my way. Dog's teeth are notoriously steeped in bacteria, a bite from a dog will normally lead to an infection, Sepsis even. Perhaps I was getting carried away with things, but Sepsis appeared to be the vogue health complication of the day, and rather worryingly can be fatal. Looking at the portly day visitor standing in his brown sandals and white socks I waited for some sort of acknowledgement of my injury, or better still an apology. Neither was forthcoming. Feeling slightly battered but not wanting an altercation, I went on my way.

On a more serious note another ball incident also involved our other four-legged friend, the horse. It was late afternoon the following month August 2012, the temperature was about twenty-five degrees; too hot to take the dogs out during the heat of the sun. I had taken my walkers out early morning and was just left with my boarders to exercise. The day before it had been twelve degrees and blowing a gale, the weather in England is nothing if not inconsistent. Sometimes it appears we are dealt all four seasons in one week. Thanks to climate change the typical Spring, Summer, Autumn and Winter seasons now appear to be merging into one. Each year we seem to experience the hottest, wettest, stormiest, driest weather since records began.

Sitting in the garden I was looking forward to the evening drawing in and bringing in the cooler air. Eventually, the shadows grew longer; the air, which was filled with the aroma of barbequed food, felt fresher but still warm. I was undecided as to where to take the boarders and couldn't decide between the beach, or a walk in the local woods. The woods, which have not yet been discovered by tourists, had become one of my summer haunts. They were quieter than the beach and the canopy of the trees makes for a more comfortable temperature in hot weather. But the advantage of the beach being that dogs would get a better run, plus there was a chance the sea may be in. What could be better than a nice refreshing dip for my crew at the end of a hot day? After careful consideration I plumped for the beach. In almost vampire-esque fashion we set about for what I assumed would be a pleasant evening walk; well that was the plan. What started off as a relaxing stroll, turned into disaster.

On the beach the weather felt comfortable and most of the holidaymakers had returned inland, the tide was quite a way out, and we were making our way out to meet the sea THEN IT HAPPENED...

Without warning a couple of reckless bareback horse riders purposely rode into the middle of my pack with a total wanton disregard. The riders must have done it for their own amusement, it certainly wasn't for my amusement or the amusement of my dogs. I'm not sure why I failed to hear a couple of horses galloping towards us, but I didn't, perhaps the direction of the breeze had carried the sound of the hooves off in a different direction. Naturally, the dogs were startled. Attempting to avoid the stampede they proceeded to disperse in several directions. This is the worst possible scenario for a dog walker to find themselves in, it's even worse than a dogfight. There was now a high risk of losing not just one dog, but multiple dogs, I needed to quickly corral them back together. Frantically I called out to them in the hope that they would re-group.

After about a minute most of the dogs had calmed down and returned to me with little hesitation. They all seemed fine, apart from Tizer, a nervous rescue female black Cocker Spaniel. She was terribly frightened by the stampede and took it upon herself to bolt back towards the direction of the car. Her owners had warned me at the consultation that she had bolted in the past, but this was several years ago, and they assured me that it would not happen again. Somewhat reluctantly I had consented to board the dog. In hindsight, I should have gone with my gut instinct and not taken the booking. But I felt sorry for the owners; due to Tizer's previous vanishing act the couple hadn't been on holiday in four years. This was because they didn't trust her with anyone, but for some unknown reason they had bestowed their trust on me, I was beginning to wish they hadn't.

My main focus was to keep the rest of the dogs together, then try and catch up with Tizer. Fit as I was there was no way I could ever catch up with a frightened dog that had just bolted. But even though I knew it was futile, I had to try. So, the remaining dogs and I attempted to run after her. Naturally, she was increasing her distance but still in sight, then suddenly right on cue Hendrix had other ideas. Rather frustratingly, he caught sight of a man with a ball launch and decided to leg it after him. Hendrix's fascination for balls had never waned. There was still no way he would come back to me once his teddy bear glass eyes had spotted a tennis ball, not even a pork chop would entice him. Naturally, Hendrix was running in the opposite direction to Tizer and at the speed of a whippet. Things were going from bad to worse. As if I wasn't stressed enough I now had my second dilemma on my hands, which dog should I chase after?

In one way it was an easy decision, I had much more chance of catching Hendrix than I did Tizer; he wasn't frightened and hopefully once he caught up with the man and ball launcher, he would come to a halt. So the remaining dogs and I changed course and proceeded to chase after Hendrix. Worryingly, by trying to catch Hendrix the distance between us and Tizer was increasing, but I had little choice in the matter. After a short time, out of breath and panting profusely, I caught up with Hendrix who by now had caught up with the ball launcher. With Hendrix now on his lead I turned round and looked towards the direction Tizer was last seen, but of course she was now completely out of sight. At this point I was scared, hot and bothered, and consumed with an unwelcome feeling of loneliness and dread. With my second wind and still hanging on to Hendrix I ran as fast as possible towards the car park with the pack (minus Tizer). I had to catch her before she reached the traffic.

That day the beach was sparsely populated, with only two women in front of me who were walking a Spaniel and a couple of Golden Retrievers. Gaining ground on them, I realised the Retrievers were my customers Molly and Max, out for a gentle walk with owner Lesley. Coincidently it was Lesley who had kindly got me the Tizer gig; she had recommended me to the owners a couple of weeks beforehand, if only she hadn't been so kind. Seeing Lesley just added to my stress. Having a customer witness me losing a dog was hardly professionalism in its glory. But perhaps she wouldn't notice me and a herd of dogs running along a quiet beach and screeching out 'Tizer, Tizer'. Who was I kidding, of course she would notice me. Overtaking her, she called out after me;

"Laura, is that Tizer that has run off? Where do you think she has gone?"

The six-million-dollar question, where was she, if only I knew. Another instance when I would have preferred anonymity over recognition. Exhausted I arrived at the dogmobile, yearning with all of my scared heart that she would be sat there, waiting for me. Sometimes if a dog bolts it will go back to the car and wait if you are lucky. But it was not to be, I was deluding myself, she wasn't in the car park, there was no sign of her on the beach, meaning the only alternative was that she had run inland. This was not good news as it meant crossing Clifton Drive, which is an extremely busy road. To say that I was panicking at this point would have been a gross understatement. If only I had picked the woods that evening.

The more often I experience fear on this level the more amazed I am at how fear, something that cannot be seen or measured has such an effect on the human brain, and in turn, the body. In these situations, the 'fight or flight' mode kicks in, activating chemicals such as adrenaline preparing our bodies to act better in a dangerous situation. All this stress is supposed to be helpful. But I never quite understand how a rapid heartbeat, trembling limbs, a dose of nausea and in my case a stomach churning with the veracity of a spin dryer, are effective tools in helping to find a dog.

I had to pull myself together and act quickly. Composing myself, I bundled the dogs that I hadn't managed to lose into the car, then proceeded to drive around looking for the elusive Tizer. After about thirty minutes of driving on the deserted streets, I threw in the towel, she was nowhere to be seen. My last redeeming hope was that she may have headed back to her home, which again is not uncommon in these situations. With a sense of cautious optimism I drove back to her house and pulled up outside, naively hoping that she was going to be sat at the front door, waiting for me. Of course, this was not the case, Tizer was not at home, what the HELL was I going to do next? All possibilities had been exhausted, it was now looking as though I was going to have to tell the owners that I had lost their beloved pet. The hand of fate was rapidly moving me towards 'check-mate'.

Getting out of the car I began to wander around calling her name. I don't really know what made me do this as I had never been in quite the same situation before, instinct maybe? Then, amazingly after a few minutes, she appeared skulking from the back alley. She must have been hiding there all the time, taking cover, obviously still scared. I was elated at this point, but I wasn't out of the woods yet, I still had to physically grab hold of her. Looking up at me with her big nervous dark eyes, she kept her distance. She was about twenty feet away from me, still scared and distrusting of me. I called her, but she wouldn't come to me. Slowly and gingerly I started inching towards her, praying to myself that she would let me go to her and put her on the lead, without running off again. I had to be gentle, any sudden movements could have a detrimental effect on proceedings.

At about one foot from her I leant down towards her, giving her soft words of encouragement. It was going well, she remained stationary, but that could all change. It was impossible to predict which way things were going to turn out, she was clearly still nervous, poor thing. Fortunately, she let me slowly go to her and clasp the lead to her collar. At that moment I was euphoric, I had gone from being cursed to being blessed in a split second. I was getting too old for all this stress, but I had to be thankful, at least I lived to see another day without my 'King' toppling over.

That evening I called the owners to put them in the picture, surprisingly they seemed accepting of the situation. In fact, they appeared relaxed about the whole thing. I, on the other hand, was not quite so relaxed and decided not to walk Tizer ever again. Main reason being I couldn't guarantee her safety; besides I didn't want to have to go through that awful experience again. The dog had now bolted a couple of times, therefore, it was highly likely that it could happen again. It's such an admirable thing to take in a rescue dog, but in my experience, there is more risk attached to some rescue dogs than non-rescue dogs.

It's not possible to know exactly how the dog has been treated in the past, and what it has been through. A lot of rescue dogs don't initially show signs of abnormal behaviour, but then later on down the line something can trigger an unexpected reaction in the dog. This is exactly what happened to a friend of mine Andy. He had been the owner of a rescue Springer Spaniel for about two years. In all that time he hadn't experienced any problems with the dog whatsoever, until one day when he put his face close to his dog to pet it. In a completely unprovoked attack the dog horrifically took a large chunk out of his nose. Andy had to undergo surgery to have his nose reconstructed and the dog had to be destroyed. Just tragic. Taking on a new rescue dog as a customer is now something that I think long and hard about.

But Summer is not all bad, and of course with a bit of planning it is possible to enjoy walks in the summer months. The best way is to take the dogs out early evening or better still early morning before the day trippers arrive. North Beach really can be quite stunning first thing on a lovely day. With blue skies, miles of beautiful golden sand, and the glistening sea gently lapping against the shoreline, away from people and the problems they bring, that's when I have to agree;

'BY HECK, I'VE GOT A GOOD JOB THIS TIME OF YEAR.'

Chapter 18

The cardinal sin - Winter 2012

Completely at the other end of the scale of good weather is of course the bad weather, which in itself presents a different set of problems for a dog walker, but in my opinion still preferable to the problems associated with hot weather.

On top of the problems with weather conditions I also have to keep a third eye out for dark coloured dogs; obvious reason being that dark coloured dogs are not as easy to see as lighter ones, especially under cover of darkness. Moses, a five-year-old miniature Schnauzer is jet black in colour, and blessed with a somewhat quirky nature. He had been on my books since early summer 2012, a lovely little dog but fairly quirky. Most dogs in my care are consistent in their behaviour but not Moses, he is a law unto himself. When picking him up from his house for doggy day care I never know what sort of mood he is going to be in, or indeed where he will be. Usually a dog excitedly waits for me by the front door, but I can never quite predict where Moses will be hanging out. Occasionally he can be found in the kitchen firmly firmly rooted to the of inside his cage, refusing to come out without the encouragement of several treats. Most of the time he is upstairs in the bedroom, again the mountain goes to Mohammed and I almost have to drag him down the stairs. His reluctance to come with me confuses me no end as once in the car, he is extremely happy to be with the gang. Then on the rare occasion, he catches me completely off guard by lurking behind the front door, lying in wait. As soon as I open the door, he scares the life out of me by making a dash for it and running straight towards the car which is always worryingly parked on an extremely busy road. I need to have my wits about me and quickly catch the little scamp before he comes to any harm.

His behaviour with the pack is also unpredictable. Sometimes he intermittently hangs around with the others and will play, to a point, but after a while he takes himself off to a quiet place and just does his own thing. Physically he makes for a very handsome dog. Owner Rick has not gone down the usual root of having his dog groomed in the typical Schnauzer fashion; as such Moses has managed to escape a 'Kaiser Bill' moustache and can sport a more natural appearance; eyelashes excluded. At about 4cm in length, his lashes look as though someone has stuck little paint brushes on the end of his eyelids; any drag queen (or Kardashian) would be proud to own such a set. Schnauzers originate from Germany and are allegedly bred with long lashes to keep the snow and other debris out of their eyes. You'd think that they must get in the way of his vision, but they don't seem to bother him, not in the slightest.

November, 2012. I will never forget the day, the weather was extremely cold, wet, and windy. As a Professional dog walker (PDW) I try not to let such things bother me, it's my job and a given that I will have to endure bad weather, complaining is not going to change it. But that month it had rained heavily almost every day and it was beginning to get me down (another record for the wettest November on record). I was looking forward to a break in the weather but it didn't seem to be happening any time soon. Although raining the proverbial 'cats and dogs' I made the call to still go on the walk, the 'rain by 7; gone by 11' rule had let me down on more than one occasion that month. So off I went on my merry way with six dogs in tow, Brece, Wasabi, Hendrix, Moses, Rocky and a couple of boarders.

Arriving at the beach, the dogs and I clambered out of the car and braced ourselves for the first brisk walk of the day. Just as I was thinking to myself how awful the weather was, it then made a turn for the worse, deteriorating even further. The wind had picked up and was now blowing wet sand into the dog's little faces, clinging to their snouts and stinging their eyes. The poor little blighters, it must have been extremely unpleasant for them, and for me for that matter. Not many dogs or people relish being freezing cold and soaked to the skin, except possibly postmen who somehow always manage to stay cheerful in the most horrid of conditions. But the upside for me is that we only need to endure the elements for an hour (if that). I usually motivate myself through the awful walks by looking forward to being back in the shelter of my home again, warm and dry and snuggled up in my dressing gown and comfy sheepskin slippers.

Apart from being uncomfortable, bad weather also means visibility is greatly impaired by the heavy rain. Although wearing a hood is a necessity, it can restrict the peripheral vision, which combined with the rain makes keeping an eye on the dogs that bit harder. All things considered, I decided that the endurance test should come to an end. Leading the retreat, we made a rapid U-turn back towards the car park. Frequently turning around, I checked that all my bedraggled dogs were still in tow. To look at them they resembled a canine terracotta army, marching on into battle. My little warriors were in a sorry state, especially Moses, his short body was completely covered in sand. The eyelashes were working though, succeeding in keeping the wet sand out of his eyes, but leaving clumps clinging to his lashes. Looking at the dishevelled dog I wondered what must have been going through his head; I imagined he was thinking, "This isn't what I signed up for."

Following a challenging struggle, I managed to get all dogs safely back into the car. Even Hendrix was glad to get back into the car on that day. After counting them all in we headed off home, I couldn't wait to be back home with more thoughts of my dressing gown and slippers. Once home, I dried the dogs off, then placed the wet towels on the radiators to air, that familiar unpleasant essence of damp-dog hovered in the air. Next I got out of my soaking wet clothes and dried myself off. Time flew by, before I knew it, it was 2.00 pm, time to prepare for the next walk of the day. Although conditions were still grim, I was encouraged that at least the wind had died down a bit. The last thing I wanted was to get another soaking, but duty called. Yet to find a coat that is completely impervious to water, I grabbed myself a second dry coat from the cloakroom. Suitably prepared, I reluctantly headed out again into the abyss of that cold November afternoon with my second batch of dogs, leaving the first lot behind, keeping warm as toast.

We landed at the beach to find the air was still bitingly cold, it almost took my breath away. With our lungs full of chilled air, we set off on the walk. Not surprisingly, the place was completely deserted, even the grey sea was withdrawing, going back out to meet the steely horizon of the sky. After about twenty minutes I finished the walk prematurely, we'd all had enough so we headed back home.

Once indoors first job was to check on my plethora of dry dogs. This is usually an easy task as when entering the house most of the dogs greet me with a tumultuous reception. They excitedly scuttle towards me, barking noisily, all the time jostling to get as close to me as possible. The welcome they shower on me is incredibly uplifting. But again I don't flatter myself that the reception is subjective, dogs will give a great welcome to just about anyone who is caring for them. I'm convinced that it is this sort of behaviour that helps reinforce man's bond with his best friend.

Moses, however, is the exception; he doesn't quite fall into the same category. By now all the dogs had appeared apart from him. This wasn't unusual behaviour, I assumed he was doing his own thing. He tended to materialise a few minutes later when things had quietened down, all in his own good time and not a minute sooner. I thought nothing of it.

I sat drinking a cup of coffee trying to warm myself up and watching a spot of TV. After about ten minutes it occurred to me that Moses had still not materialised. I began to wonder where he was so started to walk around the house looking for him and calling out his name. Still no sign, something was very wrong. At that point my stomach hit the floor with the weight of a boulder as the realisation of the situation sunk in. My calls turned into shrieks. I searched everywhere; upstairs, downstairs and in the garden but to no avail. Where the hell could he be? Possible explanations as to what must have happened flooded through my head; perhaps someone had been in the house and stolen him when I was out on my second walk. In my profession all sorts of horror stories of dogs being stolen from homes get bandied about which, to any dog owner and especially a pet sitter is always alarming to hear. I failed miserably to comprehend the situation all the while the same repetitive question repeating in my head, 'where the hell was he?'

Trying to think things through logically I finally concluded that it was unlikely that someone had come into my house to steal just one dog. It would have to be one brave person to do such a thing with my lot protecting the place. The only sensible conclusion was that I had left him on the beach after my first walk. At the time I was convinced I had counted all six dogs back into the car. However, due to the torrential conditions, my visibility was probably impaired by the weather and also my hood. In addition being dark in colour Moses camouflages against the dark interior of my car. Once in the car could he have jumped back out without me noticing? Could I really have been that unlucky? A ton of scary questions flooded through my head. Yet again, my worst nightmare appeared to be happening. As a professional dog walker (PDW), losing a customer's dog is not an option, it's not only 'checkmate', it's the cardinal sin!

With the realisation of what I assumed must have happened I headed back to the beach to begin the search for him. The weather was still relentless, driving rain stung my face, the worst possible conditions for finding a lost dog. It was at times like this that I wished I had invested in a balaclava and also in getting all the dogs electronically tagged. With poor visibility it was difficult to see or even hear anything. The place was still deserted, with only a handful of seagulls around scavenging for any tasty morsels delivered by the sea. I commenced my solitary search, running, then jogging when I tired. I was scared, but my strongest feeling was yet again one of being alone, loneliness percolated through my sorry soul. I was on my own in this, with only fear for company. It suddenly dawned on me that most pet sitters sensibly work in pairs, a business partner so to speak; covering for each other and providing support as and when needed. I, on the other hand and as usual, liked to do things the hard way and go it alone. Also being single at the time, it wasn't as if I could put a call out to a partner to help share the burden.

But I consoled myself; even if I did have a partner, it's not likely that he could have dropped everything to come and help me. Thinking things through, sometimes having someone from the opposite sex in your corner is not always an asset when it comes to doling out help and support. The potential words; 'How the hell did you manage to lose a customer's dog?' would undoubtedly add to my anxiety, but I had to admit a business partner would have been rather handy. Focusing myself I tried to think positively. I had been fortunate before when no harm had come to Tizer at the time of the horse stampede incident, perhaps I would be lucky again. But at the same time, realistically I worried that by now my good fortune must be wearing thin.

Alas, there was no sign of Moses on the flats of the beach, if he was still on the beach he had to be in the dunes; a colossal area, and impossible to see past the next dune. If I was to find him there, it would be a case of literally bumping into him and this scenario was highly unlikely. Eventually I decided to give up on that part of my search, so turned around and headed back to the car.

Once back home first thing was to call the dog warden in the unlikely hope that he had news of Moses, failing that perhaps he could assist me in the search. Secondly, I contacted the 'Lost and found dogs' group on Facebook, all the while my head was in a complete muddle. What the hell was I going to do if he didn't show up? Surely, I couldn't have lost another customer's dog, it can't have happened again? I had to keep calm, pull myself together; hysteria was never going to lead me to find him.

For the most part, I love my job and consider myself extremely fortunate to be paid to care for God's creatures. When I started up as a pet sitter, I completely understood the responsibility that I was taking on. People love their pets, after all, they are important family members. The fear of losing a customer's dog was always something in the back of my mind but on that awful day, yet again it was in the forefront of my mind, and a reality. If I didn't find Moses, there was no way I could call myself a professional pet sitter and continue looking after dogs, I would have to pack it in.

Then there was Rick, how the hell was he going to cope with having to endure the loss of his dog? How would he react to me, 'The incompetent bumbling pet sitter', would he be verbally aggressive when I broke the news to him? Would he name and shame me on social media perhaps, then go on to sue me? Rick is a lovely kind soul, but there's just no telling how someone is going to react when faced with tragedy.

While trying to plan my next steps my mobile phone suddenly beeped. I allowed myself a moment of optimism, could it be that someone had found Moses and they were calling to give me the good news? ... No, of course not, it was Rick, texting to say he was due home in an hour and asking me to drop his dog off at his house. This was all I needed! Of course, I was fully aware that he was due to return that afternoon, but he was arriving home even earlier than expected. There was now less than an hour to find Moses. Things were falling in all around me, not even time was on my side. I got myself back to the beach for a last-ditch attempt to try in earnest to find him. Naturally it was a highly unrealistic scenario that he was just going to appear and I could take him home with no one being any the wiser. In my experience life doesn't pan out like that. After about forty-five minutes of searching in vain, the daunting realisation that I was going to have to turn up at Rick's house, dogless, crept over me. It was time to face the music and break the awful news to him.

I arrived at Rick's house and parked up outside his front gate and sat there contemplating the terrible situation I found myself in. I thought about Rick and what a pleasant convivial sort of chap he is, a great customer *or at least he was.* Always friendly towards me and appreciative of everything that I did for Moses. The sort of customer who insisted on paying me if he cancelled a booking. Taking money from people to walk their dogs made me feel uncomfortable at times and I certainly couldn't cope with being paid for not walking their dogs. His insistence on remunerating me for doing nothing always lead to a long text exchange. He was adamant he paid, and I was adamant that he didn't, it usually resulted in us meeting halfway and splitting the difference.

Within a couple of minutes, Rick pulled up in his car and parked directly in front of me, accompanied by his girlfriend Adele. The couple were returning from a relaxing break at a Buddhist retreat in the Lake District. I expected he was feeling refreshed and excited about being reunited with his dog; little did he know that a reunion was not on the agenda. I now had to tell him the atrocious news; this was going to be the first time I would see him unhappy and I was the culprit. Of course, I felt worried and anxious, but somehow I felt strangely removed from the reality of the situation. It was as if I wasn't really in my own body, a bit like being in a play and acting the part of an incompetent dog walker. I wondered why I felt this detachment, but the out-of-body sensation was good in a way, it had the effect of buffering me from the enormity of the situation, enabling me to hold myself together.

Rick got out of his car; mirroring his actions I got out of mine and slowly walked towards him. For a split second, he looked happy, but it didn't take long for him to realise there was something seriously wrong. No doubt the look on my face would have given it away, and lack of dog; another big clue.

"OH MY GOD, WHAT'S HAPPENED?" he frantically shouted in my direction. I was dreading having to answer his question, but it wasn't really something I could swerve. My lips felt as if they were stuck together, I manage to prise them apart, looked down at the ground then choked on the awful words;

"Rick, I am so sorry, but I've lost Moses."

I was too afraid to make eye contact with him so continued staring at the floor. Having me gawping at him was probably the second to last thing he wanted to happen. It was done now; the Genie was out of the bottle, I was never going to be able to retract those words. After a few seconds I slowly plucked up courage and glanced towards him just in time to witness the colour drain from his face. All the benefits of his relaxing weekend lost in a flash.

Realising that something was wrong, Adele then got out of the car. Rick turned around to look at her and yelled in her direction;

"Moses has gone missing."

Adele appeared calm and silently ushered Rick into the house. Tail between my legs, I followed the couple into the kitchen whilst wondering how the hell I was going to explain myself. In all the panic I hadn't had a chance to think things through.

Like Emperor Penguins the three of us stood huddled together side by side in the modest galley-style kitchen, none of us knowing what to do or say. Time had come to a standstill. I noticed things in that kitchen that I had never spotted before and ironically focussed on a plaque fixed to the wall emblazoned with the Buddhist words of wisdom 'Let it go'. I wasn't sure that even Rick was going to be able to let this one go. Transferring my gaze from the plaque and plucking up courage I timidly focused on Rick for the second time. He stood rooted to the spot in total silence, face full of worry, with a deeply furrowed brow and tears welling up in his eyes. Seeing him in that state triggered my own tears, I couldn't hold them back any longer, they came flooding down my cheeks.

After about a minute in that oppressive atmosphere the silence was broken;

"How did it happen?"

At that moment I would have welcomed the apocalypse, but that was never going to happen. How was I going to tell this lovely man that not only had I lost his dog, but I didn't know exactly how it had happened? He didn't deserve it; nobody deserves to be told that their dog has been lost by the person who is being paid to look after it. In pathetic fashion, I told him everything that I did know, which was very little. Poised, and inwardly cowering I rehearsed his likely response in my head. Imagining dialect such as;

'Call yourself a professional pet sitter? How could you let such a thing happen?'

All of which would have been justified comments. I expected to be hit by both barrels but was astonished at his reaction. Naturally, Rick was distraught but at the same time, he was extremely understanding of my situation. He must have called on every drop of his Buddhist faith and found it in his heart to show compassion towards me. Looking at me with a sympathetic expression;

"Don't worry, it's not your fault, he's a rascal at times."

How magnanimous of him to say those thoughtful words. I had managed to lose his dog, yet there he was trying to make me feel better! I doubt that I would have been so understanding if the roles were reversed. Standing there, tears still flowing I thought that perhaps I should be coming up with a plan, just to give some sort of impression that I knew what to do in such circumstances. So I offered the suggestion that the three of should go back to the dunes to resume the search separately, thereby covering as much ground as possible. He agreed, and off we went to look for the elusive Moses. As I drove back to the beach I wondered what the atmosphere was going to be like in the privacy of Rick's car. Would the couple be angry with me by now, or would they still be in a state of shock, or maybe a bit of both?

Once at the beach, it was a relief that the weather had abated somewhat, I continued my miserable search in my designated area. After a fruitless hour of shouting and looking for the Schnauzer a little Wagtail bird decided to join me. It appeared that Moses hadn't heard my calls, but the bird had. It kept me company hovering close by, but always ahead of me. It was as if I had something that it wanted, but I had no idea what the attraction was. Never having had the pleasure of a Wagtail's company before, I felt honoured, they are usually such shy birds. Had I not been in such a panic I probably would have enjoyed its company, but as things were, I was way too distracted. As the bird and I travelled along, a strong intuitive sense crept over me; I just knew with a strong certainty that Moses wasn't going to be there, he was somewhere else. I felt as though I was searching in the wrong place and in doing so, wasting valuable time. Something was telling me that I needed to be looking for him elsewhere; but where should I be looking? There was the six-million-dollar question again. I decided to explore new grounds and returned to my car, so that I could drive around the streets to look for him. As I drove around I hoped above all hope that my intuition would send me to the right place. Whenever I saw someone I stopped to ask if they had seen a black miniature Schnauzer on the run. People were genuinely concerned but nobody had seen hide nor hair of him. Moses had vanished into thin air. After about an hour I conceded defeat, at least for the third part of the ongoing search.

Returning home, and consumed with despair, I had no idea what to do next for Moses. In times of anguish, I usually phone Anna. As Moses is one of my regulars Anna knew him quite well, hence she had an insight into his quirky nature. Anna would know what to do for the best. I called her and she answered immediately, after breaking the dreadful news to her, there was silence. My words had hit a stone wall, then after a long pause, in an assertive tone she said;

"What are you doing at home, why aren't you still out there looking for him?"

Yet another question that I didn't have the answer to. She was right though, I should have been out looking for him but in a weird way I was drawn to the inside of my house and not outside. Whether this was because I couldn't face the reality of what was happening and I just wanted to shut myself away, or there was some other unknown reason, either which I didn't know. All I really knew was that I was certain Moses wasn't on the beach.

"I don't know, I just can't get myself together, I don't know where to look for him next." I sounded quite pathetic even to my own ears. Anna continued with her firm words of advice;

"You've just got to pick yourself up, get out there and look for him until you find him."

She was right, of course, but somehow, I felt an odd resistance to her suggestion but had no idea as to why. Whilst I talked to her on the phone I restlessly paced up and down the hall, then something caught my eye.

Brece had started sniffing at the cloakroom door. Her sniffing became intense, she was getting excited, her tail beating like a drum against the dresser. This went on for about a minute then she started scratching at the door while making little yelping noises. She was onto something.

197

Something in the cloakroom had caught her attention and in a big way! I told Anna to wait a minute. With that, I opened the cloakroom door and there, nestled in a bed made from a coat that had neatly fallen onto the floor, lay a happy and comfortable Moses! My clever dog had saved the day, she had found her missing pack member!

Completely oblivious to all the heartache that had revolved around him, Moses looked up to me beneath his lashes, as if to say; 'What's all the fuss about?' Although massively relieved I was confused and couldn't quite work out how he had got himself trapped in there. Starting to join the dots together, I realised he must have sneaked into the cloakroom when I got myself a dry coat for the second walk. Unbeknown to me I had closed the door on the black dog in the dark room (another bad chess move). Moses had enjoyed his solace in the cloakroom for five hours whilst I had been on a five-hour mammoth wild goose chase. He never once made a single noise or barked the whole time I called him. Moses the maverick had a habit of barking all day long when I didn't want him to, yet when I did want him to made a noise, he turned mute! preferring to stay quiet as a mouse, comfortable in his own space away from the other dogs!

At times like this I never quite know if I have been lucky that things worked out well in the end, or unlucky that the incident happened in the first place. Whichever way, it was a great relief, a massive weight floated off my shoulders. I immediately phoned Rick and told him the good news. Naturally he was relieved beyond belief and what's more he saw the funny side of things wryly saying;

"See, I told you he can be a rascal."

I have since learnt that sometimes it is said that if a strange bird or animal comes to you when you're in desperate need, it's there to guide you; a spiritual help sent from above! Looking back on this sorry episode perhaps the little Wagtail was taking me back home to where Moses lay napping!

Chapter 19

What else could go wrong - Spring 2013

Not surprisingly there are a lot of points in the day when something can and, as mentioned, has gone horribly wrong. I am not alone in experiencing the occasional catastrophe and I take a weird sort of comfort in the fact that almost all my fellow PDWs have endured at least one gut-wrenching experience at some stage or another. But things usually work out okay in the end. The exception being one instance when the outcome for a local pair of professional pet sitters was anything but a happy one; it was disastrous. The couple were looking after a customer's Collie when it escaped from their house, ran out into the road, got knocked down by an oncoming car and tragically died from its injuries. Obviously, it's a terrible thing to happen for the dog and owners, but although I had never actually met the pet sitters in question; I felt enormous empathy for them. As animal lovers, they will undoubtedly be racked with guilt and burdened with it for the rest of their lives.

Most daily events are within the control of a pet-sitter, but some incidents are out of our hands, with probably the worst example being malevolent people purposely trying to poison dogs. In the past, there have been confirmed reports of dog haters purposely leaving meat spiked with poison in the local woods. Some unsuspecting dogs have sadly died from consuming the poisoned chalice. I know of a couple of people who have tragically lost their dogs in this manner, it's such a horrific thing to happen to a person's beloved pet.

These incidents always seem to happen in wooded areas, which is another reason why I usually prefer to walk on the beaches. Thanks to the ebb and flow of the tides, there is less chance of poison staying around for long. But even the beaches are not without hazards. The shores are frequently festooned with jellyfish and also the occasional mysterious batch of washed up palm oil; both of which on consumption are poisonous to dogs and can be fatal. Even something as innocuous as a shell on the beach can cause problems. A dog can quite easily cut its paw when coming into contact with a Razor-clam shell at high speed. As if all this wasn't enough to worry about, dog theft is also a serious concern, stories of dogs being stolen off the beach are commonplace. Presumably the dogs are enticed by a perpetrator then bundled into a get-away car. The stolen dogs are then allegedly used as bait for illegal dog fighting. It beggars belief that some people could stoop so low as to even contemplate poisoning or stealing dogs.

Something that I should have control of, but don't always, is safeguarding my customer's house keys, *my nemesis*. I find being the custodian of other people's keys to be a daunting responsibility at times. Losing a customer's key is an extremely stressful experience, not quite as bad as losing their dog, but it's up there. The hand of fate has deemed fit to separate me from a key on a couple of occasions. The moment I realise a key has gone missing, that unwelcome sinking sensation occurs in the pit of my stomach, a feeling that seems to come with the job. The biggest risk here is that I may be looking after cats whilst the owners are away, rendering me unable to get into the house to see to the cats. The key just seems to vanish into thin air, as if a bad fairy has taken it away. But I can't blame my carelessness on some mythical creature, the fact is I lose a key is because I am busy, thinking about my next task and not the job in hand. As Buddha says, I need to be mindful; when I do practice mindfulness, things tend to go a lot more smoothly, and usually without incident. But as a back-up in case my mind fails me, I have learned to ensure that the emergency contact person has a spare key.

Without a doubt my most embarrassing key faux-pas to date happened when I lost Sam Taylor's key (Tilly's owner). Coincidently it was outside Sam's house where I endured both of my 'handbrake left off' debacles. For some unknown reason, this job seemed to bring out the worse in me, it was as if I was doomed to behave in an incompetent manner around Sam's house. Sam also happens to be my hairdresser, with her salon conveniently situated approximately 200 yards from her home. On the day in question, late March 2013, I arrived at the doomed job to collect Tilly only to realise that I didn't have the door key. It was nowhere to be found; great, another elusive key!

After about a 15-minute search of the dog mobile, I gave up the ghost and decided to walk around to Sam's salon to share my latest dilemma with her. The thing about Sam is she's a rather vocal lady. In fact, in summer when approaching the salon, with the door open, it's possible to hear her dulcet tones from about a hundred yards away. I put this down to years of having to speak over the hair-dryers in order to make herself heard. Entering the salon, the noise is magnified by both the radio and the voices from the other stylists, all collectively trying to drown out the high-pitched motoring from the dryers. Once accustomed to the volume, the atmosphere is buzzing and friendly, not the sort of hairdresser environment where you may feel on edge, or scrutinised even.

Despite the racket it is a relaxing, down to earth place to have one's hair styled. A cup of coffee and a slice of banter is always on offer. In fact, things are that relaxed that Sam has even been known to use her salon's facilities to wash her pet bunny rabbit, Big Ears. Going back a few years, Big Ears was in dire need of some personal grooming himself, what better place for a rabbit coiffure than her very own salon? It was lunch time, Sam had just enough time to give Big Ears his shampoo and set, ahead of the arrival of her next customer. Not really the sort of thing that would happen in Sassoon's but at Sam's salon anything goes. Just as she was rinsing Big Ears down in one of the wash basins, her next customer arrived prematurely. Surprisingly, her client was remarkably laid back at the sight of a small mammal being washed in a basin normally associated with human heads. Taking things in her stride, the customer commented;

"Now, this is my kind of salon.'

As I walked into the cacophony on that March morning, I caught Sam in good spirits, she was in the middle of coiffuring one of her regulars, *person not rabbit*, who was seated directly opposite the entrance. I explained to Sam that I had temporarily mislaid her key, *the word 'mislaid' always sounds better than the word 'lost'*. I proceeded to ask if I could borrow hers. Without turning around, she spoke to my reflection in the mirror, and with little rebuke, granted me her key. After taking the key and returning to her house, I managed to let myself in.

Inside the hall, my eyes immediately focused on a key placed on a small occasional table. It seemed curious that my beady eye should be drawn to a key in such a manner, this required closer examination. Walking over to the table I took a closer look. My inspection concluded that it was in fact my key to Sam's house, recognisable by the remnants of an orange tag that was once inscribed with 'Tilly's name. So that's where my key was, it was on her table all the time, but how did it get there? The only feasible conclusion being that I must have accidentally dropped it on my previous visit, before getting back into the dog mobile, and somehow it had found itself in Sam's procession.

After the walk, I took Tilly home, then went back to the salon to return Sam's key. Walking back into the din I placed the key on the counter and kept Sam posted. Now cutting a different client's hair and again without turning around she spoke to my reflection. In front of a salon full of customers she blurted out;

'I found a key in my front garden the other day and wondered if it was one of yours, it's on the table in my hall."

"Oh yes I've got it thanks, Sam, and yes it was one of mine."

At first, I thought I had got away with my blunder, but no, she then drilled down, in her deafening fashion she asked;

"Just out of interest whose key is it?"

"Yours," I gingerly replied.

At this point Sam turned around, this time my response had provoked face to face dialogue. In a tone best described as irritable she exclaimed;

"Oh great, so you left the key to my front door on my front lawn?"

"Yes, that's right."

I have no idea why I thought it best to adopt such a cavalier approach to the whole thing. Perhaps subconsciously I was thinking that my casual approach at leaving her key on her open plan lawn might rub off on her. Maybe by playing the whole thing down it would influence her into thinking; 'Oh well, it's not such a big deal,' but that didn't happen. Naturally she never lets me live it down, and frequently sees fit to inform all her customers of my incompetencies. To this day I still don't know why I told her the truth, my life would have been so much easier if I had told her a white lie that day.

Customers are extremely trusting when handing over their house keys to me. Generally speaking, we leave our keys with a variety of people; workmen, decorators, and neighbours, trusting these people with the safekeeping of our keys and in turn our household possessions. But Lucy Brambell broke the mould, this was one lady who obviously didn't have a grain of trust in me.

Ms Brambell contacted me in early April 2013 in relation to looking after her cats while she was on holiday in the following month of May. In the usual fashion, I made the arrangements to go around to her house, introduce myself, get the details of her cats and find out exactly what she needed me to do. It was a lovely warm evening when I arrived at the semi-detached house at 7 pm on the dot, the agreed time. As I was complimenting myself on my punctuality, I knocked on the front door, stood there and waited for the lady of the house to materialise. There was no reply, I knocked again. I had been standing on her doorstep for a good few minutes, but nobody appeared. This seemed a tad strange, Lucy should have been expecting me. I wondered if I had got my wires crossed; it wouldn't be the first time.

After waiting for another couple of minutes I decided to go around to the side of the house to try my luck there. Surprisingly the back door was wide open, I knocked on it and shouted her name. Another long wait ensued, then a woman, whom I assumed to be Lucy, eventually appeared. She was a formidable sight; very large, heavily tanned, mid-forties, and wearing her long brunette hair loose around her shoulders. But the most striking feature about her appearance was her shorts. She was wearing possibly the shortest, tightest pink hot-pants I have ever seen on a person. The lower section of her buttocks squelched out from underneath the over-stretched pink material. It didn't bother me that she probably didn't have the right sort of figure to be wearing hot-pants. In fact, I thought it a positive that she wasn't self-conscious, quite the opposite, she was very confident in herself, the sort of person who wouldn't be afraid of their own reflection.

I explained that I was at the back door as there was no response at the front door. Expecting some sort of explanation, I was surprised when Lucy did not see fit to furnish me with one. Instead, she looked at me with a blank expression on her face, perhaps she was hard of hearing. It felt strange to ask a question and receive no reply, my feelings of uneasiness continued.

Eventually, Lucy and I embarked on a stilted conversation. As usual with a new customer I found some common ground between us. She told me, albeit reluctantly, that she was currently and coincidently working as a contract project manager at the same insurance company where I was employed. Not surprisingly, it turned out that we had some mutual contacts. This sort of thing usually helps when meeting new customers, it tends to break the ice. However, the ice was not thawing between myself and the chunky lady. In fact, the more time I spent in her company the chillier I felt. I didn't warm to her one bit, and I got the distinct sense that the feeling was mutual, it was as if she had an immediate distrust of me.

With most new customers I tend to gel with them to some extent, probably because we share a love and respect for animals, therefore there's a lot in common to talk about. Typically, people enjoy sharing information about their pets, but not Lucy, she offered absolutely no details whatsoever about her cats. Which left me with no choice but to start probing, in an

206

attempt to glean the information needed to care for her pets. This made me feel like I was intruding in some way, the long pregnant pauses between us felt peculiar. I wondered what was going through her head, what must she be thinking of me? After an upward struggle, I managed to gather just about all information required but it hadn't been easy; it was like pulling teeth. Thankfully the strained meeting was coming to an end, and as I left her house, she said she would get in touch with me nearer the time to let me know the exact dates of her holiday. But that didn't happen, I didn't hear another word from Lucy, leaving me left me to assume she had made alternative arrangements.

Several months later I was surprised when Lucy sent me a long text, the gist being she wanted me to look after her cats again. In her message, she explained that she was going to work in Edinburgh for a period of 2 months, Monday to Friday. She went on to tell me her neighbour had looked after her cats on the previous occasion, but made no apology that she had decided not to use my services, or even inform me that I had been sacked.

With a distinct lack of enthusiasm, I went around to see her for the second time to check that her requirements were still the same and to pick up her door key. Again, there was no answer from the front door, I found myself walking around to the side of the house, whereupon the back door was yet again, wide open. I knocked and called her and eventually, all in her own good time, she appeared; it was beginning to feel like I was stuck in a revolving door. Lucy stood in the kitchen whilst I stood on the doorstep. This time she was wearing a yellow mini skirt and a white cropped top.

As Lucy didn't do what is considered normal practice and invite me in to her house, I took it upon myself to walk in, uninvited. Again, there was no dialogue from her, although she watched me intensely like the proverbial hawk, which in turn made me feel like prey. I don't think I have ever felt so unwelcome in the whole of my life. Wanting to get out of there as quickly as possible I blurted out;

"Are there any changes from last time?'

She replied "No" all the while continuing her strange frosty glare. She somewhat reluctantly gave me the exact dates that she required my services. I replied that I would contact her a couple of days before she was due to leave for Edinburgh to confirm the arrangements. Still never breaking her stare, she slowly handed me her house key. I felt as though she was staring into my soul, somehow. She managed to evoke feelings of guilt in me, even though I had nothing to feel guilty about, it was all very weird. Taking the key in slow motion I then left and was more than happy to be on my way.

It was about 3 days before her trip when I received a curt message from her via social media; "I haven't heard from you and I need to know that my 'darling cats' who are very dear to me, are going to be looked after PROPERLY while I am away." I replied to the effect that I had a note in my diary to contact her the following day to confirm arrangements and that everything was in order. She pinged straight back again via social media telling me not to contact her on social media but to text her in future. Things were obviously not going too well, relations between us were poor, to say the least.

The following day I received another curt message from her, this time by text informing me that she had cancelled my services but again offered no explanation as to why. This was the second time she had wasted my time, but there was nothing I could do about it. In a way, it was a relief, I had more than a bad feeling about the woman. At the first opportunity I returned her house key; putting it through the letterbox I felt relieved; 'That's the last contact I will ever have with Lucy Brambell.' It felt good.

Chapter 20

Holidays - Summer 2013

As for all self-employed people taking a holiday is an expensive business, no money coming in but plenty going out. This is one of the reasons I don't tend to take too many days off. Other reasons are that I like to be available for my clients as often as I can, and also the planning side of things can be a logistical nightmare. Arranging a holiday for myself starts with finding a gap in my diary, then crossing the days out so that I don't take any new bookings for that period. But not wanting to let my daily regulars down, or lose them to another walker, I try to arrange cover for them. Some of my customers like to make their own arrangements in my absence, then others do not have a back-up plan and rely on me to find a suitable stand-in. Trying to find a dog lover who is available to cover is easier said than done. Fortunately I found a few excellent candidates who fitted the bill, my friend Lesley, and cousin Sharon. Up to that point I had not taken a single day off from my duties.

The handover must be executed with precision, *something that does not come naturally to me.* Details of customers' addresses, phone numbers, vet details, the diary of events (which dogs on which days) must be accurate. In addition, a customer's requirements may change from day to day so keeping the diary up to date is imperative. It is also important that I provide a thorough profile of each dog with detailed instructions on how to keep the dogs happy and safe in all situations. If only there was an app on my phone that could deal with all the minutiae.

In July 2013 I had arranged to go to London for the weekend with Nathan, my 'dog bone' benefactor who had now become a close friend. He had managed to get tickets for the England v Australia Rugby international at Twickenham, no easy feat, and something that I didn't want to miss out on. Cousin Sharon had agreed to cover for me but unfortunately, she then reneged on the arrangements. Something urgent had cropped up and she was no longer able to stand in for me. This disappointingly left me in somewhat of a predicament. I still wanted to go to London, but I couldn't let my customers down, what was I to do?

Luckily Nathan came to the rescue, he told me about a friend of his, Susan, who was also a professional dog walker. On my behalf he gave her a quick call to see if she could help; fortunately, she was free at the weekend in question and agreed to cover my dogs for me, perfect. Susan hadn't met my crew before, so it was going to be unfamiliar territory for her, meaning I definitely couldn't afford any mistakes in the arrangements.

Trying to become that meticulous person that had so often eluded me I set about arranging a complete and thorough handover. I met up with Susan on the Thursday and saturated her with information on my four dogs, giving her strict instructions on the do's and don't s. The key instruction being Haribo, a feisty female miniature Schnauzer; must not be walked with any other dogs unless it was with one of my customer's dogs. Reason being that all my other dogs had submissive temperaments and in the event of a dispute any one of them would back down to Haribo. Having a feisty dog on my books was a very rare occurrence, Haribo had manage to pass the Brece vetting stage, but I don't fully understand how. At the initial consultation Haribo arrived, tail up, moving briskly and giving out her opinions. She even snapped at Brece a couple of times. Things weren't looking good, I expected Brece to retaliate but she didn't. Instead, she looked at the little dog, turned way and then completely ignored her. Haribo was the only feisty dog that came to Heyhouses that Brece tolerated. It was as if Haribo didn't exist in Brece's eyes, which all things considered worked well. Although Haribo had her strong opinions that was as far as it went, she never actually nipped or worse bit another dog, so it was all manageable.

Having never met any of Susan's dogs, I had no idea of their temperaments, meaning it was too much of a risk to combine the two packs. Susan assured me that she was fine with all her instructions. Leaving for London on Friday morning I felt comfortable and relaxed in the knowledge that my customer's dogs were in good hands…

On the Saturday afternoon, Nathan received a call from Susan. His tone was stern, it was obvious from the way the conversation was going that something had gone wrong. I was worried. After Nathan finished the call he broke the shocking news; Haribo had managed to get herself into a fight with a dog that just happened to be a Bull Mastiff. I could hardly believe what I was hearing. Apparently, prior to the fight there had been an altercation between the pair over a water bowl at the local picturesque lake. Neither Haribo nor the Bull Mastiff backed down and a full-blown fight erupted. Naturally, Haribo came off worse. To this date I don't know where the Bull Mastiff came from, whether it was one of Susan's or just a random dog that they met on the walk. I couldn't face having that conversation. The thought of Haribo being mauled by a dog, especially such a big dog was mortifying; she didn't stand a chance. Naturally the whole ordeal took the edge off the weekend.

After the fight and requiring medical attention, Susan immediately took the battered little dog to the vets whereupon she was treated for lacerations and shock. She then made the awful call to the owners to put them in the picture and to make sure that someone would be home when she turned up with their wounded dog. Susan arrived at the owner's house with Haribo who was still in shock. Naturally, the owners were upset at the sight of their little dog, but they took the situation remarkably well, being only too aware of their dog's feisty temperament.

With hindsight, I couldn't have done things any differently, but I felt responsible, this was one of my beloved dogs that had been harmed. If I had not gone away for the weekend Haribo probably wouldn't have suffered, this fact left me feeling racked with guilt. Although physically wounded I hoped that Haribo would not be affected on the confidence stakes. In my experience a dog that has been physically attacked can also be affected mentally, in terms of confidence and their behaviour going forward with other dogs. There was no way of knowing how Haribo would fare, only time would tell.

A couple of months later I had arranged to go on a two-week holiday to Thailand, a trip that Nathan was organising. I managed the operation for covering my customers dogs, swerving Susan and calling on Lesley's help. As usual in these circumstances a few customers had made their own arrangements, leaving Lesley with about five daily regulars to cover for me.

The thing with inviting a pack of dogs to share your house is that your property may be exposed to damage from the dogs. Any destructive dogs are usually filtered out at the consultation stage, largely by relying on the customer's honesty. Of course, puppies tend to be destructive, but this sort of behaviour is not unique to the youngsters. Some adult dogs also display behavioural problems, which can manifest in the destruction of objects. In my industry, the odd incident is inevitable and par for the course.

If the occasional toy or cushion gets shredded it doesn't matter to me. But it did matter when Molly Monroe, continually munched her way through all my soft furnishings and valuables at an alarming rate. Although a mature dog at 8 years of age when it came to shredding stuff, she was probably more like 8 months. She chomped her way through a variety of stuff; toys, shoes, slippers, cushions, just about any soft inanimate object. But to be fair to Molly she only went on a chomping spree if I left the house for a short period. Of course, what I should have done when she boarded and I had to nip out was to make sure nothing soft was lying around. But as a mature dog, she caught me off guard and I completely forgot about her munching habit every single time she boarded.

One Friday evening, about a week before we were due to fly to Thailand I popped out to pick up a takeaway, leaving the dogs alone for about 10 minutes. On my return, Molly Monroe came to the door to greet me, all happy and waggy-tailed. To show her appreciation, she had brought me a present. This wasn't unusual, she always wanted to present me with the remnants of whatever it was that she had chewed. But this time, the fluffy vandal had exceeded herself, her penchant for soft furnishings appeared to have racked up a notch. With seemingly nothing else to entertain herself, she had decided to chew my passport to pieces! My heart sank when I saw the state of the valuable plastic document.

It was glaringly obvious that my passport couldn't be salvaged, about forty percent of it had been completely demolished. There was no doubt about it, a replacement was in order. The strange thing was that I wasn't annoyed, how could I berate such a happy, waggy-tailed dog? She had brought the remnants to me as a gift, with no idea of the collateral damage she had caused. Besides I had to take some responsibility myself for leaving my passport lying around.

I had taken it out of its usual safe place of my dressing table drawer to provide Nathan with my details for the flight. Rather tardily, I hadn't bothered to put it back and had left it on the kitchen worktop. But at the same time I wasn't expecting a mature Retriever to jump up onto the worktop and eat it. Perhaps Molly thought it was coated in gravy bones and couldn't resist having a little munch on it.

These things can always be sorted out, the timing could have been better though, with only a week before our trip it meant there wasn't enough time to get a replacement through the usual Post Office service. A trip to the government office in Liverpool was called for, so off we went to the big city. Fortunately getting a new passport went without a hitch, better than expected. Everything was sorted, we were going to make it to Thailand after all.

I was incredibly glad we made it to the fascinating country that is Thailand. Everywhere we went we found the Thai people to be happy, patient, helpful and respectful. I'm sure the whole Thai nation does not have all of these qualities, but the people that presented themselves to us certainly did. Nothing seemed to faze them, even rude people did not appear to offend the Thai people. The Buddhists perceive rudeness as a sign of ignorance, and an improper upbringing; and as such believe these people are to be pitied. I was in awe of so many things whilst there but the main thing that struck me was the dedication that the people demonstrate to the Buddhist faith. Shrines laden with flowers and other gifts are everywhere. Giving is a big part of the Buddhist way of life, it makes the giver feel good. Perhaps Molly was more of a Buddhist than I had realised!

A few weeks after the holiday still reminiscing about Thailand, I was sat in my lounge and sharing it with a couple of uninvited crane flies and a bunch of moths that had flown in through the back door. Just as I was thinking to myself that the place was starting to resemble 'The ugly bug ball' a knock at the front door broke my thoughts. Leaving the bugs to their explorations I got up off the sofa and went to answer the front door whereupon I was greeted by a police officer standing in front of me.

Having a policeman at my door was not a typical occurrence, in fact, it was the first time it had ever happened. Naturally, I felt worried that something awful must have happened to a family member. The policeman asked if he could come inside; not feeling as though I had many options, I consented.

With stilted mannequin movements I stepped backward to make way for him. The policeman, Brece and I stood in the hall, surrounded by an intense atmosphere. My feelings of worry increasing the whole time I was in his presence. Things felt strange, surreal. Brece, on the other hand, was quite happy and relaxed with having a member of the Lancashire Constabulary in our midst, right on cue we were treated to a performance of 'Teddy'. As usual, I grabbed her paws and showered her with kisses on her head and snout. I was pleased that she performed her party trick, it broke the atmosphere, to an extent.

Not sharing a mutual adoration of her versatility the policeman looked down at her, did and said nothing. And why would he? After all, he wasn't paying me a visit to amuse my dog, but what was he there for? Completely ignoring her performance, he said;

"I am making enquiries regarding a burglary that occurred at the abode of Lucy Brambell." *This was back in the days when the police had the resources to be able to investigate burglaries.* As one would expect, his tone was assertive.

I stood rooted to the spot, rigid, my feet felt as though they had suddenly been set in concrete. Not being able to comprehend what he was saying, somewhat dumbfounded I replied,

"Pardon?"

With that, in typical fashion, he repeated the first part of the sentence which I had heard, then eventually repeated the second part which included the daunting word 'burglary.' He continued, asking me if I knew of Lucy Brambell from Lindsay Rd St. Anne's. I couldn't think about who he was referring to at first, my mind was a complete blank. The policeman appeared to pick up on my confusion, enlightening me he gave me a brief description of her, tall with long brown hair, *he skimmed past the 'overweight' word,* adding that she had asked me to look after her cats.

After a few seconds and still confused I got a vague sense of recognition, but then I wasn't actually sure if I remembered her or just imagined an image of her. Eventually my distorted memory cleared itself up and I became certain who he was referring to. God how could I have forgotten such an unusual customer experience? It appeared that I had been incorrect in my earlier assumption that I would not be hearing from Lucy Brambell again.

The policeman continued to elaborate;

"Ms Brambell has recently been burgled, and she has given the police your name as a person who had access to her house keys."

Well, you could have knocked me down with a feather. I now appeared to be a suspect in a burglary. Of course, I knew I was innocent, but my knowledge was of no comfort to me at that point in time. And yes, I did have access to her house keys. I really wasn't sure how this one was going to pan out, would I have to go down to the station, give a statement, fingerprints perhaps? Not even Brece was going to be able to bail me out of this one.

The policeman must have realised I was worried and went on to say;

"Don't worry, madam, we know it wasn't you, but she has given your name as someone who had access to her house key and we need to follow up all leads."

It was such a relief to hear him say those words but I couldn't help wondering how he knew it wasn't me? Perhaps as a fifty-year old woman, I didn't fit the stereotypical profile of a cat burglar. He then shared his thoughts with me saying he suspected she had left her back door open and someone had just walked in and helped themselves. By this time, harbouring no loyalty to Lucy Brambell whatsoever, I told him that each time I visited her, the back door was wide open, whilst she was nowhere in sight. The policeman didn't respond to this snippet of information, instead he asked me if I had given Ms Brambell's keys to anyone else whilst they were in my possession.

"Definitely not." I was quite emphatic.

"If you don't hear from us within the week you won't be hearing from us again on this matter." With that he left.

The officer had been extremely pleasant in going about his duties and made what could have been a rather distressing experience into less of an ordeal than I initially feared it would be. He did what he could to put my mind at rest, but it wasn't at rest. Although right from the beginning I had my doubts about Lucy Brambell, I could never have envisaged that she would implicate me in the theft of her possessions. I was beginning to wish I was back in Thailand.

Chapter 21

Sick as a dog- Autumn 2013

On reflection, I consider myself relatively lucky when it comes to the health of the animals in my care, with only a couple of occasions when I have needed to take a sick dog to the vet. A few dogs have suffered bouts of sickness whilst staying with me but if the dog seems okay in itself and is not in discomfort or fed up, I don't tend to worry too much. I go by the old saying 'Sick as a Dog.' Dogs seem to have an uncanny talent for being sick in order to clean their stomachs out, without actually being ill. Sometimes they will even eat grass to bring on sickness; the dog can produce copious amounts of vomit, then carry on as normal, whilst I go around cleaning up after them. But If the sickness continues after 24 hours, then I do start to worry and do something about it.

Occasionally, dogs arrive at my house feeling under the weather but, as long as they are not too poorly, I take them in and administer any medication accordingly. The conditions are usually minor things, such as: skin complaints, sensitive stomachs, ear infections, joint problems and so forth. Occasionally I can have a few poorly dogs staying at the same time, making it crucial that I administer their medication effectively and don't get anything mixed up. At times the doggy hotel seems more like a doggy hospital, with the kitchen taking on the atmosphere of a pharmacy.

Most dogs prefer not to take their medication; I combat this by coming up with cunning ways of administering their meds. My most successful trick to date is pushing the pill into a small piece of corned beef, rolling the meat into a squidgy ball then throwing it up in the air as if it were a treat. Although the dog has just watched me put the pill in the meat, it does not think to itself; 'Hang on, there's a pill in that food,' instead, it thinks; 'Great a treat, I had better wolf it down before any of my mates get it.' The dog catches the treat mid-flight, then quickly swallows the Trojan horse down his gullet.

Then there are the dogs that arrive at Heyhouses with physical disabilities. Gucci, a visually impaired 9-year old black male Pug is a prime example. I received a phone call from the owner, Charles in Autumn 2013. During the call he warned me that Gucci was completely blind and asked if I would consider looking after him and his sibling Prada, a 7-year-old Pug. Not wanting to appear discriminatory in any way, I considered the notion, besides my heart went out to the poor little thing. Charles suggested that we met up on a dog walk to see how Gucci in particular would get along with the others, to which I agreed. I suppose understandably it was a sort of a test to see how I managed things for his blind dog. We arranged to meet up a few days later.

I immediately checked out Charles's appearance, then formed my opinions, a habit that I find unavoidable. I concluded; he was a rotund man with lots of baggy skin and folds around his face, and with a prominent set of bulbous eyes. The resemblance he bore to the pug breed was uncanny. This was not the first time that the phrase 'People look like their dogs', had crossed my mind. I have seen many similarities amongst my customers and their dogs. I have a tall slim man who owns a Whippet, a lady with long blonde hair that owns Golden Retrievers, a man with wiry hair who has a fox terrier, and a tall slender lady with silky hair who owns a Saluki, and so forth. Some people seem compelled to be attracted to a dog with similar physical characteristics to themselves; the reason for this eludes me.

After I had checked out Charles I looked down at Gucci. His appearance was a bit of a shock to me in more ways than one, but unexpectedly it was his mouth that was the main shocker and not his eyes. He possessed just one solitary tooth which stuck out of the front of his mouth at an acute angle. With no other teeth to hold his tongue in, it was left to constantly dangle out of his little mouth like a tough piece of dry old leather. He was also grossly overweight, his neck had long since disappeared under rolls of fat, leaving him to take on the appearance of a big black slug. To complete the picture, he was extremely bow-legged; in the immortal words of my grandmother;

"He couldn't stop a pig in a passage."

During the walk Charles kept Gucci leashed, acting as his eyes by steering him away from obstacles in his path. Apart from observing Gucci on that walk I did little else for him, Charles managed his Pugs, the three of them slowly followed behind me and the rest of the pack. After the walk he asked me there and then if I would be happy to look after his dogs for him. I quickly considered matters; the main change to my routine being that the pace of the walks was going to be a lot slower with Gucci on board. But that wasn't really an issue, the other dogs would still be out for the same length of time, charging about and getting a good hour of exercise.

Without even going through the formal meet and greet with Brece and following the usual steps that I take for an able-bodied dog, rather stupidly I consented to his request. This was a risk but somehow, I felt compelled to say 'yes' to him and his sorry little dog. *Not the smartest move*. Later I asked myself why I had bent the rules? I think for Charles's sake I was trying to play the whole situation down by making out that looking after a blind dog was just a matter of course; no big deal, I could cope!

A couple of weeks later as arranged Charles brought his Pugs round to my house for their holiday. Before leaving he gave me further details on Gucci's condition, elaborating that he had no eyes whatsoever. Apparently they had been removed during an operation following a severe infection in both eyes, after which his lids were then sewn together. This information left me feeling queasy to say the least and also puzzled as to why I hadn't noticed that he had no eyes when we were on our maiden walk. Perhaps it was because at the time I couldn't quite get past what was going on with his mouth. Looking at Gucci I felt sad and uncomfortable, but I suppose it was just a case of getting used to the situation, he certainly appeared to accept his lot in life; if he could, then so could I.

Charles went on to educate me; protruding eyes are a feature of the Pug breed which makes the eyes vulnerable to accidents, such as scratches from brambles and thorns. A wound to an eye can then become ulcerated and worse still, infected, whereas dogs with inset eyes are much better protected from these risks. Having looked after several Pugs at that point, in my ignorance I had never taken this fact into consideration. I have walked many a Pug in wooded areas bursting at the seams with prickly brambles, without realising the dangers to the poor Pug. Thankfully I have never had a Pug that suffered an eye injury, clearly this has been down to sheer good luck, rather than due care and diligence on my part.

Never having looked after a blind dog before I wasn't exactly sure what was in store for me. Pip, one of Anna's dogs, is also completely blind although he still has his eyes in his sockets and seems to manage remarkably well. If a dog has disabilities it does not feel self-pity and mope around, it copes with the cards it has been dealt, drawing on its other senses to help manage the best way it can. My main concern with looking after Gucci was not directed at him but at Brece. How would she react to him? There was a high possibility that he would collide into her when she was resting, and if this did happen she would be certain to give him short-change, which would inevitably leave me feeling even more sorry for the poor little dog.

For the whole of Charles's visit Brece had remained lying on the floor in the hall not moving an inch, but just watching blind Pug intently. The hall is a good vantage point, situated at the centre of the downstairs rooms and therefore a good place to see what is going on all around. Never having seen a dog with absolutely no eyes before I could tell that she didn't quite know what to make of him; more observation was required. Charles ran through the details again, then left my house with me at the helm.

After Charles's departure and on his advice, the first thing to do was show Gucci around the place, keeping him leashed so that his little bow-legs could get their bearings; we started with the garden. Despite his precarious legs he was incredibly agile, cocking his leg with the dexterity of a prima ballerina whilst emptying his bladder. On that first voyage he did a lot of relieving himself in my garden which is common for a dog when in new surroundings, but Gucci's marking his territory was excessive, I'm guessing it was a way of getting his bearings by using his own scent.

After he had completed his tour of the garden, gained a sense for the place and its obstacles and peed on everything possible, I brought him inside hoping that he wasn't going to continue to mark his territory indoors. Still on his lead he checked the downstairs rooms out, with me steering him away from obstacles. Thankfully Gucci didn't feel inclined to pee indoors.

Once I thought he had acquired a good sense of his surroundings I let him off the lead to fend for himself. As predicted, he wandered straight into Brece, who was still lying on the floor in the hall. Not surprisingly, she wasn't best pleased but then again she wasn't overly harsh either. All it warranted was a couple of gentle barks; if it had been a boisterous puppy barging into her she would have been far more ruthless. It was as if she understood that the unfortunate Pug had a disability and patience was called for. After the collision, Brece continued to watch him with her hawk eyes, never taking them off him as he slowly meandered around. The next time he wandered into her personal space she gave out a little warning growl, blind Pug immediately took the hint and changed course. Things were going better than I had expected; Brece seemed to be demonstrating a modicum of compassion which meant that I didn't have to feel too sorry for the little blind dog.

Last thing at night I took Gucci into the garden for his final toilet break of the day; keeping him on his leash in order to keep track of him. Whilst the darkness had a bearing on me, of course it meant nothing to Gucci, he was in darkness the entire time. Once again he navigated himself remarkably well, avoiding the obstacles in his path. Surprisingly he even knew when there was a step ahead of him. On his approach to the wooden steps leading onto the decking, he sensed them and stopped dead in his tracks. He then leaned forward and sniffed at the wood, with no encouragement from me he carefully ascended the steps. I have no idea how he managed this, whether it was because he could smell the wood (or his scent), or he was calling on his memory and remembered the positioning of them. It was as if he could actually see, *but I knew he couldn't as he had no eyes.*

The only weakness to his navigation skills was that occasionally, when indoors, he got himself stuck in a corner and was unable to find his way out, not dissimilar to the Duracell bunny. This carried on until I came to his rescue; a quick reset of his 'sat nav' and he was back on track. That first night I worried he might get trapped in a corner when I wasn't around to help, rendering him stuck there all night. Fortunately, this never happened; each morning when going downstairs he was always tucked up in the same bed as his brother, happy as Larry.

In fact, all things considered it was probably Prada who was the higher maintenance of the two dogs. I found Prada to be an extremely needy little Pug that required my constant attention. Grafting himself to my hip, he continually looked up at me, panting profusely the whole time. That in itself was fine had he not suffered from the worst case of halitosis that I have ever come across in my entire life. The toxic fumes of his putrid breath wafted into my face, stinging my eyes and physically drawing water, this was something that I really could have done without. I was quietly relieved when their visit came to an end and I got to hand the Pug brothers back into the loving care of Charles.

I consider myself extremely lucky in the fact that no physical accidents have happened to the dogs whilst in my care, either inside or outside of the house. In my line of business I hear of terrible atrocities happening to dogs, one of the worst being a Cavapoo who belonged to my friend Julia. Whilst on a walk with her dog who was running at a fair pace of knots it fell down a rabbit hole and broke its leg in two places. Julia heard her dog suddenly cry out and immediately ran over to find him in excruciating pain and unable to walk. She then had to carry the poor thing back to the car and take him straight to the vets. This was a wake-up call for me, *with all these wake-up calls it was a wonder I ever got any sleep*. God knows what I would do if this happened to any of my dogs, especially if it was one of the larger dogs. It would be impossible for me to carry a heavy dog and simultaneously keep track of the rest of the group. There wasn't much to be done to prevent such a tragedy, all I could do was make sure I always had my phone with me in the event of an incident. I hope I am not tempting fate but realistically the longer I do this job the higher the likelihood that one day an awful accident will happen.

Coming across so many dogs in my role as a pet sitter has made me realise just how fortunate I have been that Brece has enjoyed such rude health to date, touch wood. I have heard many tales of woe from customers who have previously owned very poorly pets. Dogs suffering from diabetes, epilepsy, diseases which were never fully diagnosed and a couple of dogs that died from multiple organ failure. So far, the only ailments Brece has suffered are a skin condition which was treated with a special shampoo, and an operation on her leg which happened following an altercation with a cat.

As with most dogs Brece has a penchant for chasing our feline friends. A dog will instinctively run after a cat; they are attracted by fast moving objects, and consider the cat as prey. Unsurprisingly the cat does not appreciate the chase. At every given opportunity Brece excitedly tears after any cat that finds itself in her vicinity. Most of the time the cat is physically and mentally quicker than she, and usually escapes by jumping over a wall or climbing a tree. I often wonder what she would do if she actually managed to catch up with a cat.

Walking out of my front gate one afternoon with her when she was about 4 years of age, I got the chance to find out. She immediately caught sight of the local ginger moggy; this was one massive cat. The instant she saw it, she pulled like mad, wrenching my arm which resulted in me having to drop the leash. Now free, she shot across the road in pursuit of the cat, thank God there was no traffic on the road at the time. She was off, on a mission, with me chasing after her. The cat, who resided at No. 4 was heading back to the safety of its home and in no time at all arrived at its front gate, quickly scurried up the drive, then calmly sat by the front door. Brece in hot pursuit also ran up the drive. Then the pivotal moment, they met face to face. Normally a cat would be hissing and displaying its claws at this point, but this was not your usual cat. Instead it remained stationary and appeared relaxed just looking up at my mad dog in silence.

I felt confident that Brece would not do anything to hurt the cat, but what would she do now she had finally caught up with it? This was a first. The answer to that question was; she did a dance! In pincer formation she started to prance about in front of the cat, repeatedly moving her front legs from side to side of the bemused animal. It was as if she wanted to play, but naturally her invitation was declined. The ginger moggy just watched her with a continual look of disdain on its face as if to say;

"You crazy dogs, what are you like?"

Sadly she had another incident with a cat in October 2013 which did not fare so well. Letting her into the back garden, in the usual manner, her beady eye immediately caught sight of a brave black cat that had wandered into 'her territory'. Cats in my garden are not a common occurrence, they tend to keep away from places where dogs reside; perhaps this cat was new to the neighbourhood and didn't know the score. As usual Brece had spotted the cat well before me. There was no chance of stopping her, she was off like a shot chasing it off her patch and desecrating my herbaceous borders in the process; all the while barking ferociously and saturating the air with her racket.

As soon as the cat realised there was a great big daft dog in its wake, it made a sharp exit by jumping over the neighbouring wall. Brece had done her work, the cat had successfully been chased off her territory, we wouldn't be getting any more trouble from that moggy. Pleased with herself she made her way back to the house. Sadly, her return journey was not quite as sprightly. Limping profusely on her right back leg she was obviously in quite a bit of discomfort and struggling to walk; this was serious. She managed to get into the house, whereupon I telephoned the vet and made an emergency appointment to get her checked out.

Arriving at the vets with my crippled Retriever we didn't have to wait too long before we were seen. The vet, a young lady in her early twenties welcomed us into the consultation room. I explained what had happened and she proceeded to physically examine Brece, after which she took an X-ray of her right back leg, whilst I waited. After about 15 minutes the young vet showed me the results.

Holding the X-ray up against the illuminated screen she explained that Brece's problem was hip dysplasia. This struck me as strange because she had a great hip score as a puppy. The vet's diagnosis confused me as I had never noticed any problems with her hips before the cat incident. To my mind the injury had been caused by overexerting herself whilst chasing the cat; I was thinking along the lines of a pulled muscle or torn ligaments.

The vet continued on her path, pointing out the image of her joints on the X-ray and highlighting little black specs that were apparently debris and the cause of her pain and discomfort. I was then informed that Brece needed to go to the vet specialists at Stamford House for a second opinion; it appeared that the diagnosis was not a definite one. Stamford House is based at St Helens, some 30 miles away. I wasn't relishing the journey one little bit as it involved a stint on the motorway but it had to be done. The following day we set off; two hours later we arrived at Stamford House, safe and sound.

After checking in we took our seat in the waiting room, eventually we were called to see the specialist. We walked (or hobbled in Brece's case) into the consulting room where we were greeted by the specialist, a tall slim man in his late thirties, with chiselled features, blue eyes and a very large prominent forehead. *Not unattractive in an extra-terrestrial sort of way.* The first thing he did was to check her previous X-ray. His examination revealed that there was nothing wrong with her hips. In fact, I recall to this day he clearly said; "She has great hips, I wish my dog's hips were as good as that."

On the one hand, it was pleasing to hear that my dog had good hips but on the other hand, I couldn't help thinking to myself; 'How come they can't read an X-ray at my local vets?' The specialist then told me that a further X-ray was required as rather annoyingly, the previous one only showed an image from her knee upwards. We had a great view of her stomach and upper leg, but not the entire leg.

The second X-ray was taken, more waiting then the results which disappointingly revealed absolutely nothing. The extra-terrestrial specialist then recommended keeping her in overnight so that further tests could be done. This involved extracting fluid from her right knee. I wasn't really sure why she needed to stay overnight but as usual in these circumstances, I said nothing and accepted the words of the expert.

The thought of leaving my dog in her new board and lodgings was an upsetting one and something that I really didn't want to be doing, I felt bad. As I left her in the consultation room, she watched me with her gold medal 'I will make you feel incredibly guilty,' eyes. My emotions were beginning to weigh me down, I was leaving her again, in a strange environment and this time she was in pain. She was bound to be worried and feeling abandoned. But I had to be realistic, lightening the load for myself, I focused on the facts: she was in the best place, it was a necessity in order to get her better, there was no other choice in the matter. The sad thing was that she wouldn't understand any of this.

The following day returning to Stamford house my mood was upbeat, excited even. I couldn't wait to see my big daft dog again, and hopefully the specialist would have a diagnosis by now and perhaps a treatment plan. More patient waiting then I finally got to see the consultant. That's when it all went a bit flat. The same extra-terrestrial vet gave me the results of the fluid tests; unfortunately they were inconclusive, we still had no diagnosis.

As with people, it seems that trying to find a diagnosis in a dog is a process of elimination, except people have the financial security of the NHS to fall back on. As a number of things had been ruled out it appeared that we were now looking at a soft tissue problem, an MRI scan was required in order to determine the exact cause of her discomfort. I had wisely invested in pet insurance when she was a pup but in my experience the pet insurance companies are not as efficient at settling claims as they are at collecting the premiums and slamming on additional 'excesses' to all claims. Acquiring a massive vet bill was something that I was trying to steer clear of.

At this point, the bill had rapidly notched up to £600. I was curious to know what the going rate for a dog MRI scan was. Putting the question to the vet, I was completely dumbfounded when he casually answered;

"£1,800." If he had said £800, it would still have been a shock but £1,800! How the hell could they justify this astronomical figure which didn't even include any treatment?

The princely sum of £1,800 kept reverberating around my head, I could hardly believe my ears. Naturally, I was uncomfortable about paying such a vast amount of money just for a scan, I shared my thoughts with the vet then left after having decided to seek a second opinion. I started asking around; a local vet, John Higgins, came highly recommended. I was reliably informed that John was a reasonably priced, old-fashioned vet with a great reputation. This was what I wanted, a hands-on vet with old-fashioned fees; a vet who knew his craft without relying on today's expensive modern technology. I decided to pay him a visit.

Walking into the waiting room of John's practice came as a bit of a shock. The reception area was small, shabby and looked as though it could do with a good clean, better still a refurb. But then, not investing in smart furnishings was probably one of the reasons that John was able to maintain his modest fees. As long as the treatment was good, the operating room sterile, then superficial sleek furnishings and décor were irrelevant.

Wearing a slightly grubby white coat John struck me as being very mature, probably in his late 70's and way past retirement age. He was almost bald apart from a horse-shoe of grey hair that surrounded his liver-spotted head. A fairly unanimated fellow with few words to share.

Without the aid of an MRI scan, John examined my injured dog. After just a few minutes he confidently diagnosed a torn cruciate ligament in her right back leg and informed me that a relatively straightforward operation was required to repair it. A few days later, first thing in the morning I took Brece back to John's to undergo her operation, and left her there.

I was quite the nervous wreck on the journey home. That dog had evoked such strong feelings of attachment in me. I surprised myself at how anxious and empty I felt without her by my side. Later in the afternoon, I received the call; I was pleased to hear that the operation had gone well and she was out of the anaesthetic; I immediately went to collect her. Upon my arrival, I checked in with the receptionist and in the usual fashion was told to take a seat. Sitting patiently in the waiting room, my stomach was in knots, I contemplated on how my poorly soldier was. She must have been confused and disoriented, and unable to understand what was happening to her or why. My nervousness continued, whilst I kept my eyes peeled on the shabby door which I was expecting her to reappear from.

After a few minutes the door opened and Brece slowly waddled towards me, accompanied by a nurse. That first sight of her was tinged with mixed emotions, part of me was delighted to see her, but at the same time I felt upset. She was obviously in quite a bit of discomfort, but focusing on the positives at least she was walking. As she got closer, I saw that her back leg was completely shaved; revealing a spindly pink limb, the flesh of which was held together with rough black bloodied stitches. I hadn't prepared myself for the sight in front of me, which resembled something off a Frankenstein set. I gave my brave soldier a very warm greeting and a pat on the back. Next, I settled the account, £470, a fraction of the fee for an MRI scan. The nurse kindly helped me carefully get Brece into my car, and we set off for home. On the return journey, I drove as slowly as possible, trying to avoid any sudden movements that may have caused her further discomfort.

Once home I settled her, she was slightly disoriented and a little sorry for herself; it was going to take time. After about eight weeks of camping out in the dining room and taking things carefully, thankfully she made a full strong recovery, never once having complained of her pain.

CHAPTER 22

TOBY – Winter 2013

Of course as a dog ages inevitably and sadly it will suffer health problems, as was the case with Toby. I was first introduced to Toby when he was two-years of age. At that time he was the most majestic, intelligent handsome black Labrador that I had ever had the pleasure of meeting, well-built, with trim physique and a large strong head. His glossy coat was predominantly black in colour apart from a slight tint of brown across the top of his head. On a bright sunny day, he positively glistened. With a slow graceful gait he carried himself in an almost regal manner and made for a very impressive dog. But the thing that I found the most striking about Toby was his intelligence. Looking into his eyes, I just knew that somehow, he had managed to acquire far more intelligence than the average dog. At times I almost felt that I was out of his league and that he understood far more than I did.

Labradors originate from Newfoundland and were recognised by the Kennel Club in 1903. The breed comes under the 'Gun-dog' category. They were originally trained to find and retrieve game on land and in water, hence their genetic fascination of water. Due to their many qualities Labradors are frequently voted the most popular dog in the UK. They also make for marvellous assistance dogs aiding people suffering from a multitude of disabilities; blindness, autism, epilepsy, and many other conditions. Emma, another black Labrador that I looked after in the past was an assistance dog to a little boy called Jack. At the age of seven Jack suddenly became deaf, and Emma was assigned to him, making Jack the first deaf child in the UK to join forces with an assistance dog.

Emma was always by Jack's side, she slept in his room at night and watched over him. I was intrigued to learn what benefits a dog can bring to a deaf child, so I asked Jack's mum who brought me up to speed; Jack couldn't hear high frequency sounds such as the alarm ringing in the mornings. When it went off Emma acted as his alarm and jumped onto his bed and gave Jack a head start to the day by washing his face with her pink salivary tongue. She also assisted in more practical ways such as delivering handwritten notes from his mother, 'breakfast ready' and such like. Emma was his alarm clock, but her main role was as a communicator between Jack and the rest of his family, passing messages to and fro.

Back to my other amazing Labrador, Toby and our early encounters. I initially started noticing him whilst going about my daily walks, regularly bumping into him with co-owner Julia. Putting an age to Julia, as we always seem compelled to do, I would say she was in her early forties. She also had a regal air about her, perhaps that's where Toby had acquired his royal demeanour.

In time Julia and I gradually got to know each other. From our chats, I gleaned that she lived with husband Tony, in a first-floor apartment, which is one of ten and formed part of a grand replica Georgian mansion. The building was erected in 1886 in the architectural style of Lytham Hall and built by one of the many rich Lancashire mill owners who retired to the resort in the 19 century. The owner died leaving no heirs. The building was then used as a male boarding school before being converted into luxury apartments in 1980. The original features of the building were preserved making for a very grand place indeed, fitting for a regal dog, such as Toby. Husband Tony worked full time, consequently, I didn't get to meet him in the early days.

Observing Toby whilst out walking I considered him to be an extremely well-trained and well-behaved dog, especially considering the fact that he was unneutered. This fact did not seem to present the usual problems associated with unneutered dogs, key one being dog aggression. Always unleashed he walked behind Julia never straying. He was accepting of all dogs that crossed his path, and obediently followed Julia's commands, not that she needed to give him many.

It crossed my mind that it must have taken a considerable amount of intense training to get a young intact Labrador to behave so impeccably. I was so impressed with Toby's behaviour that I asked Julia where he had undergone his training. To my surprise, she told me that Toby had never had any professional training, adding;

'I guess we have just been lucky.'

Julia mentioned that she was looking for someone to look after her dog. She had been offered a part-time job working as a beautician in town and asked me if I would consider having Toby for day-care.

Looking after unneutered dogs was something that I normally steered clear of, but in view of his remarkable manners, I made an exception and decided to give it a try. A couple of days later Julia and her lovely dog came to my house for the formal consultation and usual grilling from Brece. As soon as Toby entered my home, he seemed to understand what was expected of him. It was as if he knew it was some sort of test. Brece started proceedings by giving him the usual telling off just to let him know who was boss, with that he calmly looked at her as if to say;

'That's fine, I get it.'

The audition went well, Toby passed with flying colours. From then on, I had the pleasure of his company three days a week, 11 am collection from the apartment and 4 pm drop off.

Generally speaking, dogs were not permitted to reside in the apartments of the Georgian mansion but somehow Toby had managed to acquire himself a concession. This was on the understanding that there were no complaints from the other occupants, of which there were none. Quite the contrary, other residents seemed very fond of the establishment's token dog. People that we regularly bumped into were always happy to see him and frequently stopped to exchange greetings. Even the young boy that lived on the second floor and had a phobia of dogs, was fond of Toby.

The more I get to know Toby, the more I realised what a true gentle-dog he really was. In the entire time he had been in my care he had never once so much as curled his lip at another dog, although he definitely had cause. He tended to keep himself to himself when at my house, but at the same time, if other dogs wanted to play with him, he was patient and accepting of their advances.

From day one, Doug the Pug took an instant shine to Toby, he clambered all over the patient dog and constantly wanted to play. Doug looked up to Toby, in more ways than one, his large dark bulbous eyes were full of adulation for his big buddy. Sadly, I don't think the feelings were mutual, but Toby never showed irritation at the constant attention that his little pal bestowed on him. On more than one occasion I sensed that Toby was too polite to manage the situation himself, leaving me to physically remove Doug from his person, finally giving the long suffering dog some respite.

The only thing that this fabulous dog was particular about was travelling. He preferred to be in the boot of the dog mobile, and he liked to be the first dog in. If another dog was already in situ, he was reluctant to jump in, it was as if he was worried that he may disturb the other dog. Once in, he was accepting if I put another dog in the boot with him, and he didn't even mind if the dog clumsily landed on him, he never complained.

Whilst travelling in the boot, Toby was extremely calm, I never heard a peep from him. This was, however, a disadvantage as sometimes it was all too easy to forget he was there. There were a couple of occasions when I set off on a walk with all the vocal dogs, done the head count, only to realise that I was a dog down. I'd forgotten Toby and left him behind in the car. Again, he was too polite to bark and say; 'Hang on, don't forget about me here in the back'. Most of the other dogs would have been wailing like Banshees in the same situation, hence it wouldn't happen to any dog, other than Toby.

A friend, Jacqui, who often joined me on the walks christened him 'Shaft', her logic being that he was black and cool, Toby to a tee. The only thing that was perhaps not so cool about him is that being an entire dog can sometimes cause the odd problem when coming across another Labrador, of either gender (like goes to like). In stark contrast to his normal impeccable manners he usually sidled over, proudly growling as he introduced himself. This part was fine, but he immediately got over-familiar with the unsuspecting dog and started mounting it in a sort of friendly, but at the same time dominant manner.

But it was all manageable, and a small price to pay for having the privilege of looking after such a beautiful dog. There was just one more slight negative about Toby which again happened on the walks; and that was his unusual toilet habits. Avoiding the usual flats, he preferred 'A poo with a view' and liked to empty his bowels on top of the tallest, grassiest dune that he could find, or worse still a pile of nettles. I don't know why he insisted on relieving himself in such selected places, but he did, that was his thing, and again a small price to pay.

Calling on his incredible intelligence Toby always understood exactly what I was saying to him. I only had to say something once, and he got it straight away. And it wasn't just commands that he understood, he appeared to be able to compute full and varied sentences. For example, if he was sitting in the middle of the boot of the car and I wanted to put another dog in with him, I would nod in the direction of a corner and say; "Move over there Toby, so that Wasabi can get in." I only had to say it once and he immediately went to the place indicated, making room for the other dog, again without complaint. *For information on dogs understanding of language refer appendix I.*

After a couple of years of looking after Toby three days a week, I felt as though I knew him extremely well. Apart from his astounding intelligence, I knew him as a happy, serene dog. But suddenly and for no apparent reason, he seemed to go through a bit of a rut. Each time I went to collect him he appeared subdued with no interest in going for his walk, which was most unusual. Of course, being such an obedient dog, he always came with me but it took encouragement. His heart just wasn't in it, *mounting other dogs was definitely out of the question.* It was strange, he appeared to be in good health, I just couldn't work out what was wrong with him. I found myself almost wishing that he would go up to other dogs and mount them, just so that I knew he was okay.

Toby's morose mood continued for a couple of weeks at which point I decided to mention my concerns to Julia. Next time I saw her, I brought up the subject of Toby's mood. At the time Julia said very little in response to my observations, but a week later when dropping Toby off, she spoke to me, starting the conversation with;

"There is something you need to know."

In my experience dialogue of this sort is usually followed up with a negative, the negative in this instance being that Julia and husband Tony had parted ways. She had already moved out of the apartment, only returning to it occasionally. Could this be the reason for Toby's morose mood? Perhaps he was missing Julia, or just upset with the situation. Of course, there was no way of knowing for sure but I couldn't think of any other reason why Toby was not his normal self. It appeared that along with his astounding intelligence came a deep sensitivity.

After the couple's separation and whilst walking Toby sometimes I saw Julia from a distance walking along the promenade. At such times I felt slightly uncomfortable, she was alone, whilst I had the company of her dog. One such occasion we were on the beach when she spotted us and came over for a quick chat. But it was an awkward chat. As she looked down at her dog the tears started to well in her eyes, I felt for her. The next few minutes were prickly to say the least; it was a relief when she finally said her goodbyes. But how would Toby be feeling? To look at him he was forlorn, standing rooted to the spot in between the two of us.

As Julia started to walk off, I watched her for a few seconds, then turned around and slowly walked off in the opposite direction. At this point I had no idea what Toby was going to do, would he run off to join Julia, or would he stay with me? He remained sitting and mournfully watched as his owner walk away. I'm sure his heart was telling him to go with her, but his head was telling him to stay. Being so astute I think he realised he had come out with me, so he should stay with me. In the end, he turned his back on Julia, and walked towards me. It was pleasing that he made that choice, only because if he had followed Julia it would have made a sad situation all the more sadder.

In the fullness of time I saw less and less of Julia, it was now Tony (or Daddy Dog as he proudly referred to himself) that picked up the reins for all matters of Toby. I was now looking after Toby five days a week, his spirits had lifted and thankfully he returned to his normal happy self.

It was a November morning, Nathan and I were enjoying a pleasant walk along the estuary, accompanied by Toby and Nathan's two Jack Russells. The estuary walk is long and muddy in parts, it also entails crossing several stiles. Getting the terriers over the stiles was easy enough but we had messed up and not considered how we were going to get Toby over the hurdles. Being a well-built muscular dog, we soon realised we had a problem on our hands. At the first stile, Nathan strained as he lifted the bemused dog over the obstacle, before clumsily dropping him over the other side. It couldn't have been very comfortable for Toby, but in his usual style, he remained calm and did not panic as many a dog would have done. The same thing happened at the second stile, but by the time we got to the third stile Toby took matters into his own paws. He looked at me as if to say; 'I'm not going through that palaver again, sod it, I have a much better idea.'

Assessing the situation, he understood exactly what was required and jumped over the stile, clearing it perfectly. On face value, this doesn't sound like such a magnificent feat, but it entailed negotiating all four paws on the two narrow planks at different levels, on both sides of the stile. He moved more like a cat than a dog, with precision, and perfect balance, making things so much easier for us. At that moment I felt extremely proud of the black panther, there was something seriously special about this dog, I didn't know any other dog that possessed that level of ability. Toby was in a league of his own.

Later that evening when I dropped him back at his home, I asked Daddy dog (DD) about his dog's heritage. He explained that Toby's mother was a show dog whilst his father was a working dog. I'm not sure why I never knew this information before, but it certainly explained his remarkable demeanour and class. Apparently, DD had thought about 'showing' his dog but because of the brown tint on his otherwise black coat, he failed the acceptance criteria.

The interior of DD's apartment was minimal in its furnishings and pristine in its pure white décor. At least it was until the fateful day when Toby suffered an extremely unfortunate episode. On the day in question, he had been boarding with me for just one night. As arranged, I dropped him off back at the apartment the following day, after having given him his tea at my house.

Later that evening, DD called me to ask if anything unusual had happened during the day. This did not bode well, yet another string of words that is usually followed up with a negative. I replied that it had been a normal day with nothing out of the ordinary to report. As expected, the negative that had been lurking around in the conversation rose to the surface; DD had returned to his apartment that evening to find the walls were no longer pristine, they had now been redecorated in diarrhoea!

Not surprisingly DD was quite shocked at the scene in front of his eyes but pulled himself together and proceeded to clean the room up. Once the apartment had been returned to its former glory, low and behold the same thing happened again, Toby suffered yet another bout of projectile diarrhoea. I can only imagine how awful the whole ordeal must have been for all concerned. Part of me saw the funny side but I am sure DD would have struggled to find any humour on that night, no matter how hard he looked.

I have never known this to happen in a dog before and was completely confused as to the cause of the unfortunate incidents. I reflected on the day; Toby had seemed fine and in good health, then I remembered when dropping him at the apartment that evening there were remnants of dinner left in his bowl from the previous day. Entering the kitchen, in full Labrador mode he went straight over to the bowl of stale food, sniffed it, then wolfed it down in one, and that was on top of the meal he had already eaten at my house. All this food must have created some sort of chain reaction in his gut, bloat perhaps which possibly led to the unfortunate explosions.

After some period of time, DD started to see Marie, a lady who happened to live in the same apartment block, but on the ground floor with access to the front lawns. Eventually, DD sold his apartment and moved into Marie's beautifully decorated abode, along with Toby of course. This worked well for me as it meant that I didn't have to travel further to collect him. Never having owned a pet, Marie now had to get used to a dog living under her roof. Not only that, she also had to cope with me wandering in and out of her home to collect her new canine lodger.

The first thing that struck me about Marie was that she liked to keep her home in immaculate condition, not always possible when being the owner of a big furry friend. I prayed to God that Toby didn't suffer a bowel explosion in his new abode. As time marched on I think Marie got used to all the new changes in her life, she was clearly fond of her canine lodger, and cared a great deal for him. Toby was happy in his new surroundings, after all, had been given a promotion and now had access to the beautiful lawns. On a nice day, Toby loved nothing more than lying in the front garden watching the world go by, enjoying the attention and compliments from the other residents. Thankfully there was never a repeat of his low spirits.

Just before Toby's ninth birthday he started limping, slightly at first but it was gradually getting worse. Fortunately, the pain and discomfort he endured didn't appear to put him off his walks. In fact, quite the contrary he seemed to be getting even more sprightly and increasingly dominant with other dogs that crossed his path. He started running off towards other Labradors on a more frequent basis. Once he reached the object of his desire, he usually started to fervently mount the dog, much to the dismay of the other dog and owner. He had always been fond of 'dog on dog' contact but his frisky activities were on the increase. A chat with DD was called for; I put the delicate question to him and asked if he had noticed a change in Toby's behaviour on the walks, namely was he mounting dogs on a more frequent basis? I was confused when DD said that Toby didn't bother with other dogs when out walking, and he wasn't in the habit of mounting them! This left me somewhat confused, it appeared that Toby was behaving differently when with the pack, he definitely had a spring in his step when out with the gang, there were no two ways about it!

Sadly, the majestic dog's mobility continued to deteriorate but his condition did not deter his ardour, it just took him longer to get to the focus of his desire. DD took his beloved pet to the vets whereupon Toby was diagnosed with arthritis of the shoulder; a fairly common condition in large dogs.

In the past, I had heard extremely good things about the wonders of hydrotherapy treatment for dogs suffering from mobility problems. When submerged in water, the dog is no longer weight-bearing and therefore able to move its joints more freely, which greatly helps to relieve any stiffness. Also, in time, hydrotherapy can help build up muscle tone which in turn, helps to support the joints. I passed this information on to DD but Toby's vet had suggested surgery. It appeared that an operation was required which involved inserting a steel plate into Toby's leg which would relieve the pressure off his shoulder joint. This seemed a little drastic to me. I had hoped that the vet would have recommended hydrotherapy, but it was not to be. Personally, at the time, I don't think all vets were fully on board with the benefits that hydrotherapy can bring to a dog. Alternative treatments for both animals and people seem to take a long time to be accepted by the conventional professionals who naturally prefer to practice what they know.

Mid October 2013 Toby underwent the operation which appeared to go without a hitch, but of course while convalescing he had to take things easy. This meant Toby was unable to come along on the pack walks, instead he stayed at home recuperating, with daily visits from DD. Initially Toby's condition seemed to be improving but unfortunately about a month down the line his health took a turn for the worse. Toby's mobility and posture rapidly deteriorated, and to make matters worse he was now unable to pass water. In view of the seriousness of his health Toby was admitted to the Chorley Specialist Animal hospital some 25 miles away, where he remained for about a week enabling further tests to be carried out.

Several blood tests later in mid November 2013 Toby was diagnosed with an uncommonly excessive amount of testosterone in his bloodstream.

The testosterone had caused a swelling in his prostate, which was preventing him from passing water. A very rare condition, but then intact dogs are not exactly common these days. When DD gave me the update it occurred to me then that this was the likely explanation for the increase in Toby's mounting activities when out on our walks.

Whilst still at the animal hospital and now completely unable to walk, Toby also underwent a couple of scans which later revealed that the poor dog had a further four serious complications; hip dysplasia, disc spondylolysis, a bone infection, and a displaced disc. No wonder he was in such a bad way with all that going on. It was a great shame to see a once strong, majestic dog reduced to such a condition. In my ignorance, I had assumed Toby would make a good recovery after the implant operation, but instead, his health had rapidly deteriorated. I don't know if his problems were as a result of his operation, or just pure coincidence. Toby continued his stay at the animal hospital, while DD devotedly went to visit his dog every day.

During the days that ensued, Toby's testosterone levels had still not stabilised, which continued to prevent him from passing water in the usual way, therefore a catheter had to be inserted into the unfortunate dog. On top of this he wasn't eating either, not a good sign, a feeding drip was also inserted into him. This left me with a daunting image of Toby with tubes going in and out of his body. After a few days, the latest update from DD was that the catheter had started to irritate Toby, and to make matters worse his testosterone levels were still abnormally high.

The decision was finally made to castrate Toby after all these years. The operation went ahead and fortunately without complications; after which Toby's testosterone levels finally returned to normal and he was then able to pass water, unaided. This was great news, but he wasn't out of the woods yet. Toby still had all the other problems which the vet had now said could not be rectified; the prognosis was not good. To aid his suffering steroids and a massive dose of pain relief medication, including morphine, were prescribed.

On Friday, the fifth day of his hospitalisation, DD visited his dog in the usual manner. The specialist spoke to him and broke the sombre news that as there had been no improvement in his dog's condition the best thing would be to put Toby out of his misery, nothing more could be done. These are the last words that an owner wants to hear in relation to their beloved dog. But DD was not about to capitulate, he told the specialist that he was going to take Toby home over the weekend and have a think about things.

I always dreaded the day that I would lose one of my regular customer's dogs, but at the same time, of course, I knew it was inevitable. Investing emotionally in my customer's dogs was a risky thing to do, but unavoidable. As Anna always says; You can't care for animals, if you don't care about them.' It now looked as though the dreaded day was just around the corner for this incredible dog. It's such a poser to me as to why dogs have such a short longevity in comparison to humans. We get incredibly attached to them in their short lives, and love them unconditionally. God knows how DD must have been feeling, my heart went out to him.

After the long arduous weekend, and a lot of soul searching, DD decided that he wasn't going to throw in the towel and give up on his dog, he brought his dog home at the end of November. But at the same time, he was conscious that it wasn't right to keep Toby going if he had no quality of life. Toby continued his upward struggle, with his devoted owner by his side, fighting all the way.

A couple of weeks down the line, mid-December DD called me. We exchanged the usual niceties, all the while I was apprehensive, fearing the worst and wanting the conversation to fast forward, but at the same time dreading the notion that DD may have bad news. He sounded upbeat and on great form, a good sign. Then much to my relief, he gave me the excellent news that there had been an improvement in Toby's condition, his dog was now much brighter and able to walk, in a fashion. I was absolutely delighted when DD asked if he could bring his brave soldier to my house for day-care the following day.

Next morning the pair arrived. Opening the front door my first glimpse of Toby was a bit of a shock and one that I was unprepared for. Having lost an excessive amount of weight Toby was almost unrecognisable. As he hobbled passed me, I noticed that he had no use in his back right leg, he was unable to put any weight on it, meaning it was left dangling, lifeless and limp. DD followed in behind, gazing at his dog with a look of absolute adoration and pride on his face. DD always looked at his dog in that fashion, a look that I see many a time in my line of business. It's the same look that a parent gives to their small child when marvelling at how incredible their offspring is, even though the child is motionless and doing absolutely nothing. A look of pure love.

DD was extremely happy and didn't appear to be too perturbed at Toby's condition, but I suppose he'd had time to become accustomed to the situation. We stood in my hall together with the other boarders, who by now had gathered around. Looking down at Toby, thoughts went through my head along the lines of; 'My God, he looks awful and what's happened to his leg?'

As if immediately reading my mind, DD explained that the specialist didn't know what the underlying cause for the loss of use of his leg was. It could have been any one of his conditions or a combination of some or even all of them. The most likely options being that it was nerve damage, or perhaps just the fact that he was in so much pain he couldn't bear to put any weight on it. As Toby limped around the hall on his three good legs, I couldn't help thinking he was a sorry sight. But after a couple of minutes of looking at him, my thoughts slowly began to change. I was beginning to get accustomed to the shock and started to think that actually he looked quite well, especially considering the severity of his conditions. His coat was shining, his tail was wagging, and he was delighted to be back in the fold; the feeling was mutual. Doug, in particular, was ecstatic to have his old buddy back with the gang, his infatuation never waned. Doug's bulging eyes played ping-pong, continually flicking from me to Toby, then back to me again. Reading Doug's mind, I guessed he was thinking;

'Gosh, isn't this great? My old mucker is back, but where has he been, and what has happened to him?' There must have been a ton of questions going through his little black fuzzy head.

DD went on his way, leaving his beloved wobbly dog in my charge. It had been about two months since the dogs had seen each other and Doug wasted no time in grafting himself to Toby's hip. Prior to his illness, Doug's playful advances had always been politely rebuked. Back then once Doug finally got the message, he would make himself scarce by jumping up onto a chair or sofa. He always preferred to be elevated, never laying on the floor or in a dog bed. But now Doug wasn't even attempting to play with his buddy, he seemed to understand that things weren't quite right and thought it best that he stuck to him like glue. So that's what he did, he never left Toby's side, gazing up at him the whole time with his usual familiar look of adulation in his bulbous eyes.

If Toby went into another room, Doug followed suit, if Toby went outside then Doug also went outside. He never once tried to get on a chair or sofa, and didn't want to be anywhere unless it was by his buddy's side.

It was as if in his sentinel manner he wanted to show his solidarity with his pal, quite an endearing scene and one which filled my heart with joy. The day went without a hitch, DD collected his pet in the evening, then returned with him the following day for another round of doggy day-care.

Day two, Doug was delighted to see his mate again once again and wasted no time in clinging to Toby's side like a barnacle. On the third day DD called me; sadly Toby's condition had deteriorated once again. It was saddening to hear that he was in pain and also suffering a nasty stomach upset. The decision was made to keep him at the apartment, thinking that he would be better off with some peace and quiet for the foreseeable. That dog had been through so much, I just didn't know how long he could carry on the fight.

After a two-week period, and another phone call from DD, the situation was such that although Toby had recovered from his stomach upset, there was no improvement in his poorly leg. He was still grossly underweight and eating very little. Then DD said something which delighted me, echoing my earlier suggestion he told me that in a final attempt to help Toby he was going to take him for weekly hydrotherapy treatment. Music to my ears! Toby loves water and there was a chance, albeit a slim one, that the hydrotherapy could help with his conditions. A win-win situation, such great news. There was no telling if the treatment was going to be effective, as Toby's problems were so severe, but it was definitely worth a shot.

After the first session, Leanne, the therapist assessed the situation and said that as Toby's conditions were complex, it was impossible to determine if the treatment was going to be effective or not until after the fourth or fifth session. In the meantime, Toby enjoyed his swimming sessions, totally happy to be splashing around and playing with his ball.

In the water Toby had real quality of life, and DD got so much pleasure from seeing his dog happy, especially after all the suffering he had undergone.

I also got to witness Toby enjoying aqua Joie de Vivre. On the odd occasion when DD was away, I had the pleasure of taking him for his routine Monday morning appointment. It was a great outing for Toby and indeed me. Arriving at the hydrotherapy pool Toby was overcome with excitement at the prospect of diving in the water to play with his ball. Once safely strapped into his life jacket he then hurled himself in the pool, completely submerging his head under water, attempting to grab the ball, as if bobbing for apples. It was great to watch him swim and play around; his happiness was incredibly contagious. Rather strangely Toby even relished the fur drying session at the end of his swim. Bemused, I stood watching him being dried off, as he tried to catch the hot air from the dryer in his mouth. Leanne remarked that Toby was quite unique in his penchant for swallowing hot air.

By late January 2014 after the fourth session something amazing happened, Toby started putting weight on his poorly leg, albeit gingerly, but all the same he was using it. He had also built up muscle and piled on the pounds. It had been a long haul but thank god that DD did not give up on his beloved dog. To this day Toby continues to make steady progress, slowly but surely. DD firmly believes that the hydrotherapy treatment saved his life, as do I.

Chapter 23

New kids on the block - Winter 2014

By February 2014 I was exceeding my financial targets. Luckily there had been no sign of 'a catch' from my franchisor, but I decided it was time to buy myself out from the group to avoid having to pay future royalties. A financial settlement was agreed, and the transaction finalised. I was then completely independent, but still able to enjoy the benefits of the group website and discounted insurance premiums.

To help me with my new found workload, and especially to place dogs that were not well-socialised, I accrued two people to work alongside me, so-called 'host families.' A lady in her early sixties called Marion and a chap called Jimmy. Both were excellent with dogs, which meant I didn't have to worry about the animals placed in their care. When carrying out a consultation with a customer, if it transpired that their dog didn't get on particularly well with the others, or indeed Brece; I suggested putting their pet with either Marion or Jimmy, where a one to one service was provided. Assuming the customer agreed, then their pet boarded with the host. Things usually went without a hitch and I took 10% of the fee for my commission.

Marion also fulfilled house sitting jobs as and when required. Residing in a customer's house wasn't something that appealed to me but it did to Marion, her own home was a modest apartment. Any such jobs were put in her direction. I think Marion saw house sitting as a sort of upgrade in accommodation, almost like going on holiday and living in the lap of luxury with lots of lovely pets for company. The requests, albeit few and far between, were usually from affluent people who dwell in majestic homes. This type of customer usually has multiple animals and prefers the security of someone staying in their home whilst away.

Marion had moved up North from Reading several years previously where she had also worked as a professional house-sitter. She came with a good reputation and excellent references, I was lucky to have her on board. It was my job to acquire the customers, meet them, discuss their requirements then complete the service contract. At which stage and assuming everything was in order I introduced the client to Marion. House-sitting was a lucrative business. My franchisor charged £40 per day for the service but I considered this was too much and the price could not be justified. My fee was £30 per day. Once everything was in place and Marion was in situ, I had little involvement but took responsibility in the event of any problems.

I deeply regret the first house sitting job that I arranged for Marion and the position that I put her in. It was our very first assignment job back in 2011 and I was inexperienced in my new role. But in my defence, the customer had grossly misled me as to the extent of the rat infestation in her home!

At the consultation with the customer Elizabeth, she warned me that she had a couple of rats knocking about in the back garden. She owned six dogs, three rabbits and of course the rats, which she casually mentioned in passing. The house backed onto a brook and rather unwisely she kept the rabbit hutch in the back garden closely situated to the water. The rats from the brook were naturally attracted to the rabbit grain. It occurred to me that the vermin situation was not aided by the fact that the hutch was at ground level and not elevated in any way shape or form. Elizabeth understood that the rats were attracted by the rabbit food yet did nothing to rectify the situation. I found it strange that she ignored the health risk to herself and dogs, but kept my thoughts in my head. Elizabeth tried to assure me that the rats only came out at night to scavenge any grain that may have fallen out of the hutch, 'You wouldn't even know they were there!'

I provisionally booked Marion to house sit for Elizabeth. The actual booking would only be confirmed if Marion agreed to stay in a house with a rat issue and that was a highly unlikely scenario, *or so I thought.* After I left the house, I immediately made the call to Marion and put the revolting proposal to her; candidly informing her about the vermin but reiterating Elizabeth's comments;

"You won't even know they are there."

It was a certainty that Marion would decline the unattractive invitation, most people wouldn't have touched the job with a barge pole. Marion proved me wrong. I was completely startled when without hesitation she accepted the position. Being the tough old bird that she is, she resiliently replied; "Well, what I can't see, can't hurt me."

So, with that we took Elizabeth at her word and agreed to house-sit for her. Several weeks after the job I learned from Marion that Elizabeth's prediction was completely incorrect. When Marion was staying at the house she knew full well that the rats were there. The vermin, were bold as brass coming out in broad daylight, scavenging for scraps, and in their numbers, half a dozen at a time. Marion didn't even get any respite at night, when darkness fell the rats invaded the kitchen. As she lay in bed, she could hear them scratching and scuttling about. Entering the kitchen each morning, sleep deprived, she was greeted by traces of rat urine on the worktops! Although clearly not comfortable with the situation Marion barely complained; such a tough old bird.

I was fortunate to have Marion and Jimmy working alongside me. Jimmy was also a great asset. He was marvellous at looking after any new strong high maintenance dogs, which I struggled with; such dogs were put in his direction in the knowledge that they would be safe and sound. This was apart from Rocky, even though life would have been easier without Rocky on the walks, somehow I found it difficult to part ways with the lummox.

With an increasing number of people requiring pet care services, business was booming. New pet services vans were becoming prolific, popping up around town as fast as sprouting asparagus tips. People's continual improved understanding of the dog's separation anxiety issues definitely attributed to the increase in demand. There was also another factor; the RSPCA had reviewed their recommendation for the acceptable period of time in which a dog can be left alone, reducing it from 4 hours to 3 hours. These circumstances can only have benefited the pet care industry. It was almost a revelation that a new understanding of dog behaviour had landed on our doorsteps, and the timing was perfect for me and other pet sitters alike.

When I initially embarked on my business enterprise there was just a handful of local competitors. By the end of 2014 there were 59 registered pet sitters in my home-town alone. Surprisingly, the increase in local competition did not appear to provoke rivalry amongst the industry. On the contrary, relations amongst local professional dog walkers (PDWs) were generally amicable. We looked upon each other more as colleagues than rival competitors, working together and helping each other along. The same could not be said for pet sitters covering the Blackpool and surrounding areas, where relations remained fractious.

I now had customers superfluous to requirements, meaning my workload was hectic. I was always quietly pleased if a customer phoned to cancel a booking, as it alleviated the pressure somewhat, not that I was complaining. I suppose I was now in the same situation that Carol was in when she handed Wasabi over to me at the start. Established pet sitters had been extremely helpful to me when I first started by putting work my way. I now wanted to extend that kindness to other new PDWs, besides, I never knew when I would need the help of my fellow colleagues. Going forward any new enquiries were passed over to the New Kids, that was assuming they were capable and kind to the animals.

Going about my daily walks I gradually got to know most of the local PDWs. Kate was born in the area, moved away and then recently returned to Lytham to start up a combined dog walking and grooming business. I enjoyed bumping into Kate on a walk, she was great company. Our chats generally revolved around the dogs and their owners. Something that was never far from the forefront of my mind was not only Brece's mortality but the mortality of my regular customer's dogs. This was something that always concerned me. I worried not only for the owner but also for myself. By now I had built up a close bond with all of my customer's dogs, *even Rocky*. I wondered if other walkers shared my worries. During one of my conversations with Kate, I posed the question; "How do you think you will cope when one of your regulars dies?" *I was good at starting morbid conversations.*

"It has already happened, three of my customer's dogs have passed away."

Kate's bottom lip began to quiver, she was clearly sad at this point, I had managed to make her mood plummet and regretted ever bringing the subject up. Her answer surprised me. Being in the profession for longer than Kate I considered myself fortunate that none of my dogs had departed this mortal coil, thus far. There have been a few close calls, Toby being the prime example, but fortunately so far and touch wood, he has escaped the grim reaper.

Kate composed herself and took a deep intake of breath and went on to explain the demise of all three dogs; two were from natural causes but the one that sticks out in my mind, is the dog that got run over by a train. The story enfolded; the owner had been walking his dog in the local woods which back on to the edge of the railway track. The dog heard a train coming, naturally before the owner heard it. The excited dog went pelting off in the direction of the noise. Such was the dog's determination to get to the train, it managed to scramble through a small hole in the fencing and found itself on the tracks. Horrifically the dog was tragically killed by the oncoming train, leaving the owner having to retrieve his dog's body from the railway track.

Apparently, it is the responsibility of the railways to uphold the maintenance of the fencing, but the work had been neglected. Tragically at least three dogs to my knowledge have lost their lives in this unnecessary manner. There is now a sign in the woods alerting dog walkers to the dangers, *nothing like shutting the stable door after the horse has bolted.*

Jeremy is another new dog walker on the block and boyfriend to my colleague Carol. After having previously worked at the local animal sanctuary he decided to join his girlfriend in the pet sitting arena. The couple were then able to offer support to one another and also expand their business. Jeremy covers South Shore whilst Carol continues to work in Blackpool.

Jeremy is an affable young man in his late twenties and stands at about 5ft 5, slim with long hair which he wears tied back in a ponytail. With his hippy laid-back air and not too dissimilar resemblance to 'Shaggy' of Scooby-doo fame, he could easily be mistaken for a throw-back from the sixties. His loud booming voice and raucous laughter can be heard well before he is seen. Jeremy is great with his dogs and clearly loves his job; always laughing and treating them with great reverence.

Then there is Andrea, an ex-customer of mine who formerly worked for British Aerospace. In the past when I cared for her dogs, she often commented that she would also like to work with dogs at some point. Then she got her chance, in a similar fashion to me she took redundancy from Aerospace and embarked on her pet-care career, combining it with dog training, a great correlation.

'Dye's Diamond Dogs' a married couple in their early thirties suddenly appeared on my normal haunts with a large complement of hounds. Their business did not appear to have grown organically as mine had done. I am not sure how they achieved this, as I never got to know them properly. Dye is a fairly large lady, it was always a conundrum to me as to how she was the size she was, doing the work she did. The couple don't tend to be around as much nowadays, leaving me to think that perhaps they are no longer working with dogs. This tends to happen quite often, numerous people set up in this line of business but for reasons unknown to me, a lot of them fold after a short period of time. *Perhaps they have encountered checkmate in their early days.*

But the most profound dog walker to take up residence on my turf is Anna. After having lived and worked in Hereford on a country estate as an Equine therapist for a couple of multi-millionaires, she found herself in a position where she was missing her family and decided to move back up North. Her master plan was to set up her own Equine therapy business locally. In the interim, she would work as a dog walker alongside me until such time her Equine career got off the ground. With this in mind, I took on a few extra new customers for her. Once she was settled in and primed to go I passed the new dogs over to her together with a couple of my existing more high maintenance dogs!

I found myself getting into the habit of grouping my dogs in order of maintenance; high (ASBO), medium and low maintenance categories. The first ASBO that I handed to Anna was my young male Retriever, Mckenzie Monster of mud wallowing fame. Mckenzie is an incredibly strong, daft male Retriever, but lovely at the same time. He liked to play hard with Hendrix, who was the apple of his eye, showing no interest in any of the other dogs, just lucky old Hendrix.

Mckenzie Monster typically demonstrated his affection towards Hendrix by grappling him to the floor, lying on top of him, then holding him down for a considerable length of time. It worried me that his innocent play may cause an injury to Hendrix, or suffocate him even. It was extremely difficult to persuade Mckenzie not to crush his buddy as he was not good on his commands, in fact he was atrocious. This meant there was precious little I could do to stop Mckenzie wrestling with his playmate and potentially injuring him.

It wasn't all bad though, Mckenzie did have some funny habits; the most amusing being his impersonation of a dog walker. This commenced the moment we got out of the car and before I had chance to get all the dogs unleashed. Mckenzie quickly seized his opportunity; focusing on a dog that was still leashed, he grabbed the lead in his mouth then hoicked the dog for a walk.

Mckenzie thoroughly enjoyed his role as a dog walker, his favourite victim being Doug the Pug. Doug always appeared to be quite accepting of the situation, but then I don't suppose he had much say in the matter. It wasn't as if he could refuse to be dragged off, Doug was certainly no match for the powerhouse that is Mckenzie. It was always a comical sight; Doug's short bowed legs going hell for leather trying to keep up with Mckenzie's long, bouncy stride.

This crazy charismatic dog had another particularly annoying habit which happened in winter and also at the beginning of the walks. Whilst I was still clearing up at the poo station and stooped down, Mckenzie saw his chance, jumped up at me and swiped my hat off my head, exposing my messy bedraggled head of hair to the elements. He then smugly ran off with his bounty; that was assuming he didn't have a dog to walk. Trying to catch him and my hat, was like trying to catch a robber's dog. Again, I suppose it was comical, but incredibly frustrating when cold and wet.

Considering all Mckenzie's little quirks the thing that caused me the most trouble was trying to get him back into the car after a walk, he was a nightmare. Most dogs understand what is expected and just jump in. Not Mckenzie, he just didn't get it, preferring to collapse into a heap on the floor like a great big furry jelly, leaving me to lift the dead weight into the car. Even when I had managed to shove half his body in, he still didn't get it, and offered no help. Any other dog that was half-way in would have scrambled themselves into the car, not Mckenzie. I had to shove the whole of his body into the car, which did absolutely nothing for my back.

The second ASBO I handed over to Anna was a challenging cross breed, romantically named Heathcliffe but commonly called Cliffe. I have no idea what breeds Cliffe was crossed with, but he looked like an oblong on legs. Even though the owners said his recall was good, I learned the hard way that Cliffe could not be trusted when unleashed. As soon as he found himself liberated, he chased after birds, the scent of food, horses, people, just about anything, running off into the distance, never to return. It was always a case of me and the rest of the pack having to chase after him.

After several games of 'Catch me if you can' to make life that bit easier for myself I decided to always keep him on the lead. He started to come equipped with an extendable leash which enabled him a relative amount of freedom and more exercise than being on a short leash. Extendable leads are good in theory but can be somewhat tricky in practice. On lead he habitually ran off at a tangent with the strength of a baby bull. It was easy to tell when he had reached the end of the line as my arm was almost yanked out of its socket. At which point, the extended lead became a potential hazard to the other 'unleashed' dogs who may well be obliviously running full pelt towards it. On impact the lead could quite easily cut into the dog's flesh, like a wire into cheese. To have a dog injured in this manner would be catastrophic. Whenever I saw the other dogs hurtling towards the line, I dropped it like a hot potato, working on the basis that having to chase after Cliffe was a lesser evil than having a garrotted dog on my watch.

Being a sociable dog Cliffe ran up to just about everybody he set his eyes upon, with me dragging behind, hanging on the other end of the lead. Once we got to the other person of interest, I have no idea why but he usually decided to run circles around the pair of us, creating a figure of eight and entwining our legs together. This was always an awkward moment for me and probably even more awkward for the stranger whose space we had just invaded. *Still, I suppose it was a way of getting acquainted with others.*

Anna found herself with a motley crew on her hands. I thought long and hard about off-loading Rocky onto her as well, but decided against it. This was due to the fact that Rocky had calmed down slightly since Brad had plucked up the courage to have his dog neutered. I would still have classed him as a high maintenance dog but not quite on the previous ASBO level. In addition I remained extremely fond of him and he presented less of a risk to the other dogs than McKenzie, so Rocky continued to keep his place in the pack.

I was conscious of dumping the majority of my ASBOs on to Anna and felt a tad guilty in doing so. But at the same time this was how I started my baptism of fire. At the beginning of my career and not being in a position to pick and choose as I am now, I took most jobs that came my way, no matter how challenging, Rocky, Cliffe, Mckenzie to name but a few, I served my time. Also, in my defence, Anna is taller and stronger than me, and not afraid of hard work; *the antithesis of me* making her better equipped to manage the bigger dogs. But it still didn't lie easy with me.

In an attempt to balance things out for her I also passed over a few of my low maintenance dogs in her direction. These being two young Cockapoos who had been with me since puppies and were consequently well-socialised and great in the pack.

Anna was now up and running, making her own connections and acquiring new customers of her own. I also passed my new enquiries onto Anna. If she couldn't accommodate the dogs, then she passed the enquiry on to yet another two new dog walkers who had also just joined the pet carers club. One being a friend of mine, the other, a former customer who gave up a teaching career in favour of working with dogs. Pet sitting was all the rage. Surely there would come a point when the industry would become saturated, but it didn't seem to be happening any time soon. There always seemed to be plenty of work to go around.

After a 3-month period Anna was already reaching her financial targets. But she had done this the hard way by taking on just about any dog that came her way, in the same way that I had done. History was repeating itself. This meant she had more than her fair share of ASBOs on her hands, and consequently her days were fraught to say the least. When Anna gave me her daily updates and filled me in on her latest disasters it took me right back to my early days. Her conversations would start along the lines of;

"You will never guess what happened to me today?"

Or, I would start the conversation with;

"Go on then, what's gone wrong today?"

Dogs running off, dogs being ill, locking herself out of her car with multiple dogs in tow were usually the order of the day. I look forward to the day when Anna can offload some of her ASBOS in the same way that I had done. And I am sure that day can't come soon enough for Anna.

Chapter 24

That elusive business partner – 2015

Anna moving back home was a godsend to me. Not only had she taken most of my ASBOs off my hands but I now had back-up and support when needed, that elusive business partner that had been missing from the start. I was able to call on her as and when needed, which was a great comfort and support. However when Anna needed support from me I am not sure I was much of a comfort to her.

One of Anna's very own ASBOS was a one-year-old female black Pointer cross called Bonnie. Bonnie was still at the destructive stage and endowed with copious amounts of energy. Owner Sophia, of Italian origin worked full-time and rather shockingly was in the habit of muzzling her dog when she was out at work. Neither Anna nor I were comfortable with this practice as amongst other things it meant that the poor dog couldn't even have a drink water whilst trussed up. But Sophia was insistent on muzzling her dog, reason being Bonnie had managed to chew her way through two leather sofas in close succession!

Anna shared her 'muzzle' concerns with Sophia. Initially, Sophia stuck to her guns and said that she wasn't going to leave her dog unmuzzled as she didn't want to have to fork out for a fourth sofa. Anna also stuck to her guns and pointed out that by law dogs must have access to water at all times. With that Sophia decided to make a compromise by arranging for her dog to be un-muzzled at regular intervals during the day. While Sophia was out at work, some of her friends and neighbours dropped by to give Bonnie some respite from her muzzle, and a much-needed drink of water; After which Bonnie was always sadly confined back to her muzzle. Not an ideal situation but preferable to the original state of affairs.

After about six months into her pet sitting role Anna had to return to Hereford for a one-day horse therapy training course. It was vital that she passed the course in order to help get her Equine career off the ground, which was still firmly lodged on Terra firma. I agreed to cover for some of her dogs for her whilst she was away, Bonnie being one of them. All I had to do for Bonnie was to collect her, walk her, then drop her back at home, *what could be more straightforward than that?*

The day I took Bonnie for a walk was probably one of the weirdest ever, it was 2nd April, 2015. I spent most of the day feeling worried and incredibly baffled. Prior to the weird day I had seen Bonnie many times when out walking with Anna on the beach. Although Bonnie liked to burn off her energy by running at high speeds for what seemed like miles, she always returned back to the pack. In many ways she reminded me of Rocky, full of energy and destruction but lovely at the same time. All things considered I mentally put Bonnie into the medium-maintenance category.

For the most part I am relaxed when walking my pack and feel confident that they will stay close by to me. By now I knew all the dogs in my charge like the back of my hand and I had a strong bond with each and every one of them. Now left with just low maintenance dogs meant less risk of anything going wrong. This meant I was able to cherish my time spent with them without worrying about anything going wrong. Watching them play is a continual joy, a tonic, their happiness continually bounces off them and lands on me. The younger dogs constantly play fight with one another, they do this by mouthing each other. But it's not quite the case for Doug the Pug. He struggles to play with the others as he is compromised by the fact that he doesn't have much of a mouth to speak of. Doug's contribution to the play involves circling the dogs *with mouths*, barking excitedly and occasionally lifting his paw. With his less than athletic appearance and black furry uniform he looks more like a referee than a player.

Having a new dog to walk that I didn't know very well, was bound to come with a level of risk. I was going to have to keep my eyes peeled on Bonnie. I arrived at Sophia's house at the agreed time of 11 am on the weird day. Sophia has two house keys, one on loan to Anna which she gave to me. The other is kept under Sophia's front door mat for her own use. Entering the house, I looked around the place, it was apparent there was no way of keeping Bonnie away from the sofa as the place was open-plan. Apart from the front door, the downstairs was a door free zone. Bonnie immediately came bounding over to greet me, sadly wearing her muzzle which I instantly removed so that she could take a drink of water ahead of our walk.

Once on the beach and as expected Bonnie went pelting around to burn off some steam, thankfully always returning to the fold. All things considered the walk had gone well, after which I dropped Bonnie off at home and reluctantly put her muzzle back on her snout, but not before giving her a big bowl of water. I then went on my way, content in the knowledge that everything had gone to plan. Bonnie had been thoroughly exercised and she was now at home safe and sound, it was all over with, *or so I thought!*

Early that afternoon, I was surprised to receive a call from Anna who was still on her course in Hereford. I couldn't understand why she was phoning me and in doing so interrupting her studies, something did not bode well. Answering the call, Anna asked if I had walked Bonnie that morning as arranged, to which I replied that I had. I was getting more confused by the second and couldn't understand why we were having the conversation. What could have possibly gone wrong, Bonnie was home safe and sound, I had made sure of it?

During her break Anna had picked up a garbled message from Sophia who appeared to be in a state of distress. Apparently a friend of Sophia's who was on the 'muzzle rota' had called round to her house and discovered the place had been trashed. The friend made the logical assumption that Bonnie, who was now somehow unmuzzled, was the perpetrator of the damage. Before returning the call Anna asked if I would go around to check things out. She wanted to be proactive and have some positive information for Sophia before returning her call. Unfortunately being at home at the time and waiting for the imminent arrival of a customer to collect his dog, meant I was housebound for the foreseeable. I felt awful that I couldn't help Anna but all credit to her she had a back-up plan and called on our brother Dave's services. Dave coincidentally lived around the corner from Bonnie and with a spare ten minutes on his hands was able to help out. *Looking after Bonnie was turning into a family affair.*

A couple of phone calls later, Anna updated me; Dave duly went around to Bonnie's letting himself into the house by using Sophia's key from under the doormat. Once successfully inside he discovered that Bonnie had indeed managed to get her muzzle off and had clearly caused some damage. His examination of the house revealed that the level of destruction was only minimal, nothing major just a few chewed up papers and magazines. Thank God leather sofa number three was still intact!

After putting Bonnie's muzzle back on, Dave then left and placed the key back under the mat. Not long after that I received another call from Anna asking me again if I could pop round to Bonnie's to double check on things for her. Sensing that she was stressed, I felt for her, this distraction was the last thing she needed when she should have been concentrating on her course. My customer had long since been and gone by this time leaving me free to pop round. Only snag was that in between times I had somehow managed to lose Bonnie's house key!

I couldn't find the blessed thing anywhere; turning my car upside down it was nowhere to be seen. By now it was a certainty that fate was never going to reunite me with that key; a classic case of a new unfamiliar job breeding incompetency in me. In typical fashion, things were going from bad to worse. By this time, it was 4.30 pm, Sophia was due home at 5.30 pm. Anna could certainly do without having to inform her customer that I had managed to lose her house key. I tried to think things through, how the hell I was I going to get out of this mess? Then I remembered Sophia's key! That was it, I could take her key from under the mat and get another one cut, no one would be the wiser. There was just about enough time in which to execute my plan before Sophia's imminent arrival.

Arriving at Sophia's house for the second time that day, I stood by the front door, hoping that the key was under the mat where it should have been. Dave had confirmed he had put it back, but knowing the way my luck was going that day it wouldn't have surprised me if it had vanished into thin air. Gingerly lifting the mat, I was relieved to see it lying there, thank God for that. I let myself in and checked on Bonnie. She seemed fine but once again had managed to get her muzzle off and created more damage, more chewed up papers but again nothing too serious.

As time was not on my side, there was no window of opportunity to look for the muzzle, or clear up the mess. My priority was to get to the local key cutting shop before it closed. The nearest place being a quirky cobbler's on the main road in town. It was highly unlikely that there would be a parking spot nearby, meaning a walk was probably on the cards.

At about 4.50 pm I slowly pulled up outside the cobblers. Surprisingly I was granted a piece of luck; there was a nice big parking space directly outside the shop, naturally I quickly grabbed it before someone else beat me to it. I dashed towards the cobblers and arrived at the doorstep only to find it disappointedly closed. The notice in the window unreliably informed me that closing time was 5.00 pm. The cobbler had closed early, my previous 'parking space good luck' had now all been swallowed up.

Thinking on the spot I decided to get myself to the next town a couple of miles away, and try my fortune there. With a wanton disregard for speed limits, adrenaline pumping I rapidly drove round to cobbler's number two, and arrived just in time before they closed, phew! Next, all I had to do was dash back to Sophia's and put the new key under the mat. It was all rather hectic, but I allowed myself a small sense of relief; it was now looking as though another 'lost key' confession had been averted.

It was 5.20 pm when I pulled up outside Sophia's house. Simultaneously and like some sort of synchronised auto-mobile dance a brunette woman pulled up just in front of me in a white BMW. I watched as the woman elegantly stepped out of her car like some sort of model. Wearing high heels and a smart tailored blue suit, she was slim and wore her long dark hair lose around her shoulders. As she shut her car door she turned to face me. Judging by the established lines around and between her eyes I guessed she was in her late forties, Nancy Delallio sprang to mind. At this point I had never met Sophia before but I instinctively knew who she was by her olive complexion and Mediterranean looks. Being a Lancashire coastal retirement town, we don't tend to get too many dusky maidens on our shores. Looking at her my stomach churned with the realisation that she had come home early, *great*. I had hoped to execute my clandestine deed before she returned, but it was not to be. At this point my heart was pumping so fast that I felt faint. I clambered out of my battered dog mobile still wearing my scruffs and muddy wellies, feeling grossly inferior.

I Intrepidly walked towards Sophia. When about 6ft away from her I clumsily introduced myself. We embarked on a quick conversation about the destruction that Bonnie may or may not have caused. I nervously explained that I had already been in her home *which felt odd*, and could confirm that the mess was only minimal. Sophia sternly replied in a strong Italian accent;

"I will seeee for myself."

She then made her way towards the mat to retrieve her key from underneath it. At this point I was a complete nervous wreck and inwardly panicking as of course her key wasn't there, it was still in my pocket together with the new copy. As she bent down towards the mat, I blurted out;

"Oh, I have got the key, it's here."

She seemed accepting of my statement and thankfully didn't challenge me as to why I had used her key and not the spare intended for Anna. Stepping forward onto the doorstep I proceeded to unlock the door, whilst Sophia stood behind me. As Bonnie had previously been left un-muzzled there was a high probability that she may have caused even more damage by now. Would the suite still be in one piece of in several pieces by now? I had completely forgotten this snippet of information earlier, when I tried to assure Sophia that the damage was only slight. I prepared myself for the worse. The door slowly crept open onto the lounge revealing... one leather suite still intact, thank God for that!

An enthusiastic Bonnie greeted us. Sophia virtually ignored her dog; she was too preoccupied with checking her home for damage. With pursed lips and a not unexpected stern look of irritation on her face she glanced at the chewed-up papers and magazines lying around the lounge floor. Then she headed towards the kitchen, with Bonnie and I bringing up the rear. Bonnie continually lunging at the both of us, hollering and bounding around the place in her giddy excitement, again like Rocky, but not half as dangerous.

The kitchen was thankfully intact. Bonnie's enthusiasm waned slightly, and Sophia went upstairs to inspect the rest of the house, whilst I remained in the kitchen. After a few minutes, she came back downstairs, and shared the good news that the damage was only superficial. Feeling relieved that things could have been a lot worse, I thought that now was as good a time as any to mention the fact that Bonnie had managed to get her muzzle off, and lose it. With that Sophia's face dropped again, her frown lines deepened. She then embarked on her second search of her house to look for the muzzle.

Finally moving off my spot I decided it was about time to do something to help, it was the least I could do. I reflected; somehow I had managed to find myself in the home of an Italian woman, whom I had never met before, and was now searching through her possessions. It was very odd to say the least. We looked high and low for that muzzle, with Bonnie helping in our quest, but it was nowhere to be seen. After about a ten-minute search Sophia stopped in her tracks, turned around, looked at her dog, then despairingly shouted out;

"But she izzz wearing it."

This was the cherry on my cake of incompetence. All the time we were looking for Bonnie's muzzle, it was on the end of her snout. I dread to think just how stupid Sophia must have thought me, and she didn't even have the full picture of my inadequacies. Still confused I tried to figure out exactly what had happened, but just couldn't join the dots together. It was an ongoing conundrum, how could Bonnie have caused more damage when her muzzle was still on her snout, and why hadn't I noticed that she was still wearing it? Sophia looked at me in despair, nailing her colours to the mast she said;

"You avv put it on wrong, Anna knows ow to do it."

Of course, technically it was Dave who had put it on wrong, but I wasn't about to complicate matters by bringing him into the equation. I didn't even know if Sophia was aware that Dave had also been in her house, *I thought it best not to bring the subject up.*

It appeared that Anna was far more competent in such matters than I. Thankfully the ordeal was coming to an end, and no real harm had been done, excluding the damage to my self-esteem. After having made my apologies I left her house under my perpetual fog of confusion. Sitting in my car I phoned Anna to update her. Her course had now finished meaning she had time to pick over the pieces with me. The pair of us tried to establish exactly what had happened that strange day. Talking it through with her, the fog slowly lifted...

When I initially dropped Bonnie off, I had put the muzzle on her, but as pointed out by Sophia I had done so incorrectly. Anna went to pains to explain exactly how the black muzzle should have been fitted. The metal fastener must be on top of the dog's snout, and not underneath the chin, as I had positioned it. When on correctly, the muzzle is visible by the metal, when not, it morphs against the background of Bonnie's black snout, making it difficult to detect. As it was unsecured, Bonnie had managed to get it off and set about causing the damage. Then Dave arrived on the scene, found the muzzle and put it back on her, again incorrectly, but obviously better than I had, as it had remained on her snout.

When I turned up for my second visit, I was greeted by the damage, gone off at a tangent and assumed Bonnie had managed to get the muzzle off once again and shredded more papers. The true fact of the matter was that the mess lying around the place was from the first instance which Dave had discovered but left lying around as he was in a rush to leave. The whole thing was yet another classic doggy debacle. Going forward whenever I ask Anna if I can help her with anything, she briskly replies; "No, its OK thanks, I can manage."

Chapter 25

Brece the old girl - early 2016

In appearance the venerable dog still looked great. Her eyes remained clear and she still appeared to see perfectly well. But she endured some dark staining underneath both eyes, which is typical in an older dog. Her thick, fluffy coat remained in healthy condition, courtesy of the groomer. But strangely her once black nose had turned pink. Over the years the pigment appeared to have rubbed off, leaving her with a nose that resembled and behaved more like a pig's snout, which continually foraged for food and truffles.

However, without a doubt, the strangest oddity that happened to her appearance was to her fur, parts of her coat had also turned pink. Calling on my trusty friend 'Google' I learned that this sort of discolouration in an older dog is due to bodily chemical changes. She now had a nice pink tummy, and the thick fur around her ears turned a dark shade of pink. At times I wondered to myself if she was going to turn into the Pink Panther.

Physically, for a large dog of her age, she was in great health. In human years, she was now 91 years-old, so naturally showing some signs of her age. Slowing up in her mobility, and at times struggling to get up off the floor, she carried on like a creaking gate. Now no longer able to lead the pack on the walks, instead she dawdled along happy to walk at her leisure and concentrate more on exercising her pink snout as opposed to her legs.

The last of the repetitive comments that I had to tolerate whilst walking with her is without doubt the one that annoys me the most. An insensitive person will shout towards me;

'She's an old girl, isn't she?'

I found it most disconcerting when someone said these words to me, why is it that people were insistent on reminding me of her mortality? We would never dream of remarking on a person's age, face to face. It's understandably inappropriate to do so, so why is it acceptable to make such a comment about a person's dog? Usually, it was an older person who was the orator of the cutting comment. Sometimes I think people of a certain generation missed the modern school of subtlety and political correctness. With seemingly no filter or regard for the consequences of their comments, the old-school just said it how it was. In these situations, it was all I could do to stop myself responding;

"You're no spring chicken yourself."

Then there were the slightly more subtle people (younger), who politely enquired as to her age. Although they didn't physically say it, the words 'Gosh she's old, not long left now' hovered around in the air. People meant no harm by this but it taught me not to ask a dog owner how old their obviously ageing dog was. Nothing was to be gained by acquiring the information, and was just a sad reminder to the owner. But then there were the people who once in the knowledge of her age comfortingly said,

"Gosh, she's doing amazingly well."

It was surprising how these few words could make me feel so incredibly proud of her.

If anything gave her age away it was her slow and stiff gait, attributed to her arthritis. When in the car she continued to sit in the front foot well, which was far more comfortable for her than trying to scramble herself up onto a seat. It was reassuring to have her sat there watching me as I drove. Whilst quietly sat there she developed an endearing habit of giving me her paw to hold. Of course, it wasn't always safe to catch hold of it, but if at lights or stuck in traffic I was only too happy to oblige.

Sometimes whilst Brece was in the foot well, I had Haribo sat on the front seat next to me. Luckily Haribo was not mentally affected by the dog attack that she had previously endured when I was in London for that fateful weekend. Her strong personality had stood her in good stead. There were not many times when I enjoyed seeing a dog behaving in a very dominant manner. But seeing Haribo snap at the others and realising that she had not been affected by the awful ordeal, was sort of heart-warming to see. Haribo retained her 'diva dog' status and her ideas above her station, refusing to sit in the back of the car with the riff raff was one example. Whilst sat there Haribo observed Brece's paw action at close range. Diva Dog decided to replicate her moves by also giving me her paw to hold. Sometimes there were just too many paws to juggle.

To treat Brece's Arthritis, I started her off with a herbal supplement, Glucosamine with Chondroitin. It worked well at first, relieving her of some of her stiffness, but as time went by, its effectiveness seemed to wane. She needed something stronger so a quick trip to John's, and he prescribed Loxicam, a combined anti-inflammatory and painkillers. This helped her immensely, some days she was as good as new, but then other days not quite so good. After a period of time, the Loxicam also became less effective. It was as if everything I tried her with had a shelf life. Each time the effects of the treatments wore off she needed something that bit stronger.

Her arthritis continued to have a massive impact on her life-style. Besides affecting her mobility, the pain was starting to affect her physique, even the shape of her front paws began to change. Every now and then from the corner of my eye I caught sight of her paws and noticed there was something different about them, but I couldn't pin-point what it was. It was some time before it dawned on me that they had grown in size. Her once cute petite paws appeared to have expanded in width. At first, I thought they had swollen from fluid retention, as old ladies' feet tend to do. Eventually, I learned that her feet had spread out because she was putting more weight on her front legs due to the pain in her back legs. Her toes had naturally spread to carry and redistribute the excess weight on her front end. The poor thing, she must have been in quite a bit of pain, yet she still never complained and always remained happy in herself.

Brece needed more help with her condition so I decided to take her for weekly hydrotherapy at Leanne's, the same therapist that Toby frequented. Being a water fiend, I expected her to absolutely love the experience. Yet again, she proved me wrong. She was fine on our maiden journey to the hydrotherapy centre, but once we arrived it was obvious that she was suspicious of what lay ahead. Once out of the foot-well of the car she became agitated and reluctant to go inside. It took a great deal of encouragement to get her into the place. I'm not sure what concerned her about the establishment, but she was definitely not picking up a good vibe. I couldn't help feeling sorry for her. With absolutely no say in anything, she just had to do as she was told, without understanding what the hell was happening to her.

Once finally inside we were greeted by Leanne who did everything she could to try to put her at ease, but nothing worked. Brece was clearly nervous and uncomfortable in her aquatic surroundings. Leanne was wearing her black wet suit and Brece also needed to be appropriately dressed, Leanne proceeded to dress my baffled dog in a doggy life jacket, *at least she didn't have to wear a wetsuit.* Although Brece looked rather dapper in her new attire it did nothing to put her at ease. She must have been thinking; 'God what the hell is happening to me now, why am I wearing a yellow plastic coat?'

Once suitably decked out in her jacket, Leanne escorted Brece down a short ramp leading into the pool. With her tail between her legs and ears flat back she clearly wasn't happy, but she did what was expected and reluctantly crept down to the water. What was wrong with her? She was a Retriever who loves water, it was baffling. Finally, once in the water she seemed to relax a little and instinctively set about her swim, taking to it like a duck to water and finally showing signs of her Retriever heritage.

As she took her maiden length, I felt like a proud mother intensely watching her child take its first swimming lesson. Our eyes were glued to each other; mine on her out of pride, and hers on me, probably out of fear and searching for some sort of reassurance. Picking up speed things were going well, that was until she approached the end of the short pool which was probably only about 15 metres in length. I was expecting her to turn the corner ahead of the blue tiled wall, and was surprised when instead, she went crashing into it. It was as if she didn't know how to stop or turn. My heart went out to her, I imagined her to be feeling embarrassed. But she soon got the hang of it. By her second lap she had mastered the art of turning corners. After about 20 minutes her first lesson came to an end. Leanne escorted her out of the pool, released her from the yellow jacket and proceeded to towel dry her. The drying process was finished off with the aid of the doggy fur dryer. Unlike Toby she did not relish any of the drying off experience one little bit. For her après swim I had purchased a nice new red absorbent doggy dressing gown. These gowns are great for soaking up any excess water, just the ticket. Finally, her ordeal was coming to an end.

Last stage in the saga was another wardrobe change into her dapper new gown. Once in it Leanne tied the straps into a nice big gift-wrap bow across her back. Now togged up in her red robe she put me in mind of a boxer entering the ring for a big fight. 'In the red corner, we have Brece, the water loving Retriever who hates hydrotherapy.'

I wanted Brece to enjoy the sessions in the same way Toby did, but it was not to be. It was as if she associated the whole hydrotherapy experience with the environment of the vets (although not quite on the same level of fear) or the shower, both of which she still hated with a passion. It was however worth the ordeal, immediately after the first session, there was a noticeable improvement in her mobility; her stiffness was greatly relieved, her stamina increased and she was now just about able to keep up on the walks. I had been hoping for a good result but wasn't expecting it to be quite so instant.

Each time she went on one of her swimming jaunts, she continued to demonstrate great reluctance at the prospect of what lay ahead. As soon as she realised where we were headed, she became anxious. The prospect of another swim did nothing to please her. Getting her out of the car, she always tried to run off at full pelt in the opposite direction. Even though she was an old girl she still pulled like a train. It was all I could do to hang on to her and drag her into that pool.

On the other hand I was partial to the centre, it's a great little setup and I thoroughly enjoyed watching her swim. A cup of coffee was usually on offer, I sat taking my caffeine fix whilst chatting to Leanne as she worked her magic. During one of our chats, Leanne shared a story with me about another customer who travelled from Burnley to bring his Whippet for treatment. He made the 60-mile round trip on a weekly basis in an old battered car and never missed a session. Leanne explained that her customer didn't appear to have two pennies to rub together, his dog was the love of his life and his passion. Apparently, he even went without himself to ensure that his dog got the best possible treatment. Leanne threw into the conversation that she sometimes gave his dog a free session. It warms the cockles of my heart to know that there are people out there with compassion and empathy and that it's not always about the money.

The hydrotherapy sessions continued for many months to come, *much to Brece's dismay.* But eventually, like everything else, the therapy too stopped working its magic. Brece reverted to becoming less active and her back legs were beginning to give way. The common place for this to happen was the kitchen when on her way to the utility room which is a fascinating place for her. Although the smallest room in the house, it was the most attractive to Brece as it homed the fridge and waste bin. The fridge stored the fresh food whilst the bin stored the waste food, what a great place for a greedy dog to hang-out.

On the odd occasion when she was in the kitchen, and I was in a different room, I would hear her stumble. Quickly dashing through to check on her I usually found that she had invariably knocked the communal water bowl over, flooding the kitchen in the process. It always surprised me just how much ground a relatively small amount of water can cover. At times it was quite the reservoir in my kitchen. Situated by the entrance to the utility room, the bowl was turning out to be a hazard for her. I had often considered moving it, but rather tardily had never actually done anything about it.

Initially, I couldn't fathom out why she kept knocking the bowl over, in my ignorance I assumed she was just being clumsy. Then one day I witnessed one of her episodes for myself. Making a cup of tea at the time, Brece strolled into the kitchen on one of her regular pilgrimages to the utility room. I turned around as she approached the water bowl just in time to see her back-end collapse directly on top of it, the entire contents spilled all over the floor. At that exact moment somehow, the bowl flipped itself around mid-air and landed upside down making an ideal seat just in time to catch her back end as she collapsed. Now sat on her bowl and marooned in the middle of Lake Heyhouses she looked up at me as if to say;

"Gosh, what happened then?"

Casually telling her to get up, I tried to play it down, making light of the situation as one does to a child when it falls over. But my bemused dog couldn't get her strength together and struggled to stand up. I walked towards her then gave her a helping hand by lifting her back legs up and held them until she regained her strength and balance.

Once steadily back on all fours, she carried on as if nothing had happened. That moment was over for her, she was on to the next moment of her life which focused around the fridge, or the bin. But for me, the moment lingered. Naturally, I was inwardly sad to witness her collapse, and dwelled on the episode in a morose fashion for some time. If only I could be more like the dog and live for the moment, not worrying or feeling sad about a situation that had passed. One thing was for sure, it was definitely time for a change of scenery for the pesky water bowl.

In addition to her mobility problems, she had also become stone deaf, but we managed and it wasn't all bad. Being deaf did have its advantages; it gave the postman some respite and Bonfire Night was not the awful ordeal that it once was. She had also been diagnosed with a slight heart murmur. Again, this condition didn't appear to bother her either, although it was rather startling when John said she may keel over and pass out one day whilst walking. This came as a complete shock to me; I think John picked up on my concern and tried to reassure me by saying;

"But don't worry, she will probably come around and get back up again."

Of course, if it did happen, I knew I would worry; LIKE HELL, his words put the fear of God in me *old school*. I thoroughly respected John as a great vet who knew his craft, but sometimes I couldn't help thinking that his bedside manner needed a bit of tweaking. Luckily, I have not had to witness her keeling over, as yet.

And finally, to complete her medical records her front teeth appeared to have disappeared and were almost completely worn away. This confused me as it's not as if she gnawed away on bones all day long, bones are a rare treat. Unlike humans who become longer in the tooth as their gums recede, dogs appear to become shorter in the tooth.

Another stark reminder of her advancing years was that sadly, she is no longer able to get herself upstairs to my bedroom at night. It got to the point where she lost the confidence to even attempt the assault. I missed her at night beside me. On the bright side when morning came, I couldn't wait to go downstairs to be greeted by my deaf, creaking, old crock of a dog. But sometimes when I woke my feelings of excitement were outweighed by an overwhelming sense of impending doom. I worried that something awful may have happened to her during the night, the same way that I worried on that very first night as a puppy when I feared the blanket covering her cage may have starved her of oxygen. I worried about her then at the beginning of her life; and I worried about her now towards the end of her days, and many, many times in between. But touch wood, each morning I am still loyally greeted by her gorgeous fluffy face. Flamboyantly embracing her snout, I smell her fur drinking in all the endorphins and thank God, Buddha, Allah anyone else out there that I still have her for yet another day.

But there was one other thing that I could do for her, and that was to grant her a 'veteran's amnesty'. I wanted her to revel in her dotage, and to be as happy as possible, never having to feel rebuked. I made a conscious effort not to reprimand her any more, (unless she was giving a visiting dog an unnecessarily hard time). There was no point in trying to discipline her now, besides the day she didn't swipe a butty off the table, would be a very sad day indeed. That dog could now do whatever she wanted, whenever she wanted. Besides I got some sort of weird enjoyment out of watching her being naughty, I suppose I always did really.

Despite all her ailments and being a crocked up old dog, she still enjoyed a great zest for life, and was always revered as the Alpha Female in the pack, *except by Haribo*. The others continued to respect her position and she still put them in their place, as and when she needed to. Her resilience made me appreciate her all the more, she was an inspiration to me. If I felt a bit creaky or achy, I looked at her and took a leaf out of her book, making the most of what I had, as she does. She never sat there thinking; 'I wish I could keep up a bit better with the other dogs when on walks.' Instead, she thought to herself; 'The smells are great today, I wonder when I will get my next treat?'

All things considered she still looked good and I remained incredibly proud of her. So proud in fact that I decided to enter her into another dog competition. An advert had been displayed on the notice board in the local woods notifying of a forthcoming dog parade. There was a phone number for any enquiries. After a quick phone call and a conversation with the Manager of the woods I learned that the intention of the parade was to promote a positive attitude towards dogs within the woods. It was felt that there was a need for this because there had been a couple of recent reports of unscrupulous people trying to poison dogs in the woods. Meat spiked with poison had been scattered around on parts of the ground. A couple of dogs had fallen foul of the malicious actions and become sick. When the unfortunate dogs had been taken to the vets, poisoning had been confirmed. The doggy parade was going to be a defiant message to the dog haters that dogs were welcome in the woods.

The parade itself was a light-hearted affair, just a bit of fun, *at least that was the intention.* There were 6 categories; cutest bitch, waggiest tail and so forth. I asked the manager if there was going to be a veteran's category, to which I was enthusiastically told that there would be. It didn't take me long to decide that I was going to enter Brece. Personally, in my opinion, she looked much younger than her years, other people also commented on her youthful appearance. Whenever such a comment reached my ears my chest puffed up with pride, whilst a massive grin spread over my face. All this led me to believe that she would do well in the veteran's group.

The day of the parade arrived. It was a Sunday afternoon, late summer, the weather was warm. An area in one of the glens had been set aside for the extravaganza. A couple of stalls had been erected, and bunting hung from the trees to demarcate the doggy arena. Under the dappled shade of the trees, the place looked enchanting and pretty. Brece also looked pretty. Coincidently, she had been to the groomers a couple of days beforehand for her routine six weekly coiffure. Even if I say it myself, her double coat remained amazing for a dog her age, still thick and fluffy. She had scrubbed up well for the big event.

The atmosphere was friendly, dog owners chatting to each other, being sociable as they so often are. A young lady who was the owner of a local pet shop had been asked to judge the event. Even the local press had arrived to cover the occasion, *there must have been a lull in the news that week*. All entrants registered for their preferred group and the parade got underway.

Unfortunately, only a handful of dogs had entered the vet's category. In an attempt to increase the numbers, the judge reduced the entry age from the usual 10 years to 8 years, thereby opening the invitation up to more dogs. Another four dogs came forward, now increasing the number of entrants to 9. Brece and the other old codgers waited patiently for their turn, they were on last. No longer champing at the bit to run up to people and clamber all over them, Brece was calm and well-behaved. A complete contrast from her debut at the PDSA dog show all those years ago when she was a youngster. There was no longer a need for the trusty secret weapon of swede to control her this time, which was just as well as she could no longer digest it.

Finally, after all the other younger dogs had taken their 15 minutes of fame and left the stage, it was our turn. Although it was a light-hearted affair, I must admit to feeling a little apprehensive, competitive even. The 'approaching and past their sell by date' dogs and owners stepped forward. Taking the limelight, they paraded around the make-shift circuit a couple of times. I suppose in comparison to the previous sprightlier groups the veterans were a bit of a sorry sight. A couple of the dogs literally looked as though they were on their last legs; not Brece though, a little stiff in her joints, but she trotted along quite nicely. After all the parading and much deliberation, the results of the vets' group was announced. In typical reverse order; fourth place went to a black Labrador, third place went to a Beagle. Inwardly, I was quietly glad that Brece had not been placed so far as it could only mean one thing, we were runners-up or winners even, surely it would be the latter. I pondered over what our prize was going to be, a gift voucher for the pet shop, no doubt. The longer the announcements went on the more nervous and apprehensive I became. Then finally, the judge announced the runner-up position which went to a springer spaniel. I continued with my smug warm feeling now in the certain knowledge that we were the winners. The moment came, my heart skipped a beat; Then shock horror;

"And the winner of the Veteran's group is......... Lottie the 17-year old Collie!"

Almost reeling from the shock, I felt conspicuous, embarrassed and confused, all of those things. But my strongest feeling was one of transparency; it felt like people knew that I had expected my dog to win and also knew how sorely disappointed I was when she hadn't. To make matters worse the Spaniel who came second was only 8 years of age, hardly a veteran. He only qualified by the skin of his 'not so old' teeth.

I had no issue with the winner being the 17-year old ollie; that was the right decision, but I found it incredibly difficult to swallow the fact that Brece did not get placed anywhere. I knew full well I was behaving like one of those pushy parents. The sort that enters their precocious young child into talent or beauty competitions and can't cope when others don't appreciate their child's talent or beauty. I pride myself on being able to take rejection fairly well, but this resilience does not extend to accepting rejection of my dog. The only slight consolation on the day was that my friend's dog Jessie, won the 2nd place in the shiniest coat category.

Days after the shock and still reeling, I even contemplated phoning the judge to ask her how she arrived at her decision. That's how bad things were. It took me quite some time to get over the rejection, I surprised myself at how badly I had taken the whole thing. It was all just a bit of fun but why couldn't I accept it as just that? It was such a negative contrast from the PDSA dog competition all those years ago.

2016 had got off to a bad start, especially for celebrities, they were dropping like flies. The incredibly talented David Bowie led the obituaries by passing away on 10th January 2016, two days after the release of his 25th album, innovative even in death. By April 2016 and not even half way into the year we had lost, Alan Rickman, Terry Wogan, George Martin, Paul Daniels, Ronnie Corbett, David Guest, Victoria Wood, and Prince amongst many others. It was always in the back of my mind that my very own celebrity may also depart in this seemingly doomed year. With this in mind and with her 14th birthday approaching on 30thth April, I decided to celebrate the auspicious occasion. In reality, it was an excuse for the adults to have a party. Never having particularly enjoyed parties for myself, I was relishing the idea of hosting a celebration in honour of Brece. A way of deflecting the attention off me, and on to her. Pulling out all the stops, I decided to get caterers in for the big day and ordered a Japanese banquet for 25 people. The Birthday will always be etched in my mind, filed in the 'Brece' folder along with all my other great memories of her; some good, some not so good.

We were treated to a beautiful sunny day. The Magnolia was in full bloom, a fitting floral display for Princess Brece of Heyhouses. The guests started to arrive, adorning her Royal Highness with birthday presents; dog birthday cake, bowls, treats, grooming vouchers, toys, new collar, and lead. But undoubtedly the most touching gift was a helium inflated balloon emblazoned with a picture of Brece and me. I felt overwhelmed with all the gifts and even enjoyed opening them, a stark contrast to opening gifts for myself when the attention never fails to embarrass me.

Brece was on high alert for the big day. She was enjoying playing to the gallery and relishing in her many opportunities to demonstrate 'Teddy'. The caterer, a man in his late thirties, said he had never catered for a dog's birthday party before and asked if he could take pictures for his website. I was only too happy to oblige, amusing myself at the thought that a video of a 14-year old Retriever and her Japanese banquet may go viral!

Chapter 26

Must all good things come to an end?

2016

Things were going smoothly and had been doing for quite some time. Doggie dilemmas were few and far between, in fact they had ceased. Practising mindfulness and reducing numbers of ASBOs definitely contributed to this. I was now left with with my adorable regular faithfuls, Wasabi, Hendrix, Doug the Pug, Tilly, Molly and Max, Moses (thank God), Snoop, Casper, Haribo and my token ASBO Rocky, plus a few more that joined our merry band along the way.

But the group dynamics were to sadly change. Rocky's owner Brad had found happiness again with someone new, Rochelle, a beautiful brunette. In June 2016 after a whirlwind romance, the couple got married. Shortly after, they became the proud parents of a baby girl. Rochelle originated from Bolton and after the birth of their daughter she wanted to return to her roots, to be nearer to her family. Brad also wanted a change of scenery and a chance to fulfil his parental duties so he handed over the reins of his hotel empire to his partner. The couple duly moved out of the area and went to live in a rural village close to Bolton. I had assumed that the couple had found a suitable dog walker for Rocky in the village but it was not to be. I unexpectedly found out via the grape-vine that Rocky had been re-homed. Apparently the couple could not cope with both the new-born and Rocky, one of them had to go; obviously and predictably it was Rocky. Sadly, Rocky was sent to live with the owner of a kennels which was set in acres of land where he had previously boarded. Naturally, this was an emotional wrench for me. But thinking about it philosophically, but still tinged with sadness, I deduced that Rocky was now in the best home that he could be, he had the run of the fields all day long and was now where he should have been from the very beginning.

To this day I often think of Rocky, I genuinely miss him. There will always be a place in my heart for the great big lummox that is Rocky.

Another blow happened the same year when the local Council finally decided to put their spanner in the works by proposing to introduce the new dog orders. Neighbouring councils had already implemented the new dog restrictions under the Personal Space Protection Orders (PSPOs). Of course, it was only a matter of time before our local council followed suit. In early October 2016 the council announced a blueprint for their proposals. At the time, dog wardens were only authorised to distribute a fixed penalty for failure to pick up dog mess. In their infinite wisdom and mirroring other councils the local council proposed to implement new proposals;

- Increased areas where dogs must be kept on lead.
- Increased areas with a total dog exclusion.
- Restriction of the number of dogs per person to four.

Dog wardens were to be granted increased powers to issue on the spot fines for both the existing and the new dog offences. A scant map was published showing the areas where the new restrictions were to be imposed. However, the map was convoluted. With no landmarks pinpointed, it was difficult to establish where the restricted areas started and where they finished.

Of course the intention of introducing the new rules was to address the problems surrounding dogs, such as aggressive and unruly dogs and also the age-old problem of dog fouling, which is a constant irritation to all and sundry. There is no excuse for people who are aware that their dog has fouled and ignore the fact. But I doubt there isn't a dog walker alive who hasn't accidentally missed the occasional dropping. This leads me to think that the problem of uncollected mess is always going to be around to some extent. I know there have been times when I have overlooked the occasional deposit, and somebody has politely pointed out the error of my way. I continue to compensate for my omissions by picking up extra dog mess left by others, and I know that fellow PDWs are of the same ilk. To a certain extent PDW's are actually assisting the Dog Warden in helping to maintain a cleaner environment.

Dog walkers felt as though we were being penalised and that there were far more pressing issues within the community that should be addressed. It seemed as though the eyes of the world were on us, waiting to pounce if we stepped out of line. In the oppressive climate I sometimes found myself collecting the dog waste and carrying it around in a poo bag for longer than necessary. Passing the nearest bin and heading towards one further away, just so more people could see that I 'picked up'. The only flaw with this plan was that sometimes I was in a situation where I had run out of bins, leaving me with no option other than to take the poo bag home with me. One occasion, I was driving home and still had a poo bag complete with contents in my coat pocket. Unbeknown to me, somehow the poo bag fell out of my pocket and ended up underneath the accelerator-pedal. Leaving me to literally put my foot in it. Just gross.

At other times I found myself securely wrapping the poo bag around my wrist as if it was some sort of badge of honour for all to see. As I continued the walk with my vile accessory dangling from my wrist, I amused myself by making comparisons to my more affluent girlfriends with their Burberry, or Jimmy Choo handbags attached to their arms. Somehow, I very much doubt they would envy my disgusting poo handbag. My quirky revolting accessory was never going to catch on with the ladies who lunch.

Naturally, none of the Council's proposals were well received by the local dog walking community. If implemented it would mean far fewer areas where dogs would be permitted to enjoy their freedom off lead. But for a professional dog walker (PDW) who relies on walking a large group of dogs for a living it was the '4 dog per person rule' that was the killer. Although the proposals would affect me, there were many others about to be affected on a much greater scale than myself. In particular for Sam and Loz, it would be like driving a horse and carriage through their lives. The new orders would result in the couple having to refuse many of their existing customers, leading to the daunting prospect that their business may no longer be financially viable. In addition, as the couple have seven of their own dogs, it would mean that they wouldn't even be allowed to walk their own dogs together as a group. I totally agreed that dog related problems had to be addressed but my main bugbear with the council was that none of the new proposals would address any of the existing problems, it would be like taking a sledgehammer to crack a nut.

By implementing the 4 dog rule the council assumed the new restriction would address some of the problems associated with dogs. PDW's felt that this was doubtful especially with regards to the problem of dog aggression. It is a highly unlikely scenario that a PDW would have a dangerous dog in their midst, as it would make their job incredibly difficult and unsafe for all. To avoid such problems, a PDW will vet all dogs before agreeing to introduce a new dog to their pack. If it transpired that a dog has previously been involved in a fight or bitten another dog, or worse a person, then the PDW would not entertain the notion of taking it on. It is more likely to be the non-professional dog walker who is walking an aggressive dog. In my opinion and the opinion of others, the council were targeting the wrong group of people. What's worse, one aggressive dog with one person, or 7 submissive, well-trained dogs with one handler?

Naturally, there is always that section of society that does not like dogs and may even be afraid of them, especially when coming in contact with large groups of them. Nobody should be made to feel intimidated, *even if they are walking in a 'dogs allowed' area.* Some sort of reassurance needed to be made to the public that dogs walking with a PDW are safe, friendly and pose no threat to others. But presently the only way to get this message across to hesitant people is by trying to give reassurance along the lines of;

"Don't worry they are all friendly." A proper process needed to be in place, licensing perhaps, anything but not the new orders.

The proposals invoked polarising opinions in both the 'dog lovers' and the 'dog haters' camps. Somehow, a platform had been provided for dog haters to vent their views (via social media), whereas previously such people may have remained silent. It was as if a hornet's nest had been disturbed. The dog lovers were also up in arms and weren't going to take it lying down, it was an unsettling time for many people.

Historically previous new restrictions were implemented under a veil of secrecy, new by-laws appeared to sneak in under the radar without anyone realising they were about to happen. But in this instance, a member of the public found out about the new council proposals and thanks to the marvel of social media, word soon spread ahead of implementation.

On a personal note, I have customers who went about obtaining their new pet by securing my services before they even purchased their dog. If the proposals were implemented and I became financially unable to continue pet-sitting, this would effectively equate to retrospectively applying the by-laws; thus, pulling the rug out from under my customers' feet. Fellow PDWs and I wrote to the council to protest against the proposals and to appeal to their better judgement. We also encouraged our customers to write in, all of which were fully supportive and honoured our requests.

Of course, at the root of all this unrest were the PSPOs themselves. To explain the background; PSPOs were initially intended to protect people's 'Personal Space' from such things as burglary and abuse from drink or drug-related offences. They were not intended to address issues surrounding dogs. Tenuously applying the orders to dog owners was a distortion of the original purpose.

The local council headed up a working party with a view to taking their actions. Late October 2016 a meeting was held at the Town Hall to discuss the orders. In my perpetual ignorance, I had not previously appreciated that council meetings are open events to which the public are welcome to attend. By putting one's name forward prior to the meeting, concerned taxpayers were given the chance to speak out and have their say. I and several local dog walkers attended the meeting. Within the Victorian surroundings there was quite a gathering of disgruntled dog lovers, probably about thirty in total. It struck me that the council members had been clearly caught off guard, evidenced by the lack of chairs for the many attendees. The reserve stash of orange plastic chairs was called upon.

Finally seated on our out-of-context orange chairs and within the walls of the ornate but oppressive public building, the meeting got off the ground. The atmosphere felt tense, feelings were running high amongst our camp. Four people who had previously registered their intention to speak, stood up, to have their say. These being two PDWs and two other members of the public who owned six dogs a piece.

Each orator was given their 15 minutes of fame, and all spoke concisely and passionately. The councillors listened to all the concerns, then took a vote. Of the council working party consisting of six members; two councillors voted against continuing with the proposals, whilst four were in favour. This meant the proposals were to be carried forward to the next round of negotiations, a massive blow for our camp, going away from that meeting we felt worried and concerned, but not defeated.

Drastic action was required on our part, we needed to organise ourselves. The generals gathered and a strategy was formulated. First thing we did was follow the council's directive by setting up our own working party under the banner of 'Rights for Responsible Dog Walkers.' Many of our members were proactive in both the fight for our cause and also in attempting to gain collaborators. Both DEFRA (Department for environment food and rural affairs) and the Kennel Club were approached for their advice and support. Each body were in favour of freedom (within reason) for dogs off lead, and against the council's PSPO proposals.

Under the 'Freedom of Information Act' our group also approached the council to request that statistics summarising the actual complaints regarding dog offences. The council obliged and the figures were made public, revealing;

- No recorded complaints against PDWs, despite an increase in PDWs in the area.

- A handful of complaints received about aggressive dogs, *which of course had to be addressed.*
- Numerous complaints about dog fouling. The dog fouling problem attracted the largest number of complaints. Although dog fouling is simply not acceptable, the number of complaints were actually on the decline from previous years.

Under the Data Protection Act it was impossible to ascertain if the complaints came from a large section of society, or a few regular complainants. In our view the number of complaints were far less than expected and did not seem to warrant the Council's draconian proposals. The battle continued.

Our group also approached visitors from out of town, who enjoy coming to the seaside resort with their dogs and we sought their support. Shop owners who benefited from the increased revenue from visiting dog owners, were also approached. All feedback was positive and recorded on the 'Responsible Dog Owners' website, created by Brian, a key member of the group. All the while the town was continually advertised in the council's own literature as a 'Dog-friendly town.' It seemed a ludicrous state of affairs, the fact that more and more cafes and pubs were accepting of dogs, yet the places where they were allowed to exercise were about to be greatly restricted.

We continued with our plight. A Facebook page was also launched in support of 'Responsible Dog Owners Against Council Proposals.' Both dog lovers and haters aired their opinions for all to see. As emotions continued to run high in both camps it was necessary to appoint administrators to monitor the page for any personal or racist libel. Any offensive dialogue was immediately removed. A large amount of negativity was attached to individual members of the council who were vilified; at times it appeared that the council were sitting ducks, an easy target for dog fans to vent their frustrations. Later it transpired that one particular councillor said that she had actually received death threats! Things were clearly getting out of hand.

In addition to the aforementioned actions, a couple of friendly protest dog walks were arranged to support the cause for 'Responsible Dog Owners'. The more involved I became with the activities of our group, the more I became aware of something that I had not expected. This being that even within the dog lover's camp there appeared to be an underlying feeling of resentment towards people walking large groups of dogs. A couple of scathing comments had appeared on Facebook. Sam and Loz had also become conscious of the negative atmosphere. Perhaps the foundation for these feelings was that understandably some people feel uneasy when seeing large packs of dogs. More work needed to be done to alleviate people's fears that the PDW presented any type of threat to people or their dogs. After all, an increasing number of people prefer to leave their dog in a home environment as opposed to kennels when on holiday, in doing so they rely on the PDW to walk their dogs in a large group.

My colleagues and I felt as though we needed to gain support, even amongst our own camp. In an attempt to do just this Sam and Loz organised the PDW's apparel for the protest walks. This designer gear came in the form of oversized white t-shirts emblazoned with the slogan 'Support your professional dog walker.' The t-shirts were worn over our coats, I couldn't help thinking that once togged up in my attire I resembled something out of a Michelin tyre advert.

Our first organised walk took place on the town's common; a three mile stretch of grass adjacent to the sea front. A few of us arrived at the designated area ahead of the walk, wearing our PDW t-shirts with pride, only to find the green peppered in dog poo. This is already an area where dogs must be kept on lead. Therefore, the 'dog on lead' enforcement did nothing in the slightest to alleviate the problem of dog fouling. The issue here was that it was winter, many people walk their dogs early in the morning, or on their return from work in the dark. The dog fouls, the owner either doesn't see it because it's dark, or does see it and leaves it, as no one can see to object. Creative, as opposed to draconian measures, were required. Obvious suggestions would be insisting walkers take a torch with them when it is dark. Increased fines for dog fouling would also be a good deterrent.

The second walk took place on the beach. Both walks were well attended; attracting the press, radio, and local TV. Supporters were interviewed, and the interviews aired on local TV, all of which made great publicity for our cause. The plight of PDWs appeared to be given priority, each PDW was invited to speak, which was a great platform to explain how we work towards ensuring safety to all. Our presentations seemed to have a positive effect on others, and of course our fine couture must have gone some way to impress! Slowly but surely there was a camaraderie building between fellow dog walkers and professional walkers alike, and a better understanding of exactly what steps the PDWs take to make ensure their dogs are no threat to others. Hopefully, this message also reached the ears of non-dog lovers.

Things remained up in the air; it was business as usual until the council saw fit to make their decisions. There was a distinct negative feeling amongst my colleagues that the council would intransigently railroad their proposals, regardless. However, I felt a bit more optimistic, surely the council would listen to the people?

Chapter 27

The Council result 2017

It was business as usual, dog walkers continued in limbo pending the council's final decision regarding the implementation of the Personal Space Protection Orders (PSPOs). Finally, 18th May 2017 a peculiar thing happened. A meeting was held with the council committee together with a small number of members from the Responsible Dog Owner group.

Once again, it was held in the Town Hall, *this time there were enough orange plastic chairs to go around.* Top of the agenda was the council's final decisions on the PSPO proposals. Prior to the meeting I had felt optimistic that the council would see sense and not implement the new orders. But sitting there before the panel of councillors I felt daunted and suddenly not quite so optimistic. The rest of the group were also pessimistic.

We were kept waiting, whilst the council members were chunnering amongst themselves. It felt as though they were dragging things out, and in doing so increasing our anxieties. I was thinking to myself 'just get on with it, it's not the X factor results'. Finally a male representative from the council who appeared to be the head poncho stood up. The next sentences that he was about to speak were to affect the lives of many of the attendees sat before him, the atmosphere was tense. What he then said completely took the wind out of our sails!

He announced that after several meetings and discussions with the Kennel Club and DEFRA, the previous proposals had now been withdrawn. Jointly, all parties had arrived at a plausible workaround that the council considered to all intents and purposes would be beneficial to all concerned. An 'on the spot' fine was still going to be enforced in the following scenarios;

- Unruly/aggressive dogs
- Dog fouling
- Dogs in cemetery parks, children's play areas and ornamental water features.

This was an optimum result for our party, we firmly agreed with all the new enforcements. In fact, they were only marginally different to the current restrictions. There were to be no new 'dogs banned or on lead' areas, or indeed restriction of dogs per person.

Our group were delighted to hear the news but my mind wandered off when I listened to the councillor make the final announcement regarding the ornamental water features. It took me back to a time many years ago when I was walking Brece in the local public gardens. At the time she was still at her 'lunging up at people' stage.

The gardens proudly sport an ornamental pond inhabited with swans and ducks, a popular spot for people to take young children along to feed the wildlife. Brece was unleashed and happily 'Logging on' in the rose garden, preferring the aroma of dog pee to the scent of roses. I was only too aware that the ornamental water garden was close by, but I wasn't overly concerned about the risk of the lure of the water, as she was completely occupied with sniffing everything in sight with her snout.

However, she had given me a false sense of security. All of a sudden her ears pricked up, her stride lengthened, and like a rabbit out of the trap she made a dash for the pond. To set the scene; a brace of swans were relaxing on the bank enjoying the sunshine, completely oblivious to the imminent arrival of my big daft dog. To the left of the swans a couple of children accompanied by an adult were feeding some already over-fed ducks. I tried to grab her but she was far too quick for me, I didn't have a cat in hell's chance. At about 30 metres away from me I witnessed her launch herself into the mucky waters. Part of me was screaming inwardly; 'Oh, my God, the poor birds.' But then a small part was thinking; 'Ah bless her, she's going to love splashing around.'

The children outwardly screamed as the local birdlife made an early migration. Once they caught sight of the perpetrator wallowing and splashing around in the murky waters, their screams then turned to laughter. Suddenly, something to the right of the scene caught my attention. In front of the backdrop of a flamboyant flower bed stood a couple of newly-weds, posing for their wedding photos. In traditional fashion the bride was wearing a full-length white gown. She seemed relaxed and composed, completely unaware of Brece the hippopotamus, splashing around in the nearby stagnant pond.

It was fortuitous that Brece hadn't noticed the newly-weds, the call of the water had completely absorbed her attention. By this time, she was fully engaged in her swim and nice and filthy. I knew only too well that once she noticed the cortège she would undoubtedly get out of the water and make a beeline towards them.

An awful premonition flashed through my head; Brece clambering out of the mud, determinedly running towards the bride, reaching her then jumping up and covering her immaculate wedding dress in slimy rotting weeds. Brece loved to go to people; in her fluffy head people equate to attention, affection and better still the potential morsel of food. I couldn't allow her to introduce herself, it would be tantamount to ruining the wedding day, especially for the bride. On a mission, I had to get to her before she caught sight of the newly-weds. Running like the clappers, I arrived at the pond just as she slowly started to emerge from the black lagoon. She'd had her swim, her work was done, but mine was just about to start. I had to grab hold of her, and quickly.

Standing by the edge of the pond and taking on the stance of a goalkeeper, I stretched my arms and legs as wide as I could, covering as much ground as womanly possible; praying all the while that she would not clamber out of the water, pass me and score a goal by reaching the bridal party.

Fortunately, hauling herself out of the pond was a slow process; the weight of the water, sludge and weeds was holding her back. Then the inevitable happened, she spotted the happy couple and put on a spurt. She was now whimpering with excitement, *not a good sign.* I felt that all too familiar strong sense of doom in the pit of my stomach. Quickly morphing from goalkeeper to rugby player, I tackled her as she got out of the water and managed to tether her up before she got a chance to offer her congratulations to the happy couple. A big dog such as Brece can hold a lot of water and muck in a double coat, most of which seemed to come off onto me. I was wet, filthy and stunk of stagnant water, but far better me than the bride. I totally appreciated why the council would not want to have dogs visiting their ornamental ponds. I still cringe now when I think of how things could have turned out so very differently.

Back in the room; the councillor continued. In addition to the council's reasonable conclusions and also in a strange twist of fate they had now decided to completely change their rhetoric. Instead of implementing new dog restrictions, there was now going to be an increase in the number of dog-friendly areas, a complete U-turn. The powers that be now intended to promote the town as an even more dog-friendly place to visit. They wanted to be seen as being at the forefront of innovation and positivity with regards to dogs. The council had recognised the significance of the 'Paw Pound', now wanting to attract even more visitors with dogs to the area, in turn supporting the numerous cafe and restaurant businesses. The role of the dog warden was also going to change by including welfare and education. The benefits of owning and walking dogs in terms of improving mental and physical health were to be promoted.

The plight of the PDW had not been overlooked either, the four-dog limit proposal was dropped. In conjunction with the Kennel Club PDWs were to undergo some sort of free accreditation, details of which were still being discussed. Presumably, this meant some sort of policing check to ensure walkers with more than four dogs were fully competent to manage the numbers in their midst. Eureka! this was exactly what was needed. Hopefully, the accreditation would now give people reassurance that a person walking a large group of dogs was of no risk to the general public. All things considered, the council's final ruling was an incredible catharsis, we welcomed the entire content of their new proposals. The head councillor even took the unprecedented step of apologising to our group for putting us through the anguish of the past months.

Chapter 28

Skating on thin ice 2017

By now it wasn't only Brece that was showing signs of age, the years had also started to take their toll on the dog mobile. Having stood me well, and never once letting me down my car engine was beginning to burn oil at an alarming rate, even I know that's not a good sign. Finding myself in a position where I needed to spend quite a bit of money on it for one thing or another, I decided it was time for a change. Besides, I couldn't afford to have a breakdown with my precious cargo in tow.

I have no idea what I am doing when it comes to cars. With hindsight I probably should have sought the advice of someone who did, but that didn't happen. After having visited a few showrooms and considering a couple of vehicles, I finally decided on purchasing a Vauxhall Zafira from a nationwide car dealership in Blackpool.

The Zafira seemed to tick all the boxes. It was much larger than the VW Polo thus ensuring more space for the dogs. After having agreed to buy the car, the salesman and I set about completing the laborious paperwork; after which I arranged to collect the car a few days later. The day arrived, coincidentally on the same day my carpet cleaner chap Andy turned up for the routine soft furnishings spruce-up. As I was literally leaving my house on the way to the garage, I happened to mention to Andy that I was going to pick up my new car. Being of the male species he was interested and asked me what type of car I was buying. I duly told him and waited for his reply. His voice remained monotone as he calmly said;

"Oh yes, those are the ones that have been bursting into flames, it's been on the telly."

This was just great news to hear, I couldn't help wondering why I was only just hearing the information now. Going back indoors I logged on to my trusty computer and googled 'Problems with Vauxhall Zafiras.' Sure enough, the screen was populated with multiple pictures of Zafiras on fire. The first footage was taken by a mother who had managed to escape the car with her small child just before it burst into flames! Fortunately, no physical harm came to mother or child. The information went on to reveal that the root of the problem was a faulty heating system specific to the 'B' type Zafira, and not the 'A' type. At this point I didn't even know if I was in the process of buying the A or the B make, *how could I be so gormless?*

I gave the dealer a call and after much toing and froing he handed me over to his manager. I was then reliably informed that the car I was about to buy was the B type, which indeed still had a faulty heating system!! Feeling as though I was in a parallel universe, black hole even, I could hardly believe my ears. I was completely stunned that the dealership was actually prepared to sell me a car with a serious potentially life-threatening fault, and not even bother to warn me. *This is what happens when I am left to my own devices with cars.*

Needless to say, I did not purchase said vehicle. But somehow my newfound knowledge of the Zafira did not stop me impulsively purchasing another Zafira B, this time from a different dealership in Blackpool. I'm not sure why I seemed hell-bent on buying another Zafira, but there didn't seem to be too much local choice about and I as too impatient to go further afield. Also the price was reasonable, by now Zafiras probably weren't likely to be selling like 'hot' cakes! But I wasn't completely reckless, I had been assured by the new dealer that the fault with the heating system had been fixed and I was given the paperwork as evidence.

Meanwhile 3 months down the line, and still in my parallel universe, I was astonished to receive a letter from Vauxhall to say that although the fault on my car had been fixed, the fix was faulty. The letter went on to say that my car needed to be recalled for a second time. Yet again, I was that vulnerable pawn being shoved around by the hand of fate on my perpetual chessboard.

Unknowingly I had been driving around all this time in a vehicle that could have potentially burst into flames. God knows what I would have done if this had happened with a car full of dogs. There would be no way on earth I would be able to get 7 dogs out of a burning vehicle and keep them all safe on a public highway. The letter from Vauxhall explained their interim solution; if using the heating system it must be set to the full temperature. This would prevent the car from combusting! So, the options were no heat, full heat, or combustion, none of which were particularly appealing. I was left with no option other than to continue to drive my car in unsatisfactory temperatures until such time as the dealers could fit me in for the repairs. This took several months. It seemed that combustible cars that had already been sold were not a priority to the dealers.

Thanks to the council's astonishing U-turn and managing to swerve exploding cars I made it to my sixth year as a pet sitter un-hindered. My original plan was to work at my business for a period of 5 years. Although I had made a dent in reducing my mortgage, I had not achieved my financial aim and still had some way to go. This was attributed to the fact that the first two years were slow, it wasn't until the third year that I started to exceed my targets. I was beginning to feel unsure of my future; I still needed to work but at the same time I was conscious that it may be time for a change.

The main reason for my doubts being that the massive responsibility that I undertake was beginning to take its toll on me. I had dodged many a bullet and dodged checkmate on numerous occasions. Some mornings my mood was one of great apprehension. I would wake up with a feeling of impending doom that something may go horribly wrong that day. It's not so much the walking side of things that was beginning to get to me but more the unforeseen things. The chess moves that I don't see coming my way. Harping back to my days in the office, if I made a mistake the consequences were virtually non-existent and they could always be corrected. But making a mistake when caring for a customer's dog could lead to detrimental consequences and repercussions. Echoing my earlier thoughts, the longer I do the job the more chance of something going hideously wrong, teasing that hand of fate as it were. Although I know my dogs very well, I can still never 100 percent predict what might happen and how a dog will react in an unexpected scenario. How long could my good fortune prevail, was I pushing my luck too far? These questions continually reverberated around my head.

But what would I do if I didn't work with the dogs any more, and could I cope with not seeing them? What if I saw one of my ex-dogs out with someone else, how would I feel? I didn't even like it when I saw one of my ASBOs out with another walker. When this happened it always left me feeling strangely sad and forlorn. Even though I had let them go, I still missed them. I tried to imagine how I would cope if it was one of my beloved low maintenance dogs that I saw with someone else. I knew in that scenario I would feel deeply upset, jealous even.

So, here I am again, slowly pulling up to the next crossroads in my life, feeling incredibly blessed that Brece is still by my side. I don't know where my next chapter will take me, but no doubt there will be more trials, tribulations and laughs along the way. Let's just hope there are no more burglaries, ruined weddings, exploding cars, lost house keys, or even worse lost dogs.

Appendix A- Dog ability to search using magnetic fields

Quote

'There are remarkable stories of lost dogs travelling hundreds of miles, even to different countries in order to find their way home. There is now evidence to suggest that dogs are sensitive to the earths magnetic fields in a similar way to migrating birds. Research has shown that dogs have a light-sensitive molecule called Cryptochrome 1 in their retinas. It is suggested that the molecule may be used in the perception of magnetic fields. Detecting the earths magnetic fields helps the dog to orientate and navigate itself and find its way home.'

refer healthy pets.mercola. Com 2019/07/12

Appendix B- The life cycle of the puppy

Quote

'The first two weeks of a puppy's life are heavily influenced by the mother, the puppy will start to learn simple social skills, coordination, and the ranking process, but mostly they will just eat. At about three weeks they begin to open their eyes and start walking. Their sense of smell and hearing starts to develop. They begin to wag their tails, their first teeth come through and they learn to bark. The dogs learn their place in the pack from birth as they are jockeying for position whilst nursing. Dogs operate the same hierarchy as their ancestor the wolf, they are born with the pack mentality. Play is also a key part of the puppy's development; it teaches them how far they can go and when to stop. If a puppy yelps during play the other puppy will usually stop, it knows not to play quite as hard going forward, or at least it should.

Four to twelve weeks is the stage when socialisation is extremely important. The puppy needs to be introduced to other people and other dogs. Good or bad experiences will play a role in how they continue to interact with others. The puppy will go through a normal 'fear' period. In the wild, they need to learn fear to learn how to avoid it and survive it. Again, it is important that they don't have bad experiences at this stage, for example, if a broom fell on a puppy and hurt it this could lead to a fear of brooms or anything that looks similar to a broom, the dog will tend to generalise. Training should start at around nine weeks.'

Reference; Caesar's way 1/7/2019

Appendix C- Information on the dog's ability to hear

Quote:

'Canines have an amazing sense of hearing; they can also pick up twice as many different frequencies than humans. This is down to the size and positioning of their ears. The dog has eighteen muscles in the ear allowing them to rotate, tilt, raise and lower the ear. The dog's ear acts like an antenna homing in on sounds. Each ear can hear independently, and they can filter out sounds. For example, a dog can sleep through loud music but will jump up when he hears the treat bag being rustled.'

reference; petmeds.org

Appendix D – The many services the dog provides for man

Dogs are trained to work as assistance dogs that enrich the lives of their disable owners who may be blind, deaf, suffering from epilepsy, diabetes anomalies and even potential heart attacks. Some dogs can even detect other diseases such as cancer. Using their incredible sense of smell they recognise chemical changes in our bodies, created by the cancer. Currently, there is an ongoing NHS programme whereby dogs are being trained to detect cancer. Staggeringly fully trained dogs will be able to diagnose cancer immediately without the need for biopsies thus saving the NHS vital resources. Not forgetting Pets as Therapy dogs (PAT), these dogs are engaged to lift the spirits of the sick and infirm. Dogs are now also used to assist children in learning to read, some schools even own a dog. A child may lack confidence and feel uncomfortable when reading aloud in front of his peers but feels relaxed reading in front of a dog. The dog sits and listens in an attentive non-judgemental manner thus increasing the child's confidence to read aloud.

Appendix E– Why does a normally non-aggressive dog display aggression towards a frightened child?

Although dog attacks on children are few and far between, they do happen and on rare occasions can be tragically fatal. The dogs that have attacked children in the past are usually the family's own banned Pit Bull variety. It beggar's belief why people want to have this type of aggressive dog around children.

There are several reasons why an otherwise non-aggressive dog, may show aggression towards a child. Firstly, if the child is unsupervised it may be provoking the dog in a number of ways, for this reason, it's extremely important to have a placid tolerant dog in a household with children. Secondly, a young child may be wearing a nappy which instinctively attracts a dog, some dogs will try to get the nappy from an infant, which could, in turn, lead to an attack. And lastly, the child may be afraid of dogs and uncomfortable around them. It could be any one of these scenarios or a combination of all three that provokes a dog to be aggressive towards a child. The most difficult of these scenarios to manage is undoubtedly 'The frightened child' scenario. Research has revealed that fear in children creates pheromones and certain chemicals associated with stress, which in turn makes the dog nervous. The same applies to nervous adults, however for obvious reasons a child is more likely to be afraid of a dog than an adult is. At the end of the day, the dog is an animal, with big great teeth and in some cases as large as the infant, if not larger. It's no wonder that some children default to scared when confronted by a dog, especially if they haven't been socialised with dogs.

In the wild, an animal that gives off negativity is likely to pose some sort of threat. The dog's reaction to fear is a primeval instinct that is still part of his genetic make-up.

Appendix F– Why are some dogs afraid of men?

Research has not managed to come up with an explanation as to why this is, even Caesar Milan, the dog whisperer doesn't know the true reason. It's apparent the dog feels threatened in some way, but it is unclear as to why.

Quote: 'There are several theories; it may be the size and stature of a man. The deeper male voice, although personally I doubt that is the reason

313

as in my experience the dogs take up their stance before the man has uttered a word. Others think the dog is showing fear towards males because it may have been badly treated by a man in the past.

Another possibility is that as dogs are nurtured by their mothers, they are familiar with female hormones from the start of their lives. Whereas male hormones are unfamiliar to a pup and may appear threatening in some way. In my opinion the most likely reason points to scent. Such a lot of the dog's behaviour is instinctively driven by smells, the man is giving off a scent or pheromone that the dog is afraid of. But this is circumstantial and goes to show that although we still have a lot to learn about man's best friend.'

Reference – Caesar's Way by Caesar Milan

Appendix G- Information on birds migrating to the Ribble estuary

Quote:

'The extensive areas of mud flats are home to copious amounts of worms, shrimps and other creatures providing rich food for the local birdlife. Over a quarter of a million birds spend the winter on the Ribble estuary after having migrated from countries such as Russia, Iceland, Siberia, and Greenland. Apart from the Canadian Geese, the rarer birds such as Long-Eared Owls, Peregrine, Marsh Harrier and Osprey can be seen feeding in the sea supermarket. Most of the visiting birds spend the winter at the estuary, which is the third most important estuary in the UK for migrating birds. A proportion of the birds are just stopping off to refuel. These birds have flown from the Arctic and visit the estuary to feed before continuing their mammoth journey to Africa. The lake at Fairhaven situated adjacent to the estuary is home to an RSPB information bureau. On the exterior of the bureau sits an electronic information board detailing the origins of the incoming birds, the numbers, and their expected arrival date.

The arrival of the birds in their thousands is a sight to behold. After their gruelling journey, they rest in the local nature reserves situated by the sides of the estuary. During the day they flock to the estuary to feed before returning to the local nature reserves to rest. In late autumn the birds can be seen flying overhead in typical 'V' formation. It is still not fully understood how the birds accomplish their incredible journeys. Research reveals that they obtain the information they need for migration from the stars, the sun, and the earth's magnetic field. There is also some evidence to indicate that birds may also call on their sense of smell as does our friend the dog.'

Reference; www.visitlytham/RSPB.info

Appendix H- Early history of Lytham hall

Quote:

'For three centuries Benedictine monks lived in the area and farmed the surrounding land of the area where Lytham Hall now stands. The dissolution of the monasteries changed everything, and the priory was passed over to several landowners before being acquired by Cuthbert Clifton of Westby in 1606. In 1750 the hall was rebuilt into the Georgian style that we see today. The Clifton dynasty owned most of the land of Lytham St Anne's and had a great reputation for being fair landlords. They did a lot for the local community and charged very little for ground rental. Unfortunately, the Clifton family suffered financial ruin, the situation was not aided by Henry Clifton's gambling addiction and the Hall fell into a bad condition, with some of the interior and most of the exterior falling into disrepair. Chunks of masonry had fallen from the stone window frames and cracks run down the walls, most of the paint had fallen off. The Hall was sold to Guardian Royal Exchange in the 1970s, who restored the hall at a cost of 2 million pounds.'

Reference; Wikipedia

Appendix I- How many words can dogs understand?

Quote:

'Studies have shown that dogs are roughly as intelligent as a 2 year-old child and depending on the breed are able to understand approximately 165 words. MRI scanning of the dog's brain has revealed that they use the left hemisphere of their brain to compute words, as do humans. Dogs are more responsive to positive words and tones, as opposed to negative tones, which is why encouragement goes a long way when trying to train a dog.'

Reference; Dr Stanley Coren 15/9/2011

Puppies initially don't understand words, which makes it difficult to keep them safe and sound. As the puppy gets older, the number of commands it understands increases, making it easier to keep them safe. The puppy will learn to associate a command with an activity, example being; a pup is in the boot of a car and needs to keep still so that the hatch can be shut. Invariably the pup will not understand the stay command. Then in time, the pup learns that the word 'Stay' means the hatch is about to shut, and it needs to keep still, to avoid getting hurt. In contrast, an adult dog that understands multiple commands is far easier to keep safe.

Acknowledgements

After leaving school with no qualifications in English and only having read 5 books by the age of 55 years, I decided to tell my own story. Needless to say I needed all the help I could get. That help came from various patient kind friends.

Thank you to Neil for encouraging me to write in the first place. Thank you to Laura, Kay, Bennie, Diane, and Chloe, for all your time spent wading through the gobble-de-gook and trying to make sense of it all. A massive thanks to Zoe and Lynne who painstakingly read my book from cover to cover and furnished me with a full review. An extra special thankyou to my wonderful sister Bennie who has always been there for me, except perhaps when we were kids!

Lastly a sincere thankyou to all my customers for trusting me with the safe keeping of their beloved pets, not forgetting the amazing dogs themselves. And, of course, the most amazing dog of all my beautiful, strong willed Golden Retriever Brece, who has been an incredible source of amusement and asset to me over many years.